THE LIMITS OF DIVERSITY

The Limits of Diversity

How Secular and Evangelical Campuses Reproduce Inequality

Esther Chan

NEW YORK UNIVERSITY PRESS
New York

NEW YORK UNIVERSITY PRESS
New York
www.nyupress.org

Library of Congress Cataloging-in-Publication Data
Names: Chan, Esther D. author
Title: The limits of diversity : how secular and evangelical campuses reproduce inequality / Esther Chan.
Description: New York : New York University Press, [2025] | Includes bibliographical references and index.
Identifiers: LCCN 2025004511 (print) | LCCN 2025004512 (ebook) | ISBN 9781479834730 hardback | ISBN 9781479834747 paperback | ISBN 9781479834754 ebook | ISBN 9781479834792 ebook other
Subjects: LCSH: Discrimination in higher education—United States | Educational equalization—United States | Christian universities and colleges—United States
Classification: LCC LC212.42 .C526 2025 (print) | LCC LC212.42 (ebook)
LC record available at https://lccn.loc.gov/2025004511
LC ebook record available at https://lccn.loc.gov/2025004512

This book is printed on acid-free paper, and its binding materials are chosen for strength and durability. We strive to use environmentally responsible suppliers and materials to the greatest extent possible in publishing our books.

The manufacturer's authorized representative in the EU for product safety is Mare Nostrum Group B.V., Mauritskade 21D, 1091 GC Amsterdam, The Netherlands. Email: gpsr@mare-nostrum.co.uk.

Manufactured in the United States of America

10 9 8 7 6 5 4 3 2 1

Also available as an ebook

For my family

CONTENTS

Preface ix

Introduction 1

PART I. DIVERSITY FRAMEWORKS

1. Three Definitions of Diversity 31
2. Assumptions of Equality in Creed and Liberalism 54

PART II. THE LIMITS OF DIVERSITY

3. Equality Without Equity in Speech at West University 83
4. Equality Without Inclusion for LGBTQ+ Students at Christ College 106
5. Asian Americans and the Limits of Representation 130

PART III. DIVERSITY CHALLENGES AND FUTURES

6. LGBTQ+ Students 157
7. Asian American Students 181

Conclusion 207

Acknowledgments 225

Appendix: Semi-Structured Interview Guide 231

Notes 237

Bibliography 255

Index 281

About the Author 294

PREFACE

I finished writing this book prior to the second Trump administration, which immediately began to dismantle and criminalize diversity, equity, and inclusion (DEI) policies. The Trump administration directed federal agencies and bodies to upend diversity programs and remove gender pronouns and references of trans*gender and intersex peoples to erase their existence. Efforts increased to imprison and deport undocumented immigrants, framing them as criminal and fomenting broader xenophobia. Funding for research and data on diverse social groups across race, gender, sexuality, and more was removed from research agencies and databases. Once seen as a strength that companies could exploit for productivity and commercialization, diversity became anathema. Financially pressed universities risked losing much-needed funding if they chose to support their students' diversity, equity, and inclusion needs. The reach of anti-DEI policies was broad and the consequences potentially deep and long-lasting.

Anti-DEI sentiment is rooted in interlocking systems of White supremacy, patriarchy, and capitalism. These same systems are also what contributed to the failures of reconstruction after the Civil War, backlash to civil-rights-era gains and legislation, and the many other moments in history when our country has tried to free itself from its own injustice only to be forcefully pulled backward by those who have fattened themselves on injustice. Opponents of DEI frame DEI as anti-American, discriminatory to White people, and unmeritocratic. Coupled with these lies, false myths about equality, and willful ignorance of our country's shameful past and present, anti-DEI backlash is another manifestation of how those who have glutted themselves through injustice cannot imagine living in a just world.

While writing this book, there were moments when I wondered if we really needed another book critiquing diversity when the Right was gleefully doing so, but I quickly realized that the student narratives told here were necessary. They were necessary because they revealed how students were grappling with the injustices in our multifaceted world and how they knew that diversity simply was not enough despite living in an increasingly diverse world. Rather than searching misguidedly for an era of lost "greatness" in US history or acting as if our present day is a perfect world of fairness and equality, they were actively engaging past and present shortcomings in their small corner: their universities.

When I gathered data for this book during the first Trump presidency, students spoke with a mix of frustration, hope, and apathy about issues of diversity on their campuses. They were not blind to the inequitable ways diversity was being practiced on their campuses. They saw the problems with thin understandings of diversity that prioritize equal treatment over equity and numeric representation over transformational inclusion. But it was also clear that despite diversity's shortcomings, it was something they still valued and something they felt, if attached to equitable and inclusive policies and transformations, could lead to much-needed societal transformation.

This book illustrates the limits of diversity not to reach the conclusion that diversity is evil, as it is often spun by critics, but to reach the conclusion that diversity is not enough. The practices of diversity illustrated in this book reveal its tensions and limits to help us think more clearly about its generative possibilities for living in a more just world. Whether naysayers like it or not, the US is steadily marching toward becoming a majority racial minority demographic; and generation after generation is becoming more accepting of queer relationships, and more are identifying as LGTBQ+. With the growing pains of change, the future lies neither in squashing difference nor in Pollyanna celebration of difference but in ensuring that our systems grow to become more equitable.

If I conducted this study during the second Trump administration, I wonder what my students would say. I do not think they would abandon the need for diversity married to equity and inclusion. I do not think they would stop challenging their universities to do better. I do not think they would remain silent in our troubled times. They might use different terms, but the spirit is the same: Injustice and inequality rooted in our systems will never make us great.

Introduction

A voice over the library intercom tells us that the library will be closing at six. It is a warm Friday evening in October, and I am grateful that Kyle, a student of color involved in his university's diversity leadership, has made the time to speak to me. I pause my recorder, and we find a bench in the library's quad to continue speaking about his experiences of diversity at West University's campus.[1] Throughout our interview, Kyle speaks eloquently, jumping from references to Jordan Peele's *Get Out* and Christina Sharpe's *In the Wake* to performing spoken word when discussing issues of diversity on campus. Kyle describes the difficult tensions over free speech and hate speech that preoccupy the university in light of Donald Trump's election as president in 2016 and the death of a Charlottesville protester just months before our interview. He feels that the university does not approach issues of diversity and speech with equity in mind but rather treats all perspectives as equally valid. Kyle often finds himself at odds with how West University frames diversity even though he works for their DEI (diversity, equity, and inclusion) office.

I meet with Genesis at Christ College, a small evangelical Christian college located in a metropolitan West Coast city.[2] Genesis, who is racially White and identifies as a lesbian, wears an oversized sweater over a skirt and leggings. Using she/her pronouns and they/them pronouns, Genesis serves on the leadership of the LGBTQ+ student organization at Christ College, aptly named Harbor, to provide a safe place for LGBTQ+ students. Although Christ College recognizes Harbor as an officially registered student group, the university's broader policies fail to promote inclusion outside this found space. Genesis and other Harbor leaders seek to change the housing system and remove the college's negative theological statements around sexuality to ensure the safety and inclusion of LGBTQ+ students. Although Christ College purports to support diversity, its administrators resist changing the university's policies toward LGBTQ+ students by citing their donors and denomination.

It is a chilly Saturday morning when Jason and I meet at the student union at Christ College. Jason wears a cozy white fleece for the gray day. Jason is a second-generation Asian American and is part of an Asian American organization on campus. Due to the small size of their group on the campus and busy schedules, the Asian American student organization Jason is part of no longer meets regularly. He feels the loss of this group acutely as it is one of the few spaces where he feels comfortable in a predominantly racially White university. Even though Jason considers diversity as encompassing all types of differences, he does not think Asian Americans are really considered part of "diversity" on campus. Nearly 40 percent of Christ College's student body is made up of racialized minorities, and Christ College is an advocate of racial reconciliation. Yet, there is something amiss about Asian American inclusion in diversity not only at Christ College but also perhaps at other universities. Jason thinks this has to do with the perceived numeric overrepresentation and success of Asian Americans in higher education despite their status as a racial minority in the United States.

Kyle, Genesis, and Jason are several of the seventy-eight students I interviewed at West University and Christ College from the fall of 2017 to the spring of 2018. They are students with different demographic backgrounds and various social identities who are involved in different parts of student life at their universities. Kyle works within one of his university's recognized leadership positions that aims to foster diversity on campus. Genesis is a member of an LGBTQ+ student organization; Jason is involved in an Asian American student group. Each of the populations at the core of this book—diversity leaders, LGBTQ+ students, and Asian Americans—manifest different relationships to diversity in higher education, helping us understand the limitations of current dominant approaches to diversity.

On campus, universities rely heavily on students in diversity leadership positions to promote diversity, but these student leaders must operate within the constraints of their university structure. Students in university diversity leadership positions differ from those who may primarily act as activists through other avenues on their campus, such as through student organizing, by opting to be part of the university's sanctioned positions. Further, some of these diversity leadership positions are paid positions, thus potentially cleaving students in these leadership positions closer to the university's diversity discourse and practices. These student leaders, like Kyle, must contend with how to manage their obligations to the university while also advocating for their own visions of diversity, equity, and inclusion, which may be at odds with their university's official stances and policies.

Sexuality and gender identity are also increasingly salient to discussions of diversity. University diversity statements often include gender identity and sexuality in their definitions of diversity. This is even the case at some religious universities, which may include LGBTQ+ students in diversity and nondiscrimination statements even as they advance policies and pedagogies that exclude them.[3] This tension is reflected at Christ College, where Genesis and their peers labor to bring greater inclusion for LGBTQ+ students. Proponents of DEI bans, such as those put in place in the state of Florida, describe diversity programs as a means to indoctrinate students with supposedly anti-American and deviant perspectives that they argue are found in critical race theory and gender theories.[4] Issues of gender and sexuality are therefore closely related to discussions of diversity, but they remain understudied in research that focuses on diversity in higher education.[5]

Although a racialized minority in the United States, Asian Americans are often considered overrepresented in higher education, raising questions of their inclusion given that diversity is often tied to underrepresented racialized minorities.[6] Jason's uncertainty about whether Asian Americans are really considered part of "diversity" on campus reflects this tension over racial diversity and numeric representation. Further, Asian Americans were recently at the heart of the *Students for Fair Admissions v. Harvard* and the *Students for Fair Admissions v. UNC* court cases, which led to the end of race-conscious affirmative action policies on college campuses. Their status as a racial minority that is "overrepresented" in pockets of higher education and as a "racial mascot" in ending affirmative action make Asian Americans especially important in understanding how diversity is identified and practiced.[7]

This book highlights three approaches to diversity and examines key flashpoints around issues of speech, race, and gender identity and sexuality to demonstrate the limits and possibilities of these different diversity frameworks for equity and inclusion. I examine the experiences and perceptions of students employed in diversity leadership, LGBTQ+ students, and Asian Americans to show how secular and religious universities' use of dominant diversity frameworks and their associated practices reproduce inequality along multiple lines of social difference. Students' views of diversity sometimes reflected their universities', but they also challenged their universities' inequality regimes by critically engaging their universities' approaches to diversity and working to bring equity and inclusion for themselves.

The dominant approach to diversity—*diversity as difference*—reproduces inequality in that it operates from an assumption of abstract equality that "flattens" social groups and perspectives. Universities and students who hold this view start from the position that different social groups exist as equals and therefore all peoples should be subjected to the same processes or forms of evaluation. However, diversity as difference is impossible for universities to implement in practice. This is because people, in reality, do not start from equal positions and, inevitably, private evangelical and public secular universities must make decisions about which groups to prioritize within their organizational and cultural constraints. These decisions often reinscribe the views, positions, and organizational structures that favor or center the dominant groups.

A second approach to diversity understands diversity through *numeric metrics* and *representation*. Universities produce numbers about diversity, and students also sometimes view their representation and inclusion in diversity on their campuses through their numbers and visual cues. However, diversity as numerical can reproduce inequality when interpreted through a cultural lens that amplifies inequitable understandings of diversity. This is because numbers are not neutral, despite often creating a veneer of neutrality or greater objectivity. The trouble with thinking about diversity as numeric lies in the interpretation of numbers. Numbers can give groups legitimacy and point out inequalities, but people can also interpret numbers in ways that denigrate groups and uphold systems of inequality.

Against and sometimes with these two views, the students I interviewed articulated an alternative approach to diversity as difference and diversity as numeric. A third understanding of diversity, as a means to righting *power disparities and creating equity*, offers the most promising approach to establishing diversity on campus. It highlights the need for organizational *and* cultural changes with the goal of bringing about equity and inclusion. These organizational and cultural changes, however, are often incomplete. Universities that hold a power and equity view often do so in tension with the other perspectives and under the unique constraints of their university contexts, thereby making it difficult to create an equitable and inclusive environment. Students with an equity and power view of diversity challenge their universities to continually think about *who* and *what* education is for, thus helping us envision how universities can move from inequality regimes to equity regimes.

Universities as Inequality Regimes

In this book, I argue that universities' dominant approaches and practices of diversity reflect inequality regimes. The sociologist and theorist Joan Acker defines *inequality regimes* as "loosely interrelated practices, processes, actions, and meanings that result in and maintain class, gender, and racial inequalities."[8] Acker specifically describes inequality regimes in relationship to class, gender, and race, but she also notes that inequality regimes create and maintain inequality for other forms of social difference.[9] This book illustrates how universities act as inequality regimes toward multiple forms of social difference through their organizational discourses, practices, and policies around *diversity*.

Unlike an inequality regime, an *equity regime* is oriented around meanings, practices, and processes that institutionalize equity across social differences.[10] Here, it is important to clarify that equity is different from equality. Indeed, one of the biggest shortcomings of current dominant understandings of diversity as difference and diversity as numeric is that they are rooted in a commitment to *abstract equality* among social groups that is divorced from historical and current social injustices. Abstract equality is embedded in liberal and neoliberal meanings and practices that denude groups of their unique histories of inequalities to maintain the "sameness" of these groups such that an equal playing field among groups is assumed a priori.[11] Thus, it is "abstract" because equality between groups does not exist in reality. This manifests itself in subjecting unequal groups to the same policies, practices, and resources, which results in the perpetuation of social inequality and injustice.

Unlike equality, equity is oriented toward addressing the institutional and historical processes and practices that have created an unequal playing field.[12] Equality remains "the long-term goal of a just society," such that people regardless of their social differences have the same access to resources and opportunities, but equity recognizes that this moment has not yet arrived and will not arrive until the forces that create and perpetuate the unequal playing field are remediated.[13] Ultimately, an equity regime is oriented toward historical, economic, social, cultural, and institutional forces with the goal of creating a truly more equal world. For universities to become equity regimes, they need to not only understand diversity's meanings, practices, tensions, and limits on different college campuses and across different types of social differences but also to reject the aspects of diversity ideology that do not lead us to a more equitable and equal world.

Universities are not and have never been neutral to inequality. They play a key role in various forms of stratification, even as education is often described as a great equalizer for socioeconomic inequality.[14] While there is empirical evidence to suggest that obtaining a college degree helps people overcome their less-advantaged economic or class origins, sociologists also explain how various organizational, social, and cultural practices act as mechanisms *within* colleges that reproduce inequality.[15] For example, the sociologists Elizabeth Armstrong and Laura Hamilton show how gender and class inequality is reproduced through partying during college.[16] Anthony Abraham Jack demonstrates how elite universities reproduce class and racial inequality through university practices and cultural norms.[17] Blake Silver illustrates how racial and gender inequality is reproduced as students embody and are policed to maintain stereotypical gendered and racialized behaviors.[18]

What these studies reveal is that universities are not neutral in their organizational and cultural practices and processes. This should not be surprising, as universities were created to educate elite White, Protestant, heterosexual, cisgender men. Scholars describe these histories and sedimented practices and processes in different ways. The sociologist Victor Ray describes these practices and processes that maintain racial inequality in organizations as "racialized organizations."[19] In the context of education more specifically, scholars describe these institutions as having "historic scaffolds of Whiteness" and being imbued with "White institutional presence."[20] These terms describe the way educational institutions were created for White people and how White cultural practices, norms, and epistemologies became and continue to be the norm. Other scholars describe organizations as "gendered" and "heterosexualized," referring to how organizational culture, practices, and processes create gender inequality and reinforce heteronormativity.[21] In various ways, these scholars all point out the invisible organizational histories, practices, processes, and norms that favor certain groups while creating various forms of inequality and disadvantage for other groups. Universities are therefore inequality regimes that, importantly, stratify along *multiple lines of difference.*

A key way that universities become inequality regimes is through diversity regimes. The sociologist James Thomas defines diversity regimes as "the organizational meanings and practices that institutionalize a commitment to diversity."[22] Diversity regimes create and obscure inequality through the language and practice of "diversity." Notably, Thomas's account primarily focuses on how the language of and practices of diversity act as a mechanism for reproducing *racial inequality* in higher education. He argues that diversity regimes obscure racial inequality by "flattening" diversity through the inclusion of all sorts of difference, creating false equivalences between different kinds of social groups and social experiences of marginalization. I also observed this kind of "flattening" but to different ends. Diversity regimes do more than reproduce racial inequality: they are important for reproducing inequalities of all sorts and making sense of diversity struggles on campus.

As we will see, universities act as inequality regimes that perpetuate inequality along multiple lines of social difference through their approaches to diversity. To understand how diversity evolved to "flatten" across social differences and (re)produce various forms of social inequality, it is necessary to understand some of the history of diversity policies and rhetoric in higher education.

Diversity as Race and Beyond in Higher Education

Diversity discourse gained prominence in US higher education after a landmark Supreme Court ruling, *University of California Regents v. Bakke* (1978), upended universities' affirmative action admission practices.[23] Allan Bakke, a thirty-five-year-old White man, sued the University of California after being twice denied admission to the

University of California, Davis, School of Medicine. Bakke argued that the university's affirmative action policies unfairly rejected him on the basis of race. The university's admissions policies designated a number of seats for racialized minority students. The university defended itself by arguing that its policies were necessary to address current and historical racial inequality, increase the number of physicians who were not traditionally represented in the medical profession, improve healthcare services for underserved communities, and create a diverse student body for mutual educational edification.[24] In finding against the university, the *Bakke* ruling transformed how racial diversity in higher education was framed.

First, the Supreme Court ruled that racial quotas were unconstitutional. But while the court prohibited racial quotas, universities persisted in thinking about racial diversity in *numerical* terms. Indeed, universities' attempts to obtain a "critical mass" of racialized minorities was a primary point of contention in subsequent court cases.[25] Second, in the *Bakke* decision, Justice Lewis Powell Jr. articulated what became known as the *diversity rationale*—the view that race can be considered in college admissions as long as it enhances the learning environment by creating a diverse student body.[26]

Although the University of California provided various reasons for its admissions policies, the educational benefits of diversity became the *only* legitimate reason race could be considered in admissions. In breaking from earlier framings of affirmative action that emphasized remedial action, such as through racial quotas, for historical discrimination and exclusionary laws and policies, Powell's opinion detached the inequalities that racialized minorities faced from history.[27] Rather than validating the university's claims that its admissions policies redressed historical wrongs, Powell argued that the approach placed an undue burden on White students who were innocent of any wrongdoing.[28]

In repeated challenges to affirmative action, the courts defended race-conscious admissions by emphasizing the diversity rationale. In 2023, however, the US Supreme Court's ruling in *Students for Fair Admissions v. Harvard* and *Students for Fair Admissions v. UNC* made race-conscious affirmative action practices on colleges inadmissible. The diversity rationale was found wanting. In a post–affirmative action world, scholars and activists are beset with the difficult task of reimagining diversity and creating alternatives to diversity discourse that can lead to social equity in college settings.

Yet, for many years, various scholars have demonstrated how an emphasis on diversity fails to bring about racial equity on college campuses. The sociologist Sarah Mayorga-Gallo argues that diversity is a type of *racial ideology* that helps people make sense of the material conditions and social relationships of racial groups. Diversity is a racial ideology that is White-centric, allowing systems of White supremacy to persist.[29] In saying "systems of White supremacy," I am not referring to individuals in white hoods touting narratives of White superiority but rather how people who are racialized as White have created structures that continue to systemically privilege their material success, psychological well-being, and epistemic standpoints while exploiting and dehumanizing Black and Indigenous people and people of color.[30]

Diversity and the diversity rationale as racial ideologies allow White people to claim that they appreciate racial difference without critically engaging with, let alone addressing, persistent systems of racial inequality.[31] The language of racial diversity allows White people and people in positions of power to create a veneer of racial harmony while simultaneously invalidating real experiences of discrimination and structural inequality.[32] By obscuring the social structures and historical inequality that shape the outcomes of different racial groups, the racial ideology of diversity allows a person to claim that they are not racist while ignoring how racist policies and systems continue to shape life outcomes.[33] In these different ways, diversity centers White people's material well-being, emotional responses to racial inequality, and discursive justifications for existing and persisting racial inequality.

Diversity as racial ideology thus makes invisible persistent systemic racial inequality and sustains systemic White supremacy, but focusing on diversity as *racial ideology* fails to recognize how "diversity" as a term is so capacious that it also includes social identities beyond race, such as gender identity, sexuality, religion, and more, including even inconsequential social differences.[34] In higher education, the expansion of diversity to include other social categories can be directly linked to the *Bakke* court case's diversity rationale, Reagan-era promises to dismantle affirmative action, and the growth of managerial perspectives of diversity that emphasized diversity's value in promoting productivity in organizations.[35] This big-tent approach to diversity demoted the interests of legally protected groups, which had originally been included in affirmative action campaigns because of their history of exclusion, in favor of including other types of social difference under the umbrella of diversity.[36]

Even before the 2023 Supreme Court rulings, then, a growing chorus of voices had critiqued the ability of diversity to capture the complexities of historical and systemic inequality faced by different groups.[37] In designing this study, I wanted to explore the limitations and potential of diversity discourse and practices across a range of settings in higher education, encompassing the experiences of students with different kinds of claims to a "diverse" identity. To do this, I interviewed students who either participated in diversity leadership or identified as Asian American or LGBTQ+ at a public secular university (West University) and a private evangelical Christian college (Christ College). Notably, these universities are situated in states that had bans on affirmative action even before the recent Supreme Court decision.

I draw on West University and Christ College's similarities and differences to show how contextual factors lend to specific conflicts over diversity. Contextual factors, such as a university's composition (or numerical representation of groups), a university's organizational structure (such as having a DEI office, having student organizations, being public or private), and culture (the embedded beliefs, values, assumptions, and ways of thinking that shape behavior) are important to the experiences of minoritized students.[38] They are also important to how students make sense of diversity, its possibilities, and its shortcomings.

In the following sections, I describe background information from conversations in the sociology of religion, Asian Americans, and gender and sexuality and how this study contributes to these conversations. This will help us make sense of how diversity and inequality regimes currently operate on US campuses and how they can be transformed.

Religion and Managing Diversity

Evangelical Christian colleges are becoming increasingly racially diverse.[39] Indeed, some Christian colleges have become majority minority institutions where racialized minorities outnumber White students.[40] Like their secular counterparts, they express a commitment to diversity; some have also employed high-level diversity administrators and created diversity offices. Despite these advances, evangelical Christian colleges often have a fraught racial history of opposing efforts toward racial integration and imposing color-blind approaches to racial tensions on their campuses.[41]

Evangelical Christians often draw on *racial reconciliation* to address issues of race. Racial reconciliation emphasizes interpersonal relationships and unity through faith rather than political engagement to bring social change.[42] Racial reconciliation, moreover, promotes a color-blind approach to race by overshadowing the significance of race in favor of shared religious identity. This combination—downplaying racial inequality and emphasizing the individual over sticky systems—is neither color-blind nor race neutral. Instead, it reflects a White racial worldview that maintains White racial dominance and racial inequality in evangelical Christianity.[43] Those who may argue for a different approach to race—one that recognizes racial injustice and the need for political action—may find their perspectives suppressed in favor for racial reconciliation.[44] Racial reconciliation is also prominent on Christian campuses, where students may learn about the importance of racial reconciliation as part of valuing diversity without addressing broader systems of Whiteness and racial injustice.[45]

Most scholarly studies of diversity discourse and practices in Christian higher education, like studies on diversity in secular colleges, focus on race to the exclusion of other forms of social difference.[46] The exception to this involves the status of LGBTQ+ individuals. Popular accounts of both Christian colleges and conservative Christian denominations often present evangelical Christians as being at odds with LGBTQ+ groups, but issues of gender and sexuality are complex and intersect with religion in ways that do not fit easy popular narratives.[47] Christians hold multiple views on sexuality and gender identity.[48] The sociologist Dawne Moon and colleagues, for example, find that LGBTQ+ conservative Christians are able to challenge the gender binary by putting forth new narratives that draw on religious authority.[49] For example, LGBTQ+ Christians may argue that God created and intended sex/gender spectra and that humanly created sex/gender binaries are not essential to the teachings of Christianity. At the same time, religious organizations often construct cisgendered realities, making it difficult for nonbinary and trans* individuals to be fully included, regardless of the aforementioned perspectives.[50] This cisgendering or cisnormativity refers to how people who experience congruence between their embodiment of gender and sex and what they were assigned at birth are culturally and institutionally constructed as the norm at the erasure of trans* and nonbinary identities.[51] Religion, therefore, offers discursive resources and organizational practices for constraining and empowering gender identity and sexuality, as it does for race.

Ideas of "the secular," like religious commitments, also structure ways of understanding and managing race, gender, and sexuality. Saba Mahmood's study of minorities in Egypt shows how secular governance produces new minority identities, and the contributors to a recent volume edited by Jonathan Kahn and Vincent Lloyd explore how secular forces discipline race.[52] Joan Scott argues that gender is a key way secular actors draw lines between religion and secularism while overshadowing the long history of gender inequality in secular institutions and societies and the continued ways that it exists.[53] These studies indicate that the secular is not neutral to race or gender but instead, like religion, plays a role in constituting gender and sexuality through cultural discourse and organizational practices.

A focus on how the secular extends and constrains racial identities, gender identities, and sexuality is understudied and undertheorized. This is largely a consequence of what Charles Taylor calls "subtraction stories" that have shaped imaginaries of the secular, turning the secular into anything that is no longer considered religion, rather than recognizing the secular as its own system of sacreds and taboos that cannot be divorced from forms of governance.[54] A focus on subtraction stories, moreover, fails to recognize how distinctions between religion and the secular are actively constructed and often in opposition to one another, even as scholars note that secularism has distinctly Western Christian roots.[55] Studies on secular governance often focus on how religion is reoriented rather than how other social categories such as race, gender identity, and sexuality are managed and transformed through secular institutions and contexts.[56]

In this book, I extend scholarship on religion and secularity by comparing diversity discourse and practice in evangelical Christian and secular contexts, particularly how diversity intersects with organizational structure to constrain possibilities of diversity, equity, and inclusion. I show that students are critical of both secular and evangelical approaches to diversity as difference and diversity as numeric. While diversity discourse takes different forms on secular and Christian campuses, students recognize a shared assumption of abstract equality. While universities may try to maintain equality among diverse groups, this practice of diversity as equality among differences is not implemented in practice.

Asian Americans in Higher Education

When popular news outlets focus on Asian Americans at *elite* universities, it is easy for the public to believe that Asian Americans are overrepresented in higher education writ large.[57] However, this myopic focus on elite universities overshadows the reality that Asian Americans make up only around 6 to 7 percent of the US population and around 6 percent of overall college enrollment.[58] The majority of Asian American college students attend nonselective colleges, and their collegiate enrollment is concentrated in less than ten states.[59] It is true, however, that Asian Americans have the highest collegiate enrollment rate and graduation rate among racial groups in the US.[60] Further, over 50 percent of Asian Americans have a baccalaureate degree or higher, in comparison to only around 30 percent of the overall US population.[61]

The relative success of Asian Americans has inspired public and scholarly attempts to explain their educational outcomes, many of which lean on structural and cultural arguments. Structural arguments point to selection patterns in immigration, such as Asian Americans' use of H1-B visas, which prioritize immigrants in specialty occupations, to explain their relative success. The sociologists Jennifer Lee and Min Zhou put forth the idea of "hyper-selectivity" to describe immigrant populations that have above-average educational attainment in comparison to their sending country and their host country. For example, in 2010, half of Chinese immigrants in the US had a bachelor's degree, in comparison to only 4 percent of adults in China and around 30 percent of adults in the US.[62] Asian American success in higher education may reflect these patterns, as parental education and socioeconomic status are often strong predictors of children's educational outcomes.[63]

The educational outcomes of Asian Americans and their purported overrepresentation in higher education is often tied to the *model minority myth*, the idea that Asian Americans have gained success, and even surpassed White people in some outcomes, through cultural values that emphasize self-discipline, hard work, and education.[64] The model minority myth rose in tandem with the culture of poverty narrative in the 1960s.[65] Emphasizing the experiences of poor Puerto Ricans and Mexicans, the anthropologist Oscar Lewis argued that these groups had developed a culture of poverty that included dependency, feelings of fatalism, the inability to defer gratification, and hostility toward institutions.[66] Compared to the culture of poverty, the model minority myth held up Asian Americans as a group that had developed a superior set of cultural values that allowed them to get ahead.[67] Both the model minority myth and the culture of poverty narrative thus explained poverty and socioeconomic attainment through essentialist cultural values rather than systemic inequality and how culture is linked to broader institutions.

Myths like the model minority play a key role in producing racial hierarchies in the United States. The political scientist Claire J. Kim argues that cultural interpretations, like the model minority myth, are part of a process of racial triangulation that creates a racial hierarchy situating Asian Americans between Black and White people.[68] Racial triangulation places Asian Americans ahead of Black people, culturally, but still excludes them from political and civic arenas dominated by White people. This mirrors other conversations about racial hierarchies in the United States in light of the country's shifting demographics. The sociologist Eduardo Bonilla-Silva argues that East Asian Americans and other light-skinned racialized minorities will become an "honorary White" group that creates a buffer between White people and a "collective Black" group made up of Black people, dark-skinned racialized minorities, and Southeast Asian Americans.[69] The model minority myth and processes of racial triangulation ultimately maintain the racial status quo that keeps White people in positions of structural advantage and dominance.

The model minority myth also misrepresents Asian Americans as monolithically successful, despite well-documented differences in educational attainment, earnings, and poverty rates between groups with different national origins and immigration histories.[70] Some Asian ethnic groups may benefit from greater support for and during higher education but may not be included in support programs and policies to increase diversity due to their racialization as "Asian American" and the model minority myth.[71] For example, in supporting diversity, the National Science Foundation (NSF) does not consider Asian Americans and Pacific Islanders as an "underrepresented minority" in STEM (science, technology, engineering, and mathematics). Disaggregating the "Asian American" category, however, reveals ethnic disparities in STEM indicating that some Asian American and Pacific Islander groups would benefit from NSF support.[72] Therefore, while Asian Americans as a "race" may be included in diversity statements, policies may nonetheless dismiss them as monolithically successful, creating mixed messages regarding where they fit into diversity discourse and policies in higher education.

Asian Americans' educational outcomes, numerical representation, centrality to recent affirmative action court cases, and status as the "model minority" (even when acknowledged as a myth) raise important questions about where Asian Americans fit in existing diversity discourse and policies. Despite this, Asian Americans are surprisingly missing in studies explicitly focusing on *diversity* in higher education even as studies have examined Asian American experiences in colleges more broadly.[73] We ought to study Asian Americans in diversity discourse and practices for two reasons. First, although scholars have shown that diversity discourse obscures racial inequality, diversity discourse is still used for racial equity aims, and early diversity discourse was explicitly remedial.[74] Asian Americans are therefore a crucial case to study because they are racial minorities even though they exceed the average American in educational attainment as an aggregate. Second, the place of Asian Americans in the US racial hierarchy makes them a vital group to study for understanding the racial limits and possibilities of diversity. By examining Asian Americans, we can see how and to what extent diversity discourse and practices reproduce or challenge the existing racial hierarchy.

This book shows that Asian Americans approach their inclusion in diversity discourse with ambivalence, turning to their numerical representation and the model minority myth to make sense of their inclusion or exclusion from policies. Students' narratives reveal how diversity discourse and a focus on numeric metrics may insidiously refer to a racial hierarchy. Asian Americans may exclude themselves from campus diversity discourse and practices because of their academic success and numerical representation, at times using language that valorizes their own culture and performance over those of other racialized minorities. When Asian Americans (and others) rely on aspects of the model minority myth to explain why they should or should not be included in diversity discourse and policies, they engage in the process of racial triangulation. Diversity discourse and practices, in other words, can also reify the US racial hierarchy and maintain systemic White supremacy through racial triangulation.

LGBTQ+ in Higher Education

Although the LGBTQ+ population has become more visible on college campuses in the past decades, how many students identify as LGBTQ+ remains unclear. Universities typically do not include statistics on LGTBQ+ students in their demographics, and few universities collect data on sexual orientation and gender identity beyond a gender binary.[75] This uncertainty has several sources. Because LGBTQ+ identities were long underresearched, survey developers lacked a set of best practices related to these demographics. Asking demographic questions related to gender identity or sexuality could potentially out students and risk their exposure to homophobic or trans*phobic administrators, faculty, and students.[76] Furthermore, survey questions and response categories often inadequately capture the spectrum and complexity of gender identities and sexual orientations, and terms for these identities change and evolve rapidly.[77] These challenges have made it difficult to operationalize gender identity and sexuality on surveys.

Over the past decade, some universities have begun collecting more data on gender identity and sexuality.[78] For example, the University of Iowa was the first public institution to ask about gender identity and sexual orientation on its application, doing so in 2012.[79] More recently, the Common Application made changes to allow applicants to select "another legal sex" when asking about their legal sex and to select their own pronouns, but the Common Application does not ask questions about sexual orientation.[80] Asking about sexual orientation in applications, however, could aid universities in targeted recruiting in ways similar to recruitment efforts to increase racial diversity.[81]

From the end of the first decade of the twenty-first century through the second decade, large national surveys on college students began asking students about their sexual identity and gender identity.[82] Data from the American College Health Association estimate that 7.2 percent of college students in 2010 identified as lesbian, gay, or bisexual.[83] More recently, analysis of the Cooperative Institutional Research Program's Freshman Survey suggests that 8.5 percent of first-year college students are on the queer spectrum. The 2017 National Survey of Student Engagement suggests that a little over 5 percent are on the queer spectrum and a little less than 1 percent are on the trans* spectrum.[84] Whatever their specific numbers, LGBTQ+ students make up a significant and growing minority on college campuses. More people are identifying as LGBTQ+, with one in five Gen Z adults (people born between 1997 and 2003) identifying as LGBTQ+.[85] In 2020, nearly 10 percent of youth ages thirteen to seventeen identified as LGBTQ+.[86]

Despite growing public acceptance, LGBTQ+ students continue to experience discrimination and chilly campus climates, which shape their retention, educational outcomes, mental health, wellness, and more.[87] Advocates and scholars continue to argue for more data on LGBTQ+ students that track their outcomes, retention, and experiences of the campus climate, but data collection on this population remains uneven. Given the significance of quantification in *racial* diversity discourse and the importance of numerical representation for creating a healthier campus climate for minoritized groups, we need to consider how and to what extent quantifying diversity and numerical representation is significant to other social groups under the diversity umbrella, such as LGBTQ+ students, and what are the consequences of quantifying.[88]

The experience of LGBTQ+ students at conservative religious universities is of particular interest for this study. Students at these universities may face significant barriers to inclusion that LGBTQ+ students at secular universities do not, whether because of theologically conservative teachings on sexual orientation or because of lifestyle expectations that may prohibit same-sex relationships.[89] Religious universities may also apply for waivers to Title IX, the federal statute that prohibits discrimination in educational institutions on the basis of sex.[90] After the Obama administration expanded Title IX protections to include trans* identities, more Christian colleges and universities applied for waivers.[91] Title IX was rolled back under the Trump administration and expanded again under the Biden administration to include gender identity and sexual orientation.[92] Religious universities' ability to gain exemptions to Title IX through the Office of Civil Rights and the Department of Education make them not only culturally different in their religious orientation but also structurally different in their permission to discriminate.

Recent surveys suggest that 12 percent of students on Christian colleges do not identify as heterosexual, 30 percent have experienced non-heterosexual attraction, and 2 percent identify as outside the gender binary.[93] LGBTQ+ individuals attending religious universities struggle with isolation, institutionalized homophobic and/or trans*phobic policies, and possible expulsion, and they often report feeling afraid, experience bullying, and remain closeted. A sizable minority have reported being exposed to conversion therapy from mental health professionals when seeking help.[94] In a random sample of colleges in the Council for Christian Colleges and Universities (CCCU)—a consortium of over 185 evangelical Christian colleges and universities in the United States and internationally of which Christ College in this study is affiliated—researchers found that all included explicit bans on homosexual relations.[95] Furthermore, the majority of CCCU campuses do not have LGBTQ+ student groups.[96] Perhaps surprisingly, 45 percent of Christian universities more broadly have officially recognized LGBTQ+ student groups, and 55 percent included sexual orientation in nondiscrimination statements.[97] Yet, simultaneously, 79 percent of Christian colleges officially hold theologically conservative views on marriage and sexuality.[98] Therefore, LGBTQ+ students may face mixed messages about their inclusion through conflicting policies and organizational affordances. This raises important questions about how diversity and inclusion are imagined vis-à-vis university organizational structures, policies, and culture.

While LGBTQ+ students at Christian colleges face unique challenges, LGBTQ+ students at secular universities also struggle with chilly campus climates and lower educational outcomes.[99] When LGBTQ+ students encounter harassment, microaggressions, and chilly campus climates, this can negatively affect their academic performance and increase dropout rates and absenteeism.[100] This suggests that both secular and evangelical contexts are failing at cultivating greater inclusion for LGBTQ+ students. The reasons for this probably differ; however, little research has compared LGBTQ+ students on secular and religious campuses to examine the different or similar ways religious and secular universities may be creating exclusion or inclusion through diversity discourse and policies.

Given these factors, it is important to understand how LGBTQ+ individuals conceive of themselves in relationship to burgeoning diversity discourse and policies on religious and secular campuses for several reasons. First, as described earlier, existing scholarship on diversity discourse has tended to focus on *racial diversity* and how the language of diversity fails to create racial equity.[101] We know less about how other types of difference fit into the landscape of diversity discourse and the impact of diversity discourse on equity and inclusion for those groups. This is especially important because scholarly criticisms of diversity discourse often charge that a capacious understanding of diversity flattens group differences and obscures possibilities of *racial equity* without considering how diversity discourse may also fail (or succeed) in bringing equity to other groups.[102]

My findings show that LGBTQ+ students experience exclusion in different ways on secular and evangelical Christian colleges. At West University, their safety (and the safety of other minoritized groups) may be deprioritized in the name of preserving free speech on campus. Even though the university has made organizational changes for LGBTQ+ students, these remain incomplete across the campus. At Christ College, LGBTQ+ students are met with homophobic and trans*phobic policies. Students feel that the university prioritizes its donors and denominational affiliation over the safety of LGBTQ+ students. Ultimately, both campuses require reorientations in their organizational practices, policies, and culture if they are to achieve true inclusion for these students.

University Contexts

West University and Christ College share some similarities and differences that help us understand the limits of diversity. Table I.1 compares West University and Christ College's most salient attributes. West

University is a large land-grant university located in a state that banned affirmative action through a statewide proposition long before the Supreme Court's recent 2023 ruling. It is part of a consortium of public state universities that guarantee admission to top graduating high school students in the state while also providing a "local path" to mitigate inequality of education across high schools. West University enrolls approximately thirty thousand undergraduates. The undergraduate student body is composed of approximately 4 percent African Americans, 20 percent Hispanics, 34 percent Asian Americans, 27 percent White people, and 15 percent international students. Asian Americans, in other words, are the largest population on the campus. West University also ranks as one of the top fifty LGBTQ+-friendly campuses and has a center for LGBTQ+ students with professional staff members, multiple LGBTQ+ student groups, and housing specifically for LGBTQ+ students. West University's diversity statement and community values include various identities including race, ethnicity, gender identity, and sexual orientation, among others. West University also has a high-ranking DEI administrator and DEI office with ample opportunities for students to engage with diversity initiatives sponsored by the university. Outside of the DEI office, other offices on the campus promote dialoguing across difference and social justice. Students may apply to work in the DEI office and these other offices, engaging in event planning, facilitating conversations, and offering peer guidance.

Founded in the late nineteenth century, Christ College is a private university affiliated with an evangelical denomination. Christ College's creed maintains hallmarks of evangelicalism, such as belief in the authority of the Bible, the death and resurrection of Jesus Christ, and the importance of evangelizing. As mentioned earlier, Christ College is part of the CCCU. While Christ College does not require that its students attend weekly religious services, students are required to take courses on Christianity as part of their core curriculum. Like West University, Christ College has a high-ranking DEI administrator and DEI office. Christ College also has various centers on campus that support racial and ethnic minority students and is known as a strong proponent of racial reconciliation, with a center focusing specifically on racial reconciliation. Students may work for these centers in capacities of event planning, discussion facilitation, and ministry.

TABLE I.1. West University and Christ College's Attributes

	West University	Christ College
University type	Public	Private
Religious affiliation	None	Evangelical denomination
Full-time undergraduate enrollment	30,000	3,500
Percentage women[a]	53	67
Percentage undergraduates of color[b]	58	40
Percentage in-state	91	60
Tuition and fees (not including room and board)	In-state: $12,500 Out-of-state: $40,000	$40,000
Cost of room and board	$15,000	$12,000
Percentage awarded need-based financial aid, year 1	50	75
Percentage of freshmen in on-campus housing	97	92
Percentage of all undergraduates in on-campus housing	45	54
Number of applicants	80,000	4,000
Percentage accepted	17	85
Mean SAT (out of 1600)	1350	1160
Percentage graduating in 5 years	89	67
Student to faculty ratio	18 to 1	13 to 1
DEI office(s) and officer(s)	Y	Y
LGBTQ+ student group(s)	Y	Y
LGBTQ+ housing	Y	N
Racial and ethnic student group(s)	Y	Y
Racial and ethnic housing	Y	N

Note: This information was taken from university and peer university common data sets and websites. Summaries of attributes are elided across participating universities and peer universities to maintain university confidentiality. Numbers also reflect those from 2020.

a Nonbinary identities not provided in university common data sets.

b Percentage undergraduates of color does not include international students.

Approximately thirty-five hundred undergraduate students are enrolled at Christ College. Approximately 40 percent of the university is made up of racial and ethnic minorities. The incoming 2017 freshmen class was made up of around 11 percent Asian Americans, 16 percent Hispanics, and 5 percent African American students. While Christ College is not a public university, it is similar to West University in that it is also located in a state that passed a proposition banning affirmative action. Christ College also has student groups that coalesce around race, ethnicity, and other identities and interests. Like West University, some of these student groups host large cultural events for the campus. While Asian Americans at Christ College make up a visibly smaller group than they do at West University, they are nonetheless overrepresented in both universities, since Asian Americans only make up around 6 to 7 percent of the US population.[103] Christ College is also unique among CCCU campuses in having a recognized LGBTQ+ student organization, but it fits well into broader trends that show that a sizable minority of Christian colleges have recognized LGBTQ+ student organizations even as they maintain theological statements against same-sex relationships.[104]

I chose West University and Christ College to elucidate key differences and similarities that may affect experiences of diversity on college campuses. The *public and private nature* of these universities can shape diversity discourse and policies. As recipients of state and federal funding, public universities must abide by certain laws regarding nondiscrimination practices. Public universities can face litigation and lose funding if they violate these statutes. Some Christian colleges refuse federal aid, including financial aid for students, to avoid federal oversight.[105] Religious universities may also apply for and receive exemptions to certain civil rights laws, such as Title IX. Christ College receives federal financial assistance. In 2021, Christ College was included in a class-action lawsuit against the US Department of Education asking the courts to end Title IX exemptions. Overall, these structural differences can affect how and why diversity policies are implemented on campus as well as which groups are the focus of diversity initiatives.

The differences in *secular and evangelical context* are useful for elucidating how lines of difference are imagined and limited. At the time of the study, both universities had DEI administrators and offices, diversity leadership positions for students, and student groups that coalesced around racial or ethnic identity and gender identity and sexuality. (Christ College recently folded its DEI office into a broader student support office.) As scholarship suggests that both religious and secular institutions provide discursive ways of managing race and group differences, examining how these cultural resources are manifested in universities with *organizational similarities* (e.g., student organizations, diversity leadership positions) provides insight into how culture (religious and secular) might intersect with these organizational practices to produce different perspectives, practices, and experiences of diversity.[106] Furthermore, examining different groups—those that coalesce around race and those that coalesce around sexuality and gender identity—allows us to observe the limitations of religious and secular frameworks of diversity.

Numerical representation, also known as "compositional diversity," matters for diversity and campus climate. Although both universities may be racially diverse, they differ in which population is the largest numerically. White students are the majority at Christ College, while Asian American students are the largest population of the racial groups at West University. The difference in the largest racial populations on the two campuses is important for calibrating how numerical representation matters for issues of diversity and inclusion. Comparing the experiences of Asian Americans who are the largest population on a college campus with Asian Americans who are not allows us to examine how students interpret numerical representation in relationship to diversity discourse. Finally, keeping an eye on numerical representation and narratives of representation is important for understanding the limits of numerical representation for the inclusion not only of racial minorities but also of LGBTQ+ students.

Data and Methods

The arguments laid out in this book are built on the seventy-eight interviews I conducted with students who identify as Asian Americans or LGBTQ+ or who participated in diversity leadership at West University and Christ College during the 2017–18 academic school year. In addition to these interviews, I conducted several observations on both campuses among various student groups. Given my limited access to the groups across the universities, my analysis focuses on the interviews while drawing on my participant observations sparingly. I also interviewed a handful of faculty and staff at the helm of diversity work on their campuses, who provided useful background information on their universities. While their voices are important, I center those of the students to examine lived experiences of diversity and inclusion. On both campuses, I recruited students involved in diversity initiatives, LGBTQ+ student organizations, and Asian American organizations for interviews. While the majority of students interviewed at both colleges were currently enrolled, I also interviewed several recent graduates.

Both universities' DEI offices were founded within three years of when I conducted my research, making the offices relatively young. These offices emphasize diversity, equity, and inclusion in their branding, and both were created in response to controversies on campus. Students explained to me that an insensitive event at West University led to protests by student groups of color, who demanded a diversity office. At Christ College, a coalition of students of color released a petition for a diversity office to respond to systemic and historical discrimination on campus. Both universities responded by creating DEI offices and high-level administrative positions.

At West University, the DEI office provides funding for student groups and campus programs. In addition to hiring full-time professional staff in the DEI office, the university hires students to lead programs on campus as part of a student diversity board. These hired students described their responsibilities as communicating campus needs to the staff members, heading different projects and events, overseeing funding, and performing community outreach to students. These diversity student leaders are highly visible and listed on the DEI office's website. Besides the student diversity board, which acted as part of the DEI office, staffed dialogue groups and social-justice-oriented groups employ students to provide student leadership in diversity efforts by hosting intergroup dialogues on campus and addressing conflicts when they arise in dormitories. I recruited the student leaders directly via email and through snowball sampling. At West University, I interviewed a total of eleven diversity student leaders, all paid employees of the university.

The DEI office at Christ College employs a high-level staff member; however, the office is smaller and does not have teams and subdivisions as West University does, nor does it employ student leaders. Rather, students participate in other staff-facilitated programs that have a longer history on the campus. Programs that facilitate racial reconciliation and multicultural community on the campus were over a decade old when I started my fieldwork, and it is these offices that provide students with paid and unpaid diversity leadership opportunities. Student leadership emphasizing diversity and belonging is also oriented around student ministry and dormitory life. Although student leaders do not need to identify as Christian to apply or serve, some students interviewed felt that the university may still exercise religious discrimination in hiring students in contexts that involve providing Christian spiritual support. Unlike West University, where student leaders could be easily found on websites, some programs provided online information about student leaders, while the majority did not. I contacted the staff in these programs, who invited student leaders to participate in my study, after which I used snowball sampling. I interviewed a total of thirteen diversity student leaders at Christ College.[107]

While both universities have LGBTQ+ groups, the organization and number of groups differ. At West University, multiple LGBTQ+ groups exist, coalescing around racial and ethnic identities, religion, and specific interests, such as health and art. LGBTQ+ groups may also affiliate themselves with a broader coalition board, which hosts events and provides general programming. Iterations of this board have existed for several decades. West University also has a LGBTQ+ center, and many LGBTQ+ groups use its facilities and host their meetings there. Meanwhile, Harbor is the only LGBTQ+ group that exists on Christ College. Harbor only received official recognition within the preceding seven years of when I conducted this study, having previously been denied official status twice and meeting "underground" for several years. Due to the lack of a LGBTQ+ center at Christ College, I chose to interview students at West University who were primarily affiliated with student LGBTQ+ groups.

I recruited broadly through the LGBTQ+ coalition board and affiliated groups at West University. I emailed student groups affiliated with the coalition, requesting interviews and help to recruit for interviews. I was also able to conduct some participant observations with a religious LGBTQ+ student group at West University and recruited through my attendance. I interviewed a total of seventeen LGBTQ+ students involved with various LGBTQ+ groups affiliated with the coalition board at West University. At Christ College, leaders of Harbor notified their students of my study. Using a mix of snowball sampling and purposive sampling, I interviewed a total of twelve LGBTQ+ students from Harbor at Christ College.

Asian Americans make up the largest population on the campus at West University. The university has many Asian American ethnic affinity groups, ranging from general cultural clubs to those that emphasize very specific interests such as lion dance, martial arts, anime, and more. I recruited students through Asian Americans at West (AAW), one of the largest East Asian American student organizations on campus. Although AAW caters predominantly to an East Asian ethnic identity, the group advertises itself as pan-Asian, and its leadership reflects a diversity of Asian ethnicities and other racial or ethnic identities. AAW hosts general student-body mixers, which range from social to educational, participates in community service, and organizes cultural activities, such as Lunar New Year festivals and an annual cultural night that exhibits dance and Asian American history. I interviewed a total of seventeen students from AAW.

I recruited Asian American students at Christ College from various Asian ethnic student groups and primarily through snowball sampling. Due to the relatively small Asian American population at Christ College, I recruited from two East Asian student groups to maintain congruity with AAW. It should also be noted that, while AAW was very active, the Asian American groups at Christ College were struggling to meet regularly. During my time at the university, the groups did not hold any body meetings despite leaders discussing the possibility. Students attributed this to busy schedules and low numbers. I interviewed a total of eight Asian American students at Christ College. The majority of Asian American students interviewed at both universities were second-generation Asian Americans.

Terminology

I use the terms "queer" and "trans*" in addition to "LGBTQ+" and other terms my interviewees used. Some of these identities and terms readers may be more familiar with, such as "lesbian," "gay," and "bisexual." "Queer" marks the destabilization of gender and sexuality, moving beyond binaries of gender as well as heteronormativity and homonormativity.[108] "Queer" can therefore apply to both gender identity and sexuality. The asterisk at the end of "trans*" reflects the spectrum and various representation of different trans* identities, including those who identify as transgender, transitioning, and more.[109] Readers will also notice that if students specified various pronouns (e.g., she/they), I use both without prioritizing one over the other.

Despite the different ethnic identities recruited in my Asian American sample, I have chosen to refer to these students as "Asian American" collectively. I recognize that my sample includes a range of Asian ethnic identities that are not limited to East Asian identities, although these were the majority. Many scholars point to the dangers of examining Asian Americans at large without attending to their ethnic differences.[110] I have nevertheless chosen to refer to my sample as Asian Americans primarily because of how diversity is often associated with racial and panethnic categories rather than with specific ethnic categories. In other words, while a student may identify as Chinese, Korean, Thai, Vietnamese, or another Asian ethnic identity, they will largely be viewed, particularly in university statistics, as Asian. I discuss students' specific ethnic identities when it is relevant for understanding their narratives. Similarly, readers will notice that outside of discussing my Asian American sample, I often refer to students of various racial and ethnic identities as "students of color" and provide their racial or ethnic identity when it is relevant for understanding their narratives. I have chosen to do this to maintain the confidentiality of my participants—some of whom were quite visible on their campuses.

Finally, scholars of education usually call secular universities "nonsectarian" to describe the relationship between an educational institution and a religious institution, such that nonsectarian schools are those that are not affiliated with a particular religion. On the one hand, West University is nonsectarian in the sense that it is not affiliated with a religion. Christ College is sectarian in that it is affiliated with a Christian denomination. The term "nonsectarian," however, is primarily useful for describing an organizational configuration between a college and a religious body and less useful for describing the principles by which a school manages difference. Because of this, "secular" is a more accurate description, as it encompasses not only institutional configurations but also cultural ideals. Since I am interested in the cultural discourse of secularism and diversity and how it intersects with public and private contexts, I use the term "secular," rather than "nonsectarian," throughout this book.

Book Overview

The ensuing chapters of this book are divided into three parts. Part 1 explores the discursive contours of diversity on campus. Chapter 1 describes the three views of diversity—*diversity as difference*, *diversity as numerically quantifiable*, and *diversity as power and equity*. Chapter 2 moves away from how students define diversity in the abstract to how students respond to two diversity statements: one from a secular framework and the other from an evangelical Christian framework. Students' critiques of these frameworks suggest that there is an assumption of equality among "differences" in secular and evangelical frameworks of diversity.

Part 2 moves away from abstract frameworks of diversity to interrogate how the universities and students applied these frameworks in different settings and to different dilemmas on their campuses. Chapter 3 focuses on how diversity student leaders struggled in their aspirations for diversity as equity and diversity as difference through issues of speech at West University. Chapter 4 focuses on how LGBTQ+ students struggled for equity and inclusion at Christ College, including students' rejection of the idea of freedom of religion as a basis for discriminating against LGBTQ+ students. In chapter 5, we move away from specific flash points on West University and Christ College to examine the pitfalls of numerical representation as revealed through Asian American students' narratives of inclusion. Together, these chapters reveal the shortcomings and inequitable consequences of diversity as difference and numerical representation.

Part 3 focuses on LGBTQ+ students and Asian American students, examining the challenges and futures of diversity, equity, and inclusion for these groups. Finally, the concluding chapter provides some broad recommendations for how secular and evangelical Christian universities can move toward equity and inclusion.

PART I

Diversity Frameworks

1

Three Definitions of Diversity

I meet Erin at one of the common eateries at West University. Her dark hair, pulled back in a bun, is streaked with highlights. She wears a stylish black romper and bronze studs. Erin is a South Asian cisgender woman who plans and facilitates discussions on the campus as part of her role in diversity leadership. During our interview, she speaks confidently about how she measures diversity: "Whenever I consider, 'Is this space diverse?,' I always consider how many people there look like me. And that's in the sense of not looking like me specifically, not like South Asian or not like dark skin—just how many people there inhabit racialized bodies? How many people there are people of color? How many people there subvert traditional ideas of what their bodies should look like? Are there disabled folks? Are there LGBTQ folks and all of those things?" Erin's perspective captures two aspects of diversity: visibility and quantifiability. Diversity is something that can be perceived and counted.

Across state borders at Christ College, Reese laughs frequently and ironically as we discuss diversity. Wearing a bright blue hoodie with a flannel jacket over it, Reese makes me think of Joseph and his technicolor dream coat. Reese, who uses he/him and they/them pronouns, is a gay student of color involved with Harbor, the LGBTQ+ student group at Christ College. Reese shakes their head and gestures to the space we sit in as we speak about diversity and the experiences of LGBTQ+ students at Christ College:

> So, I think diversity is less of people of the dominant categories. At least less of their voice and more of their listening and more of their stepping back and just acknowledging. And I think diversity and equity are tied together. Like, I'm way past the point of equality. 'Cause like, no, I don't want equality. I want equity [*laughs*]. And diversity needs to happen on both a social and institutional level—like you can't just have one and ex-

pect the other to change by itself. . . . And it's not just like the ratio of LGBTQ students to straight students or White students to students of color. It's not just a number. It's work.

Reese emphasizes diversity's relationship to equity and power. They purposefully and adamantly eschew counting diversity as a number or ratio. Diversity, they assert, is the work that brings about institutional and social change.

Despite the apparent differences in Erin's and Reese's definitions of diversity, they also share similarities. Both students implicitly recognize that diversity is about difference—differences among social representation and identities. That difference can be seen and counted, but diversity is potentially much more than that. Diversity is also about transforming relations of power among different groups to produce social and institutional changes.

This chapter lays the foundation for the rest of this book by presenting how diversity is understood among students in diversity leadership, Asian Americans, and LGBTQ+ students at West University and Christ College. While we focus on students' definitions in this chapter, we will see later that universities also promote some of these definitions over others. How diversity is defined plays an important role in how people and institutions address inequality.[1] Scholarly studies of public definitions of diversity similarly emphasize difference, particularly social differences.[2] In a study of Fortune 1000 employees, for example, David Embrick found that respondents often discussed diversity through a laundry list of differences, including nonsensical ones, such as pet ownership or fashion choices.[3] Differences like cat or dog ownership dilute the meaning of diversity by detracting from how diversity can meaningfully refer to policies and practices aimed to bring about greater inclusion and equity for historically marginalized groups.

Students define diversity through frameworks of difference, numerical representation, and power and equity. Table 1.1 presents an overview of these different definitions and their implications. This chapter largely focuses on the "Features" row, with the other rows discussed when necessary. Subsequent chapters illustrate the implications of these features for organizational practices, inclusion, and equity. When students define diversity as difference, they reflect a flattened view of diversity that

TABLE 1.1. Features and Implications of Diversity as Difference, Numerical Representation, and Power and Equity

	Diversity as difference	Diversity as numerical representation	Diversity as power and equity (power analysis frame of diversity)
Features	• Diversity is a matter of social differences, including recognizable social categories, such as race, as well as differences in worldviews, culture, and perspectives. • Operates on an assumption of abstract equality among social differences. • Often justified on the diversity rationale.	• Diversity is quantifiable. • Can be (to a certain extent) visibly calculated or perceived. • Draws on language of majorities and minorities, probabilities of potential contact between groups, and numerical measures. • Operates on an assumption of abstract equality by making social difference quantifiable.	• Diversity is about recognizing historical and contemporary forms of social inequality that are embedded in social and cultural structures. • The goal of diversity is to bring greater equity to marginalized social groups and to transform relationships of power. • Rejects the assumption of abstract equality among social groups and across social difference.
Organizational indicators and practices	• Diversity statements. • Diversity offices. • Diversity officers and administrators. • Student organizations for all sorts of social difference. • Student organizations have equal access to university space. • University funding opportunities.	• Diversity statistics. • Diversity offices. • Student organizations for all sorts of social difference.	• Diversity statements. • Diversity offices that center equity. • Diversity officers and administrators. • Diversity statistics described through lenses of equity. • Student organizations for marginalized populations. • Changes to the university's structures and culture that bring about greater inclusion and equity.
Implications for inclusion	• All groups are considered equal and are assumed to have equal access to the campus. • Student organizations are available for different types of difference. • Exclusion in public and private universities has different legal ramifications.	• Some social groups are quantified, while others are not. • Some groups will gravitate toward numeric measures as a sign of inclusion, while other social groups will not. • Emphasizing visual cues makes invisible certain groups and intersections.	• Inclusion is not separable from equity and requires changes in the university's organizational structure and culture. • Exposes the normative assumptions about the ideal student embedded in the university's structure and culture that make inclusion incomplete or impossible.
Implications for equity	• Equity is not a concern. Rather, organizations focus on demonstrating and managing abstract equality among groups. • If equity is considered, it is done through bureaucratic means or within existing university limits that may reinforce social inequality rather than mitigate it.	• Numeric measurements of diversity can potentially support calls for equity. • Numeric measurements can perpetuate inequality by masking persistent inequalities on the campus and by suggesting that quantification is the best practice for measuring outcomes. • Interpretations of numeric measures can perpetuate inequality by creating inaccurate explanations about representation or outcome metrics, thereby preventing the equitable distribution of resources.	• Equity is a primary concern and must be addressed in relationship to diversity and inclusion. • Equity must be part of the organizational structure and culture. This means recognizing the normative assumptions of the university structure and culture and changing power relations.

equalizes social categories, backgrounds, and perspectives as "diversity."[4] When students discuss diversity through numbers, diversity becomes something that is quantifiable and often relies on visual cues to quickly gauge diversity. Other students recognize that a concept of diversity as difference is not enough to drive change. Rather, true diversity recognizes power imbalances and seeks systemic transformations that lead to greater equity. The sociologist Natasha Warikoo has termed this approach to diversity a "power analysis frame."[5] I use this term interchangeably with the idea of diversity as power and equity.

Although I present and discuss these three diversity frameworks separately, it is important to note that overlaps exist among these three. For example, all these understandings of diversity incorporate some understanding of diversity as difference. Those who use quantitative approaches to diversity can articulate aspects of a power analysis frame, and those who use a power analysis frame may argue for numeric measures of diversity that can support the need for structural changes. Students are capable of drawing on these different understandings simultaneously and in response to different situations. Therefore, it is best to understand these different definitions of diversity and their implications on inclusion and equity as ideal types that help us understand the contours, limits, and consequences of diversity discourse.[6] Teasing them apart allows us to examine each of the frameworks' implications for inclusion and equity, including their capacity to uphold or challenge the university as an inequality regime.

Diversity as Difference

The majority of students at West University and Christ College (sixty-two of the seventy-eight students) defined diversity as difference or one of its synonyms. Such differences included specific identities, such as race, gender identity, sexual orientation, and religion. Of these specific identities, over 60 percent discussed diversity in relationship to race and ethnicity. Race was the most frequently mentioned identity, second only in frequency to the idea of "difference." Around one-fourth mentioned LGBTQ+ identities. Approximately another quarter of my respondents defined diversity through the idea that "everyone comes from a different background," as did another quarter who described diversity as including "different views and beliefs." Diversity as difference, then, incorporates recognizable social categories as well as various perspectives and backgrounds. Diversity as difference is capacious enough as a framework that students sometimes described diversity as *all* possibilities of difference.

Students' recitation of "diverse" identities frequently echoed university diversity statements. Consider Freya's definition of diversity: "I think diversity is being inclusive of being all different sorts of backgrounds and identities, including gender, race, ability, sexual orientation, all the other different identities one can be, I suppose, and really making an active effort to include different people and to be aware of all the different identities people might come across. I think of just a melting pot." Freya, a queer cisgender woman of color, is a recent graduate of West University and was involved with West University's LGBTQ+ student groups as an undergraduate. She begins by defining diversity as the inclusion of different backgrounds and identities, emphasizing identities such as "gender, race, ability, sexual orientation" as examples. Recognizing that these identities can be limitless, she includes "all the other different identities one can be." The varieties of difference are key to Freya's definition of diversity. Indeed, she uses the word "different" four times in her quote.

Freya also draws on the well-known metaphor of the "melting pot." The idea that the United States is a "melting pot" is an old one that scholars have drawn on and critiqued for decades.[7] Often associated with immigration, the metaphor evokes the image of blending together social differences. The reality, however, is that immigrants to the US have often been forced to conform to the Anglo majority.[8] Freya was the only respondent to discuss diversity in relationship to a "melting pot"; however, two students drew on alternative food metaphors to explain diversity. Joyce, an Asian American cisgender woman involved with Asian Americans at West (AAW), described diversity as a pizza: "I think of diversity as when a whole of something is made up of different parts. So, there's like different groups, not just one pizza that's just bread. It's a pizza with peppers, mushrooms, a bunch of different things." Meanwhile, Helena, a Japanese American cisgender woman and a diversity leader at Christ College, pointed to different brands of chips to think about diversity:

> I define diversity as multiple different options. So, say if it's potato chips, a diverse amount of potato chips would be Lay's, Pringles, Cheetos, etcetera. You have all of that. Diversity would also be the same. You have like black, white, red, something like that. And I think if you happen to have one over the other, you can't help it if there's a sale on Pringles today or you just have an excessive amount of Pringles, but it's like you are still bringing in who you are, and it's better to have at least one there than the other. If you look at people [as a] group, it can get harder. Like, you only have me to represent Japan. That doesn't work, but I can do my best. It's better that I'm here than not, I think.

Rather than considering diversity as some kind of melting pot, these students consider the contributions of different social groups as discrete, rather than porous. Within this framework, Helena's reference to the distribution of different groups, or potato chips in her example, as something a person "can't help" is notable. In describing the greater presence of a chip's brand over another as the consequence of a "sale," she acknowledges that other forces and factors shape numerical representation, but she suggests that there is nothing to be done about those forces. We will turn to numerical diversity later in this chapter. In general, however, students did not draw on old metaphors or produce new ones to describe diversity.

While students like Freya discussed diversity in relation to enumerated identities and social groups, students also frequently perceived diversity as different beliefs and perspectives. Giselle, also a recent graduate of West University who was involved with AAW, asserted such a perspective: "I think diversity is the opportunity to, I guess, be exposed and have a greater understanding of different people and culture and attitudes and beliefs. And it's really broad, so I think everyone's idea of diversity is very different. I think a lot of people when they first think of diversity, they think first of ethnicity and nationality, but for me, I think diversity is those other things too that aren't necessarily . . . up front. It's going to be about attitudes, beliefs, and ideas." Rather than emphasizing a social category like race, Giselle considers diversity as "different people" and focuses on culture, attitudes, and beliefs. Although she recognizes that people normally think of ethnicity and nationality when they hear the term "diversity," she thinks diversity is not "up front."

By contrasting identities that are "up front" with a person's "attitudes, beliefs, and ideas," she recognizes that there is something instinctually visual about diversity even as her comments also encompass aspects of diversity that may be more discursive in nature. For Giselle, diversity is not only about social identities but also about one's views and beliefs.

When describing diversity as difference, students often relied on the *diversity rationale*—the view that diversity provides educational benefits—to justify why being exposed to difference was important and necessary.[9] Madelyn, an Asian American cisgender woman involved with AAW, put it succinctly: "I think diversity is both good and important because it brings many different aspects to the table. And in that we can learn from each other." Similarly, Tessa, a White, queer, cisgender woman who serves in diversity leadership at West University, stated, "I think diversity in experiences. And I think, by saying 'experiences,' you can encompass race and ethnicity. You encompass being, for example . . . commuter students—we're talking about nontraditional students who maybe have children, right? Bringing people from all those experiences together, that to me, helps create . . . diversity of thought—where we're engaging different people to actually question their previous beliefs, to maybe learn a thing or two that's different." Tessa's and Madelyn's views of diversity emphasize the importance of learning and being exposed to different views and thoughts. Tessa describes diversity through experiences, explicitly stating that the notion of experiences would encompass people's race and ethnicity. In this sense, Tessa is like the many others in my study who considered diversity as racial or ethnic difference. At the same time, however, Tessa ties this to specific experiences and diversity of thought, which ultimately allows people to learn from one another. For Tessa, then, diversity of thought is intimately connected to people's social identities and associated experiences.

At Christ College, Peter, a biracial Asian American cisgender man, explains how diversity helped him grow personally:

> I think it's important for growth, and I think, speaking from my experience—like, I've moved around a lot, and everywhere I move to, I will meet people who will come from different backgrounds, who come from different places than me, and that's really helped. I mean, it's challenged me at times, but it's helped me deconstruct things that needed to

> be but also helped me hold onto the things that were important to me. So, just for my personal growth and learning to be more open-minded and I guess living in community with people who are different from myself and having respect for other people.

Peter was born in Japan and spent over a decade of his life living in a rural area there before he moved to a city in the US. The switch from rural Japan to a private Christian high school in a bustling, diverse US city left an impression on Peter as to the benefits of diversity. The cultural differences challenged Peter and helped him "deconstruct" things in his life, which he later explained to me were things related to his conservative Christian upbringing. For Peter, being exposed to differences allowed him to grow personally.

Another group of students discussed diversity in relationship to "culture." "Culture" is a term that is related to, but distinct from, race.[10] Sociological definitions of race define it as a social construct that often emphasizes similar physical traits but is the product of social processes, power dynamics, and different historical moments.[11] In contrast, sociologists typically understand culture as customs, language, beliefs, tastes, values, and collective memories that are dynamically developed by social groups.[12] Culture can therefore be attached to racial and ethnic groups inasmuch as they are social groups, but culture can also be created by nonracialized social groups, such as gamers, punk rock musicians, religious movements, and sororities. In other words, culture's relationship with diversity is vague and capacious enough to indicate race while providing for other forms of social difference.

The Asian Americans I interviewed often mentioned "culture" in addition to "race" and "ethnicity," but the term rarely came up in my discussions with LGBTQ+ students and students in diversity leadership. For example, Steven, an Asian American cisgender man involved with AAW, defines diversity as "a wide array of different sort of things within . . . some sort of context": "There's diversity of ideas or, I guess, experiences. . . . Yeah, cultural, racial diversity, just means drawing from [a] lot of different sources in whatever sort of category." Similarly, David, an Asian American cisgender man at Christ College involved with an Asian American student organization, explained, "I think diversity can be in the context of race, culture, location, and all these different factors. Really, as a whole, I think it's all those factors together, but I think there's definitely different parts of diversity, like racial diversity or cultural diversity and . . . just different upbringings, I would say." Steven's and David's views of diversity draw on elements discussed earlier, such as the diversity of ideas as well as race. Even as they order their comments in ways that suggest that race and culture are distinct, both also use "culture" and "race" as interchangeable when it comes to diversity.

Why might "culture" be more salient to Asian Americans than to the diversity leaders and LGBTQ+ students? Although "race," "ethnicity," and "culture" are related but separate concepts, university policies on diversity sometimes use the terms interchangeably. For example, race-based groups at West University and Christ College are sometimes called "cultural organizations," adding to the fungibility of race, ethnicity, and culture. It is therefore not surprising that students in these "cultural" organizations sometimes call on "culture" in defining diversity. Students in the Asian American organizations on both campuses certainly understood themselves as not only a social group but also a cultural group where students of Asian ethnic descent could come together, while also providing a space for students who are not Asian to engage in elements of Asian culture. Indeed, students in these Asian American organizations held "cultural" nights or festivals that celebrated parts of their ethnic heritage, such as the Lunar New Year.

Of the very small minority of students involved with LGBTQ+ organizations or diversity leadership who mentioned "culture" as part of their definitions of diversity, all were students of color. But here, too, they were a statistical minority: the majority of students of color who were involved in diversity leadership programs and LGBTQ+ organizations did not talk about "culture." It is possible that they avoid the term because "culture" evokes old but persistent explanations of racial inequality that attribute inequality in life outcomes to pathological cultures rather than systemic injustices.[13] Indeed, in the US, particularly in the era of color-blind racism, commentators sometimes use the language of "culture" to invoke race while deflecting overtly racist discourse.[14] These students, in other words, may simultaneously be aware of the importance of culture to different racial or ethnic groups and of how political pundits, popular media, and some scholars have constructed some groups as pathological through "culture." As we will see in chapters 5 and 7, describing diversity as culture has consequences for how Asian Americans consider their numerical representation and inclusion in diversity on their campuses.

Overall, when students defined diversity as difference, they saw diversity as encompassing various social identities, backgrounds, and discursive perspectives. The frame of diversity as difference ultimately flattens social differences, backgrounds, and perspectives and reflects an assumption of abstract equality. This flattening suggests that all types of social difference, backgrounds, and worldviews are equally "diversity" and denudes them of their present and past histories of social inequality and stratification.[15]

Diversity as Numerical Representation

Numbers are a central part of how universities posture themselves as diverse.[16] Some students, too, defined diversity through numeric metrics. Scholars argue that numerical diversity, also known as "compositional diversity," is one of the key elements to a university's campus climate.[17] Numerical diversity or compositional diversity refers to the number of a certain group within the university's population.[18] Compositional diversity is important for minoritized students, in that meeting others like themselves can create a sense of community and shape their educational outcomes.[19] At the same time, relying on compositional diversity is one of the fastest ways for an institution, including a university, to measure diversity without necessarily transforming its organizational policies and practices.[20]

Natalie, a White cisgender woman who identifies as lesbian and is involved with a LGBTQ+ organization at West University, placed mathematics at the center of diversity: "I like to define it [diversity] in mathematical ways. It's like the chance that any two people in the group are different in a certain way, whether it be in race, gender, or different things, but the chance that any two are different, like randomly picked out of the group . . . but along many different lines of difference, if that makes sense." Although Natalie draws on the ubiquitous narrative of difference, she situates different identities in a diverse space through an understanding of mathematical probabilities. The idea of diversity as the probability of encounter requires one to know the composition of differences. To calculate this probability, we would need to know all the salient differences and their permutations to create a denominator from which a probability of encounter could be computed. The permutation of a group's differences could be endless; the framework assumes that all "lines of differences" can be identified and are meaningful in the same way. In this way, quantifying diversity also "flattens" social differences by suggesting that all types of differences can be understood through numeric metrics.

Natalie is not the only student to incorporate the language of quantification into her understanding of diversity. Ian, an Asian American cisgender man involved with an Asian American organization at Christ College, also described diversity through numerical terms: "I feel like diversity is kind of like when you look at a population, there's an equal ratio of different races, but not only the presence of different races to add to the diversity but also an understanding among all the races of each other's cultures and their mind-sets. I think that's what truly embodies diversity because just having—if you have, say, African Americans, Koreans, and White people together, they're all by themselves. They're all separate entities, but if they were all to understand one another, it would add more to the meaning of diversity in general." Ian defines diversity through the language of ratios. At the same time, he is clear that these ratios of different racial groups should be equal. Ian combines his numeric understanding of diversity with the idea of exchange among different racial groups, such that diversity fosters greater understanding across groups. Ian is, in effect, drawing on numerical understandings as well as aspects of the diversity rationale in which learning from others is central to diversity.

Leon, an Asian American cisgender man who identifies as gay and is involved in an Asian American organization at Christ College, begins by equivocating on a definition of diversity but ultimately turns to thinking of diversity in quantitative terms: "I don't really have a definition of it [diversity]; however, I would like to just walk into a room and see a majority of POC [people of color] and a speckle of White people. I see diversity as like, 'Oh, there's a group of Asians, but they're not all [the same] Asians. Some are Vietnamese, some are Korean.' That's what diversity is to me—generalizing a group from their looks, but they all have different backgrounds." Leon, like Natalie and Ian, draws on notions of diversity in terms of difference. His emphasis on surveying a room and considering the population's composition also echoes Erin's view presented at the beginning of this chapter. Both Leon and Erin underscore numerical representation, as counted by visible markers of difference. Leon considers diversity to exist when the majority of a group's members are people of color from various ethnicities. Erin also evaluated diversity in relation to the number of people who do not fit the norm, asking, "How many people there inhabit racialized bodies? How many people there are people of color? How many people there subvert traditional ideas of what their bodies should look like?" Helena's metaphor of the chips also fits into this framework.

These students' views of diversity include the narrative of diversity as difference discussed earlier, but they emphasize the most visibly perceivable and quantifiable aspects of difference, even if just in vague superlatives of majorities and minorities. Students describe walking into a room and perceiving if the majority of people in the space are people of color. The quantity of students of color, then, becomes a way to measure whether a space is diverse. But considering diversity through numerical thinking—such as minorities and majorities, descriptive statistics, and quotas—has its pitfalls. When students rely on their ability to visibly perceive and vaguely count identities as an index for diversity, they privilege identities that are visible through physical and cultural markers while subsuming identities that may be invisible.

For example, several students described having a mental illness as an important part of their intersectional identities, but their mental health status was not known to me until they offered this information. If I entered a room thinking only of visible forms of difference, I might not immediately consider diversity in mental health status, focusing instead on physical manifestations of difference, such as race or gender identity. If, on the other hand, I entered a space centered on discussing mental health, I might assume that there are people with diverse mental health statuses in the room. Even so, I might not know attendees' specific mental health statuses, and I would find it difficult to make a numerical calculation about who is represented. I might, however, be able to reasonably count gendered and racialized bodies in that space and consider the space diverse on the basis of what I perceive. As beings who make snap judgments about the people we see, we are not likely to depart from a perception-based notion of diversity (at least not completely).[21]

It is nonetheless important to recognize that perception-based diversity hides other social categories and that seeing and perceiving majorities and minorities go hand in hand.

Counting bodies is a provenance of what Michel Foucault calls "biopolitics" and, as such, is subject to institutional powers.[22] Although Foucault originally applied the term "biopolitics" to government bodies that count and regulate their populations, organizations like universities also make regulative decisions about their populations that shape their distribution of resources. Each year, universities collect and share data on their student bodies for the Common Data Set. The data collected in the Common Data Set reflect standardized items and draw on data standards from the US Department of Education. The Common Data Set provides demographic information on race and gender as well as other important information regarding graduation rates and cost of attendance. What is ultimately included in these data sets is a matter of deliberation, including feedback from participating universities and an advisory board.[23]

The Common Application, which a variety of colleges have adopted in their admission process, is another example of how what is measured and quantified changes over time. The producers of the Common Application recently opted to include nonbinary measures of gender identity but declined to collect data on sexuality due to the possibility of outing students.[24] For a group to be recognized as a social category and, thus, countable is a complex and contested process that often includes a mix of opposition activism and working with people in power.[25] Indeed, in the process of counting, institutions may create social categories—social identities that take on an ontological life of their own—as people begin to identify with these categories.[26] Making something a measurable category can create a group and make visible the invisible.

Diversity as Power and Equity

The majority of the students I spoke to at West University and Christ College defined diversity in relationship to difference and numerical representation. An important subset, however, also discussed diversity through what Natasha Warikoo calls a "power analysis framework." She defines a power analysis approach to diversity as "one that views the significance of race in society according to unequal power relations between groups. In particular it emphasizes the ways power operates through racial inequality. This perspective is consistent with a view of race as inherently based in group struggles for power. Those who see race through this frame often come to believe that individuals should actively resist the racial ideologies and injustices they perceive, as part of the broader goal of working toward racial justice and equality."[27] Although this perspective emphasizes unequal power relationships between *racial* groups, such a framework can be applied beyond race, where unequal power relations are also at work. One can easily replace race with gender identity or sexuality and ascertain the relevance of struggles of power and equality in Warikoo's definition. What is significant about this view among the students in my study is that it is a conception of diversity that moves beyond specific identities to relationships of power.

At West University, nearly half of the student leaders involved in diversity initiatives and nearly 30 percent of LGBTQ+ students discussed diversity through a power analysis framework. Alex, a White gender-nonconforming gay student involved in diversity leadership, discussed diversity in relationship to equity, using New York City as an example: "I'd like to think that diversity goes hand in hand with equity, but that's not always true. There can be diversity even if it's not equitable. . . . New York is very diverse, but it's still not equitable. If we compared statistics and think about it quantitatively, even though there is good representation of high and low class, we know that the low class is less privileged than the upper class. So, there's diversity there, and they're interacting and moving in the same space. . . . It's diverse, but it's not equitable." Alex hopes that diversity and equity go together, but they recognize that this is not always the case. When I ask what equity means to them, Alex explains that equity is "equal access" and that "each person regardless of their identity or their ability has access to the same goods and services." Alex's account also notably critiques numerical measures of diversity. They note that one can certainly quantify and look at statistics to observe differences in representation, but that does not get at issues of power and privilege. The power analysis frame of diversity critiques both diversity as difference and diversity as numerical representation.

Similarly, Dani, a queer student of color at West University, described diversity in terms of equity and reallocating resources:

> I define diversity by making sure diversity is equitable, not just equal. And that's like an apparent problem I see almost on a daily basis when talking about diversity or especially when talking about marginalized communities or talking about privileges. Whereas people with privilege, I've seen tend to gravitate more to treating people equal already, but that discounts, ignores the history of being oppressed and being disadvantaged from a long time ago. And so, already people are starting off at different levels, and if you just start with equal treatment, that just perpetuates and continues on the cycle of oppression. . . . It maintains those and solves nothing. If we really wanted to be diverse and really want to [have] justice, . . . then we should have equitable education, meaning that . . . resources are allocated to the most marginalized and then making sure they are on the same footing as different groups on campus.

Like Alex, Dani thinks that "real" diversity must be equitable. To them, equality is not enough because equality does not recognize forms of systematic and historical disadvantage that have left groups of people marginalized. Both Alex and Dani reject the abstract equality inherent in notions of diversity as difference and diversity as numerical representation. They argue that treating disadvantaged groups the same as advantaged groups does nothing to address the consequences and persistence of inequality. For Alex and Dani, equity is more than ensuring equal access to resources on campus; it requires providing resources for marginalized populations so that they might be on equal footing with other students.[28]

Students contrasted this approach to diversity with tokenism. The term "token" first arose in the 1970s as a way to describe women in professions dominated by men but has since spread to describe other settings and other types of minoritized identities.[29] Scholars consider minorities as tokens when they make up 15 percent or less of a largely homogeneous population. Such populations are likely to feel ostracized and isolated not only because of their numeric size but also because dominant groups may exclude them, treating them more as "symbols rather than individuals."[30] Students draw on the term to describe the presence of minorities in largely homogeneous groups that provide the illusion of diversity without deeper changes to the dominant culture, structure, and systems of power and status. By drawing on a power analysis frame of diversity to critique tokenism, students criticized diversity as numerical representation.

Wesley, a biracial Asian American who identifies as queer and serves in diversity leadership at West University, put it succinctly: "I think the fact that it's [diversity's] used as a token or like an image. I think really the hurtful things are when it is used to hide inequalities." Fred, a White, gay, cisgender man involved with a LGBTQ+ organization at West University, also described the tokenizing of minorities as a potential downside of university approaches to diversity:

> One bad thing about diversity can be when it becomes just fulfilling a quota and, like, when you treat people as tokens, like, "Oh, we just need to get more people of color. We need to get more queer people in this group." Then it becomes forced, and then I think you . . . might not treat them as fully with respect. You might just treat them as a check box, but that's not because of diversity itself. That's just the way it can be approached, and I think people just have to be aware when they're talking, like, "We need to be more diverse," to be careful not to do it like that.

In Fred's perspective, the goal of diversity is problematic when people interpret it as akin to filling quotas or checking boxes about different identities. Fred feels that when organizations and people implement diversity measures with those priorities, they may treat minoritized individuals not with respect but rather as a means to an end of appearing diverse.

Brett, a queer nonbinary student from an LGBTQ+ organization at West University, offered similar comments on diversity and tokens, particularly within corporate structure: "I mean, diversity is one of those things that can often be very easily tokenized. If we're talking about diversity within or in corporate settings, it can often be used as a pacification tool as opposed to effecting any real change in the company's structures or setting. So, in that way, I can see diversity as something that is symbolically helpful, but materially very little can actually change within it, just being diverse in itself." Like the other students quoted earlier, Brett sees the possibility of tokenizing minorities as a pitfall of diversity measures. Brett describes diversity as a "pacification tool" rather than something that might bring about material change. When I asked Brett to expand on what they meant by this, they explained,

> So often I think diversity is used by people who would be more critical of those systems to then go on and accept them because they look better, like, they look like a more equitable system for minorities, which is not actually true, right? We can have female CEOs who are just as advancing their classist views. . . . Like, making something more diverse itself I don't think leads to material change like we want it to. I think material change takes a lot longer and is a lot more systemic and effort, so then a group can use diversity as this pacifier against those who would be in a position who would be morally inclined to make those systems more equitable.

Brett explains that when an organization appears to be diverse, people may simply accept it without attempting to make it more equitable. They use the example of a female CEO, who, as a minority, adds diversity to the world of male CEOs but who nonetheless advances an agenda that does not challenge inequitable systems. Brett argues that diversity fails when minorities are included without any broader changes that bring about equity. This, to Brett, reflects tokenism and pacification rather than true diversity.

At Christ College, far fewer students defined diversity in relationship to a power analysis framework. Those who did were either involved with the university's diversity leadership or part of Harbor, Christ College's LGBTQ+ student group. Tom, a White, gay, cisgender man involved in Harbor, described the need to keep equity in mind when trying to make a space diverse. He described this in relation to integration efforts in the 1960s:

> It's hard because if it's [diversity's] not done, I guess with equity in mind, you can end up harming people. . . . Like, when schools were integrated from the '60s to the '80s, if you are a Black student coming into the integrated high school, you were still having a horrible time 'cause . . . it was kind of a botched integration. Like, the act of diversification is really, really difficult, and when it's not done right, it can end up harming people that . . . are supposed to be being empowered. . . . You can't just have a bunch of cis straight White men making all the decisions.

Tom feels that implementing diversity without equity can produce destructive outcomes. Tom uses the example of Black students entering a White high school with the goal of integration. As he explains, if Black students do not have power in that space, they will have a "horrible time." Tom goes on to describe the need to have minorities in positions of power to make decisions and change institutions, arguing against only having "cis straight White men" in positions of power.

Dana, a biracial, queer, cisgender woman who served in diversity leadership at Christ College, also drew on a power analysis frame to describe diversity as a "seat at the table":

> How do I define diversity? Mmm. I really love Solange's *A Seat at the Table*. I think it's hard to put words. I love metaphor, especially. So, I just love that term, and I think John Perkins uses it too. Just a seat at the table of recognizing that not everyone is given similar access. . . . But, yeah, I think it acknowledges that there's differences, and there are ways that we have othered people, but diversity calls us to look and see who is given the most power and privilege and isn't given a seat at the table and how to invite them in.

During her time at Christ College, Dana was involved with diversity leadership, facilitating discussions on race. Dana draws on the imagery of a "seat at the table," a term she attributes both to the performer Solange Knowles and to John Perkins, a Black evangelical leader, who has used it in discussions of racial reconciliation. To her, having a "seat at the table" means recognizing and addressing the fact that people who have been othered have had less access due to differences in power and privilege.

Dana clarifies that "having a seat at the table" is not about tokenism: "Tokenism. Like, even me saying 'we inviting'—that's a position of power in of itself. And so, I think when it's at its worst, diversity is asking . . . a lot of vulnerability and to teach, and that can just be exhausting and burn people out. And also [it] is a way to take knowledge and power and vulnerability to empower people who already have power, you know. I think diversity at its best is a seat at the table. I think of that as a round table. There's no head, and it's just talking and conversation and creativity." Dana critiques her own views of diversity while trying to clarify her power analysis frame of diversity. In opposing tokenism and using minorities to educate people in power, she criticizes the diversity rationale that often undergirds the diversity as difference framework. For her, a truly diverse table would not be stratified by power. There is no head at this table, no unequal balances of power. Instead, this "table" is a round table in which people are equal and no group is exploited for the interests of another.

That fewer students at Christ College described diversity in a power analysis framework as compared to students at West University may reflect the trenchant focus on individualism in White evangelicalism. The sociologists Michael Emerson and Christian Smith found in their study on Black and White evangelicals that White evangelicals focus on individualistic solutions to racial tensions, while Black evangelicals see the need for structural and institutional changes.[31] Christ College is a predominantly White university. Although Christ College has expressed a commitment to racial reconciliation, the concept in itself, with its emphasis on relationships between individuals and forgiveness, is a White framing of racial inequality that focuses on individual actions rather than systemic change.[32]

Despite growing concerns about racial diversity at Christian colleges, many Christian colleges, including Christ College, have developed diversity frameworks that do not include an acknowledgment of structural inequality and power relationships. Indeed, scholarship on students attending evangelical Christian colleges show that students of color and White students both value a process of racial reconciliation to address racial tensions, but students of color differ from their White counterparts in that they want to center issues of race within religious organizations.[33] Put differently, neither White students nor White leaders of Christian colleges see the necessity of addressing and centering issues of racial inequality within religious organizations. The lack of recognition of structural inequalities reflects the obstinate centrality of individualism among White evangelicals and reinforces systemic White supremacy on these campuses.

I completed my research nearly two decades after Emerson and Smith's work. Since then, scholarship has continued to show that racial reconciliation remains the dominant frame for understanding racial inequality among evangelicals. This is seen across congregations as well as evangelical Christian colleges.[34] To the extent that the racial reconciliation approach reinscribes Whiteness, it may be preventing students on Christian colleges—even students of color—from developing a power analysis frame of diversity.[35]

Two other aspects of the sample deserve comment. First, all of the students who described diversity in a power analysis framework, at either college, either worked in diversity leadership positions or were involved with LGBTQ+ organizations. Students involved in diversity leadership may be more exposed to ideas of equity and structural change because their positions work directly with the institution's structure. There may also be a selection effect at play: students who become leaders in diversity initiatives may already be more attuned to discussions of diversity that focus on equity. Students involved in LGBTQ+ organizations on campus may be exposed to power analysis frameworks through the activist nature of these clubs, which seek not only to provide a safe space for LGBTQ+ students to meet but also to provide services and advocacy for students. Indeed, Jonathan Coley's study on LGBTQ+ students on Christian campuses demonstrates that students often develop activist identities as they participate in these organizations, which provide them the tools for power analysis thinking.[36]

It is also notable that none of the Asian Americans interviewed on either of the campuses described diversity through a power analysis framework.[37] There are several plausible reasons for this. The majority of Asian Americans in my study are second generation. They are the children of immigrants whose families probably migrated to the US after the 1965 Hart-Celler Act. Although Asian Americans have lived in the US prior to the late twentieth century, more recent immigrants may not be aware of the history of Asian American exclusion, such as the Chinese Exclusion Act of 1882 or the Asiatic Barred Zones Act of 1917. Asian American students' lack of a power analysis framework may also reflect the absence of learning about Asian American history and the United States' racist immigration policies in their education.[38]

Nevertheless, the Asian American students at West University, in particular, are involved in exactly the types of ethnic organizations and coethnic relationships that the scholars Monica Trieu and Hana Lee have suggested may encourage Asian Americans to develop a critical consciousness.[39] AAW, for instance, has held events to educate its members on Asian American history and problems with the model minority myth in stereotyping. The fact that these activities do not seem to have sparked a power analysis framework of diversity may suggest that more is needed than learning about history. It may require the articulation of one's racial or ethnic history within a power analysis framework to help students move toward a critical engagement of power differences in race relationships in the United States.

Three Views of Diversity and Inequality Regimes

Students at West University and Christ College defined diversity in three ways: diversity as difference, diversity as numerical representation, and diversity as power and equity. Diversity as difference is the most common way that students define diversity, reflecting a well-known and established way of defining diversity across the United States and in different sectors.[40] Diversity as difference—as students defined it—encompasses various social identities and cultures as well as discursive perspectives and worldviews. Diversity as difference suggests that the items listed in definitions of diversity are all part of what counts as "diversity." Students' views help us understand how the university works as an inequality regime.

First, diversity as difference operates under a sense of abstract equality that flattens different groups and social perspectives by denuding them of histories of inequality that remain today. When students define diversity as difference, they fail to recognize these histories of inequality, and they do not discuss diversity in relationship to issues of equity and power for marginalized groups. Second, when students invoke diversity as difference, they also implicitly justify the presence of diversity through the diversity rationale—the view that diversity is beneficial because it allows people to learn from one another. This too fails to recognize how the educational benefits of diversity are unevenly and inequitably distributed and can contribute to the university as an inequality regime by naming social differences for the purposes of education rather than to ameliorate social injustices.[41]

Students invoke two different understandings of diversity as numerical representation. On the one hand, students rely on numerical metrics that allow them to describe diversity through the language of majorities, minorities, probabilities, overrepresentation, and underrepresentation. On the other hand, students describe this type of diversity on the basis of quick visuals that allow them to approximate the presence of majorities and minorities in a space. One does not, in other words, need to crunch numbers to understand diversity in this way. Students can simply perceive it quickly, based on visual cues that prioritize visible forms of diversity. But calibrating diversity on the basis of visual cues may make invisible certain groups, whose presence then become difficult for students to quantify. For example, studies show that students struggle to identify class diversity on their campuses.[42]

These ways of understanding diversity can walk the tightrope between equality and equity, thus perpetuating or resisting how the university operates as an inequality regime. When students quantify, they flatten groups so that they can supposedly all be operationalized and measured, so that numeric information can be generated. This is an act of abstract equality that can be found when diversity is understood as difference. At the same time, numbers can be used to help students understand issues of equity. For example, the language of underrepresentation may be indicative of a broader systemic issue. Students can also call for quantifying for equitable reasons, such as for recognition of their group or to gather data for equity reasons. Therefore, quantifying diversity sits uneasily between equality and equity. And as we will see in chapter 5, one of the biggest pitfalls of quantification is that numbers do not exist neutrally. Numeric metrics need to be *interpreted*, and those interpretations can reproduce inequality even if done in the name of equity.

Finally, a minority of students—none of them Asian American—articulated definitions of diversity through an equity and power lens. This power analysis framework suggests that diversity is not simply or only about social differences but is about histories of and persistent social inequality. Notably, students who held this perspective called for structural changes that recognize imbalances of power as well as cultural changes within their universities. Students directly denounced views of diversity as abstract equality by calling for diversity as equity. They also criticized the idea of diversity as something that can be numerically quantified when they contrasted the idea of tokens with a power analysis understanding of diversity. In many ways, then, this perspective on diversity critiqued the other forms. But while those students who hold a power-aware perspective of diversity are likely to resist the perpetuation of inequality regimes on their campuses, they are also constrained within their university contexts. Indeed, as we will see later in the book, students struggle to balance competing diversity claims. Implementing a power analysis frame of diversity requires continued vigilance, outer and inner examination, and indefatigable dreaming of better futures. In chapter 2, we move to specific ways that students respond to equality and equity in secular and evangelical Christian diversity statements.

2

Assumptions of Equality in Creed and Liberalism

"Is this your only copy?" Tom asks me as he scrutinizes the two diversity statements before him. "I'm very visual in my thinking." I tell him to go ahead and mark up the page. We spend the next ten minutes dissecting diversity statements from a hypothetical secular university and a hypothetical evangelical Christian college.

Tom is a White, gay, cisgender man involved in Harbor, Christ College's LGBTQ+ student group. Tom, who grew up in a Christian home, now identifies as an atheist. We draw diagrams as we consider forgiveness and reconciliation in the evangelical college's diversity statement. Tom explains, "I'm very pro-forgiveness even if the other person doesn't ask for forgiveness. I think that forgiveness can help you heal even if it doesn't do anything for them [the offending party]. But in situations of oppression [*Tom begins drawing the diagram*], you have the oppressor and the oppressed person, who is a square, and then you have God. You oppress the person, and then you also sinned against God. So if you get forgiven by God, that's good. You're at like half of the battle, but you also haven't done anything to relieve the oppression."

I nod. "Let me try to rearticulate." I take out my pen and add to Tom's diagram. "It's kind of like: this is fine [*I draw a vague circle around the vertical line between God and humans*], but then the problem is that there are structures beneath this [*I draw squiggly lines beneath the horizontal human-human relationship*] that are enabling this sort of oppression, right?"

Tom nods enthusiastically. "Yes!"

"So, it's not enough to say, 'Okay, forgive,' on this horizontal level if you're not doing anything to break this apart?" I point to the human-human horizontal with squiggles of structural oppression.

"Yes! Totally!"

Tom's diagram, representing the limits of forgiveness, argues that an emphasis on forgiveness as primarily a spiritual act does not address broader societal issues. Tom focuses specifically on the relationship between the oppressor and the oppressed, explaining that the evangelical emphasis on forgiveness does not do anything to "relieve oppression."

Tom and I continue to discuss the statements. Tom feels that if someone is discriminated against, it would be more difficult to demand accountability at the hypothetical evangelical Christian college because of the emphasis on forgiveness. Tom compares the language of the two statements throughout the documents. He feels that evangelical Christians would be uncomfortable with the language of tolerance and pluralism in the secular diversity statement. Tom thoughtfully pauses as he considers the secular statement. Although he prefers the secular diversity statement, he notes that the secular statement has problems as well. He wonders if the language in the statement means "respect[ing] people who are racist."

Tom's evaluation of the statements points to some of the major issues that arose for students in their evaluations of diversity statements from a hypothetical secular university and evangelical Christian college. This chapter investigates those student responses.[1] These diversity statements present explicit definitions and aspirations for diversity from a religious (evangelical Christian) and a secular framework. Because it is methodologically difficult to compare how students assess secular and religious languages of diversity, presenting students with an evangelical Christian diversity statement *and* a secular statement brings into relief the secularity and religious frameworks of the two statements, thus allowing us to examine both. People throughout history have actively engaged in constructing "religion" and "secular" as categories and institutionalizing them differently in the public and private spheres.[2] As a result, these categories are co-constructed and co-constituted in institutional patterns and practices in society. Critically examining how students respond to religious and secular diversity statements helps uncover the assumptions of these frameworks as students evaluate them together.

Institutional diversity statements are also important because they reflect how universities describe diversity for a public audience and may come from high-level administrative officials in the university.[3] Statements reflect the political, historical, and social situatedness of diversity discourse and are performances of self-image.[4] The statements used in this study are a conglomerate of official diversity statements from various institutions similar to West University and Christ College.[5]

I gave my respondents the following statements:

1. We believe that diversity is critical to the pluralistic university and can broaden and deepen the educational experience and the scholarly environment. We seek to foster open-mindedness, understanding, compassion, and inclusiveness among individuals and groups. We are committed to ensuring freedom of expression and dialogue, in a respectful and civil manner, on the spectrum of views held by our varied and diverse campus communities. We acknowledge society carries historical and divisive biases based on race, ethnicity, sex, gender identity, age, disability, sexual orientation, religion, and political beliefs. Therefore, we seek to foster understanding and tolerance among individuals and groups, and we promote awareness through education and constructive strategies for resolving conflict.
2. We seek to embody Christ's teachings of love and inclusivity across boundaries of racial, ethnic, gender, socioeconomic, class, age, ability, religious, and other expressions of human difference. Living out the calling and mission of Christ means living within diversity and practicing inclusion on our campus. We believe that all people, without exception, bear the image of God. Because sin has marred each individual, Christ, in His great love, chose to die on the cross for the sake of every person so that all may receive forgiveness for sin and be reconciled to God. Our pursuit of diversity involves fulfilling Christ's command to love our neighbors as ourselves. In submitting to the Lordship of Christ, we seek to eliminate attitudes of superiority.

The first statement reflects the diversity statement of a hypothetical secular university, and the second reflects the diversity statement of a hypothetical evangelical Christian college.

Students' responses to these "official" diversity statements allow us to see how they critically engage institutional diversity discourse and how they draw on the diversity definitions identified in chapter 1 in affirming or challenging the statements. Here, I focus on students' *cri-*

tiques of the evangelical and secular statements. This means that we focus on the voices of students who were critical of these statements. In doing so, I recognize that I am not sharing the voices of the many students who felt that the evangelical and secular frameworks ultimately wanted the same thing. This, however, does not deter from my broader argument. Indeed, by demonstrating that students critiqued *both* statements for failing to consider issues of equity, I show that *both* secular and evangelical approaches to diversity operate from a similar assumption of abstract equality. In other words, just as some students felt the hypothetical universities wanted the same things through uniquely secular or religious language, student critiques also show that both secular *and* evangelical language of diversity work through a similar appeal to equality.

Overall, student critiques suggest that both statements ultimately rely on an assumption of abstract equality in articulating diversity as difference. This insistence on abstract equality, whether voiced in secular or evangelical language, contributes to the way universities operate as inequality regimes. Secular and evangelical language can obfuscate equity for marginalized groups with religious creed and secular ideals. In challenging these statements, students drew on a power and equity approach to diversity to describe the shortcomings of religious and secular language of diversity.

Equality in Christian Creed

Understanding students' critiques of the evangelical diversity statement requires a brief detour through the narratives of students who defined diversity through explicitly religious language. This is to help us establish a "baseline" to compare students' criticisms. Most of the students who identified as Christian or attended Christ College did not draw on religion in defining diversity. Around 10 percent of the students on both campuses mentioned religion as part of their definitions of diversity, but only two students—both diversity leaders at Christ College—approached diversity in relationship to their Christian faith. For both students, diversity is intimately connected to God's intentions in creation. Mike, a White, heterosexual, cisgender man, explains, "I think diversity for me is the image of God in all people. And I think everyone carries different pieces of who God is in the way that they're made, so I think diversity is when all those different pieces are represented and just an understanding that the more diversity we have, the more we can see God." Mike considers diversity in relationship to the "image of God." In his perspective, every person reflects different aspects of who God is, and diversity allows people to see more of God.

Amy, a White, heterosexual, cisgender woman who takes pride in being a woman in STEM, explains diversity in relationship to God, creation, and evolution, saying, "I would define diversity, as a biology major first, as biodiversity within creation. I'm Christian, so I call it 'creation'—that we look around and we can see that all life forms are diverse. . . . My Christian perspective is that diversity is the very fabric of creation, that God has continually prioritized diversity in his creation. That's how I read stories like the Tower of Babel. I see diversity continually affirmed, continually affirmed throughout the process of evolution and various mechanisms of creation. I see diversity affirmed and affirmed and affirmed." While not using the idea of the "image of God," Amy's perspective holds that God created diversity and that God affirms diversity through the many life forms on Earth.

Amy's and Mike's focus on God's role in diversity emphasizes the value of diversity and each human being. Notably, their definitions of diversity could also be understood through the view of *diversity as difference*, even though they use religious language to describe and affirm the value of differences. They see difference as part of God's creation and what it means for humans to be made in the "image of God." Their evangelical Christian definitions of diversity do not engage with issues of power and equity. Rather, their definitions of diversity celebrate and affirm diversity, seeing all peoples as equally reflecting God's image and creativity. This celebratory and affirming approach not only is found among evangelical Christians but reflects a broader social approach to diversity and race in which inequality is overshadowed.[6] I present Mike's and Amy's Christian framings of diversity to suggest that explicit religious definitions of diversity reveal an understanding of diversity as difference that operates with an assumption of abstract equality among differences that is rooted in God's plan, God's image, and God's creation. In other words, Christian framings of diversity are similar to secular framings of diversity that assume equality among different groups.

Now we turn to students' critiques of the evangelical diversity statement to see how students observed equality operating through religious language in ways that deter equity. First, students drew on a power analysis framework and their own experiences at Christ College to argue that the evangelical diversity statement fails to engage with historical and persistent social inequalities. It should be noted that while these students rarely criticized the idea of equality per se, their focus on histories of inequality and oppression reveals an implicit rejection of abstract equality. Using a power analysis frame of diversity, students criticized the evangelical Christian language of love, reconciliation, and forgiveness for failing to lead to equitable actions.

Second, while students' rejection of equality was sometimes more implicit than overt, students explicitly identified the language of sin as a way of creating a veneer of equality that did not recognize the very real fact that there are oppressors and oppressed, perpetrators and victims. They felt that the language of sin does away with these distinctions, making everyone equal. This stands in the way of creating an equitable world. Third, students criticized the evangelical diversity statement for reflecting a White racial perspective. Recognizing the history of systemic White supremacy within evangelical Christianity, students felt that this history, and its persistence into the present, needed to be addressed.

Missing a Power Analysis Frame

A power analysis frame of diversity recognizes the importance of historical oppression and the inequitable distribution of power among groups.[7] This framework is most apparent in students' awareness of the diversity statement's silence on histories of oppression and the need to change society's structures. Given the prevalence of the power analysis frame among diversity student leaders and LGBTQ+ students, it was also mostly these students who described this missing framework. A handful of Asian American students also voiced this assessment. Students attuned to a power-aware understanding of diversity saw the lack of recognition of historical oppression as a glaring omission in the evangelical statement; they welcomed its acknowledgment in the secular statement.

Beatrice, a biracial student leader from Christ College who identifies as a cisgender woman and heterosexual, explained why she prefers the secular diversity statement over the evangelical statement. She draws on a power analysis definition of diversity:

> This part [in the secular diversity statement] is really important to me: "We acknowledge society carries historical and divisive biases based on race, ethnicity, sex, gender identity, age, disability," all of that. . . . That's the main thing missing from the religious statement, because I think, especially at Christian universities, there's a message of positivity. . . . "We're going to move forward and spread God's love" and all of that, but the problem with that is that you don't acknowledge that there are real problems that are continuing. . . . We've defined the problem [in the secular statement], we know the problem has happened in the past, we know it's still happening, and we're trying to be constructive about it and teaching about it, so we can move forward. Whereas, the religious statement, it seems more stuck, 'cause we've been hearing this for decades, . . . and it's again evading the problem. It's focusing on positivity and spreading God's love, but it's not actually acknowledging the problem.

Beatrice contrasts the secular diversity statement's emphasis on historical and divisive biases with what she perceives as the excessively positive message of the evangelical Christian diversity statement. What she sees in the statement is an unhelpful emphasis on spreading God's love that does not acknowledge the historical problems that continue to this day. Reflecting the love of God is a common mantra among evangelical Christians, but Beatrice argues that evangelical institutions, including colleges, often pontificate on the importance of spreading God's love without challenging the legacies of historical and systemic inequality.

Sam, a White cisgender man who works in diversity student leadership at Christ College, also felt that the Christian diversity statement did not adequately address issues of history, instead falling into the Christian mantras of reconciliation:

> The [evangelical] one has a whole bunch of issues. . . . So have you read the book *Dear White Christians* by any chance? One of the things the author talks about is the idea that when White folk engage in reconciliation studies, they pursue freedom without righting the wrongs that have been committed. And so, they almost demand it. So they say, "If you're angry

> at me, that's not right. You're not participating in reconciliation," but . . . they're not changing the consequences of history. And I feel like almost to an extent the [evangelical statement] is doing that, because it almost feels like it's pushing for "we need to forgive each other and sing songs together and be happy."

Like Beatrice, Sam feels that the statement tries to be positive—"sing songs together and be happy"—when what is really needed is to address the "consequences of history." Sam draws on Jennifer Harvey's *Dear White Christians* to describe his problem with Christian approaches to reconciliation. In this book, Harvey argues for the need to move beyond racial reconciliation to a paradigm of reparations. Drawing on Harvey's work, Sam lambasts the reconciliation framework for allowing White people to demand reconciliation rather than addressing the consequences of systemic racism. Through a power analysis approach to diversity, Sam recognizes how racial reconciliation emphasizes individual relationships over structural change and religious identity over racial identity.

Daniel, an Asian American student at Christ College who identifies as a cisgender man, felt that focusing on forgiveness failed to engage with society's problems:

> I grew up in the Christian faith, so I like putting Christ's love and intention as the ambition for doing that. . . . But I also see a lot of problems with it. . . . A lot of people say that Christ tells you to do stuff and when you don't do it, you are excused from not doing it because Christ forgives all sins, so it creates an excuse. Like, people who lie all the time go to Christ and say, "I'm sorry," but it doesn't change the fact that they're still lying every single day. So, it's just another thing on the list that they have to ask forgiveness for, not actually solve problems that are actually affecting people in various ways.

As a Christian, Daniel affirms the teachings of Christ to love others and seeks to root his motivations in Christ, but he also notes how aspects of Christian creed can prevent meaningful change and action. He thinks forgiveness can act as an excuse, such that one does not change their behavior or try to fix a society's problems. Like Tom at the beginning of this chapter, Daniel senses that forgiveness can be a problem if it prevents people from working toward meaningful change.

These creedal beliefs, such as love and racial reconciliation, deflect from the difficult work of addressing systemic inequality. Scholars have shown repeatedly that racial reconciliation fails to address issues of inequality and injustice and may in fact suppress those who want to engage in systemic change.[8] Love discourse, too, deflects from systemic change by emphasizing feelings toward marginalized people rather than engaging in the difficult work of social change.[9] When love discourse is propagated by people in power, it becomes a way of centering the emotions of the dominant group and their standpoints and deflecting difficult work.

Sin and the Impossibility of Equality

In addition to describing the lack of a power analysis framework that recognized inequality, students focused on the language of sin to describe how the Christian evangelical statement operates from an assumption of abstract equality among peoples. The language of sin creates a veneer of equality in which all people are equally sinners, but this overshadows the reality that there are perpetrators and victims, oppressors and oppressed. While this assessment overlaps with the power analysis framework described earlier, students' emphasis on the language of sin allows us to see the ramifications of a theological term for equality and equity.

Tessa, a diversity student leader at West University who is White and identifies as a queer, cisgender woman, explained,

> My immediate reaction is that the religious statement has no mention of sexual orientation, and a lot of the language—like every individual sins, all of our sins are equal—a lot of that language I have seen in the context of "All of our sins are equal, so if you accept that your homosexuality is as bad as murder, . . . is [as] bad as lying, but if you accept that your homosexuality is a sin and you renounce it, then you can go to heaven too." I'm skeptical of the way in which the rhetoric of God's love will be applied to individuals. . . . It doesn't specifically say sexual orientation, and that's something that has been an issue with different parts of Christianity in the present and the past.

After mentioning the lack of sexual orientation in the evangelical statement, Tessa immediately moves to discussing how evangelicals typically see homosexuality as a sin that is equivalent in its baseness to murder and lying, because all "sins are equal." The path to acceptance, then, is conditional on people renouncing their sin, in this case, their homosexuality. She is ultimately skeptical of God's love rhetoric in conjunction with this language of sin because some Christians reject groups, such as LGBTQ+ individuals, on the basis of the language of sin.

Dani, a queer student of color from West University, felt similarly, stating, "This [secular] one includes history. This [Christian] one doesn't. This [Christian] one's more like, 'Oh, we treat everyone equal,' and probably low down, low key, they're like, 'No, you're not equal.' . . . Um, 'because sin has marred each individual, God chose to die on the cross for the sake of every person,' which that has not been practiced historically. There has been the use of religion against different communities of color, and without acknowledging that, it's really almost hurtful, if you understand the history." Dani points out how the Christian statement is about "treat[ing] everyone equal" by suggesting that *all* have sinned and how God died on the cross for *every* person. However, Dani rejects this abstract equality by noting that Christian institutions have fallen short of extending that grace to everyone. For Dani, the evangelical diversity statement is wanting not just because the creedal language of sin does not equalize but also because historically, White people used religion against people of color and equalizing statements were not truly applied.

Similarly, Alex, a gender-nonconforming gay student who serves in diversity leadership at West University, noted,

> Immediately, when I read the Christian one, it's like I want to think that it has the same parts as the first one, but there's so much tied up with this idea of sin. . . . It says, "because sin has marred each individual." It makes me wonder historically, especially through Christianity, more people or marginalized groups of people have often been accused of being more sinful than the next person. So it makes me wonder, "Okay, if sin has marred each individual, then we should all be equal." But I feel like it doesn't really operate that way.

The language of sin, Alex notes, has a lot of baggage. On the one hand, if everyone has sinned, it seems to suggest that everyone is equal, but Alex observes that some are perceived as more sinful than others. In Alex's perspective, the diversity statement's assumption of equality in the language of sin is historically inaccurate.

Rae, who uses she/her and they/them pronouns and is part of Harbor at Christ College, also described their issue with the language of sin and equality, couching this within a power analysis framework:

> In the first statement from the non-Christian university, it acknowledges a lot of the problems with society, like how people might be discriminated against based on all these different things due to biases that are created by our society. And the Christian university statement seems to be . . . kind of saying, you know, "Oh, we love everybody equally, and we're all sinners, so we're all flawed." And I think this can be viewed as kind of implying that if people don't conform to their particular definition of normal, they might be more flawed than somebody else. . . . And I think that is kind of a challenging way to try and confront diversity.

Rae contrasts what they see as the power analysis framework in the secular diversity statement with the language of sin and love in the evangelical Christian diversity statement. They emphasize how the evangelical diversity statement's declaration of the universal nature of sin, while nominally promoting the view of loving all people equally, makes it difficult to address harm. Rae does not think this is the right way to approach—or, as they put it, confront—issues of diversity.

Beatrice, a Christ College student leader whom we met earlier, preferred the secular statement for how it acknowledged history and discussed her difficulties with the Christian diversity statement because of its elision between sin and perpetrating harm:

> Okay, so the mentioning of sin is supposed to be an equalizer, but it's doing the opposite. Because in discussions of race especially, there's definitely a perpetrator, like there's definitely an aggressor, and it's almost like it's trying to spread that sin to everyone, like, "Now we're equal. We're all going to share the problem," but not acknowledging that it was very one-sided for a great amount of history. . . . This line, "In submitting to

> the lordship of Christ, we seek to eliminate attitudes of superiority," . . . a lot of Christian superiority comes from believing that White men are the chosen ones, you know? White men's burden, all American history, and everything, and it just seems like the wrong way to implement that when it's automatically pairing that with attitudes of superiority.

For Beatrice, the fundamental flaw of the evangelical statement is that it fails to acknowledge that perpetrators and victims are not equal. After critiquing the language of sin in relationship to equality and racial oppression, she reflects on the line about "eliminating attitudes of superiority." Given that White men have historically viewed themselves as the chosen ones and other peoples as their burden, Beatrice sees this phrasing as deeply problematic. The phrasing implies that the burden of needing to eradicate attitudes of superiority is shared equally when, she argues, historically it was White people who believed they were superior to other racial groups.

These students' critiques of the language of sin consistently invoke the assumption of abstract equality between groups. Some students drew on a power analysis framework to critique this perspective, arguing that Christians have historically not applied this abstract equality to different groups. They felt that the language of sin obfuscates how people have marginalized, oppressed, and been perpetrators against others. When used in a university diversity statement, the language of sin and God's grace perpetuates the university as an inequality regime by favoring abstract equality between privileged and oppressed groups. These students reject the language of sin because it attempts to equalize people and is blind to power and equity. In chapter 4, we will see some of the contradictions of this equalizing in the treatment of LGBTQ+ students on Christ College.

The Standpoint of Whiteness

Students also considered whose standpoint was represented when evaluating the evangelical diversity statement. Specifically, students felt that the diversity statement reflected a White racial perspective that ultimately needs to be addressed. Dana, a biracial student who identifies as a queer, cisgender woman, was formerly in diversity leadership. She described the evangelical diversity statement in language that echoes Beatrice's and Tom's, but she also linked histories of inequality to the use of religion by White people: "I think there's definitely this kumbaya feeling of 'Oh, we're all God created.' . . . There's really, really great theology in the *imago dei*, but I think it can take on some colonistic ideals of 'Well, White people are the most successful. They have the most money, and so obviously, we're chosen, God's chosen.' I heard a lot of that language. . . . 'Well, everything happens for a reason. . . . Oh, we're all the human race. God created all of us equally,' but then they aren't willing to look at sociological economic injustices." Dana describes the evangelical statement as being overly "kumbaya." Notably, she affirms the theology of *imago dei*—the idea that every person is created in the image of God. Mike also drew on this term when defining diversity through a Christian framework; however, Dana notes that historically, a colonial interpretation of *imago dei* has justified White people as God's chosen people. While Dana appreciates the "really, really great theology" of *imago dei*, she rejects its appropriateness for a diversity statement, given what she perceives as the centrality of the concept to White people's oppression of peoples of color.

Other students also recognized the role of Christianity in perpetuating systemic White supremacy, such that equality among racial groups did not, and still does not, exist. Daniel, a cisgender Asian American man attending Christ College, notes, "[The] church for a long time championed the idea that White people were better than Black people, people of darker skin, that they were subservient, that they were part of the creatures that man was supposed to dominate, so that has a long history in the church. The church tries to wipe it away, sweep it under the rug, but its effects are still there. Like, it's predominantly been a White-dominated institution. It has used religion as a guise for inexcusable and inhumane things. That's kind of like what Western culture does."

Randy, a gay Asian American student who participated in AAW as well as an LGBTQ+ group at West University, also explained his troubles with the Christian diversity statement:

> But the problem for me, at least, with the second [Christian] one is . . . a historical notion of imperialism and the Crusades and the missionaries and the White man's burden of "Oh, all God's children are savages, and

> therefore, they need to be christened" and whatnot, and that's what happened to the Native Americans; that's what happened to the Chinese. . . . So when missionaries came, it's like they used the notion that God was this compassionate, . . . benevolent being. . . . What happened was that they were taking power from them, but they were just using God's name to do that. . . . [The secular statement] says that "We acknowledge society carries historical and diverse biases," and I think that is what is lacking from [the Christian one]. Because the thing is [the Christian diversity statement] kind of just assumes that . . . this religion didn't do anything wrong or that the people who follow this religion didn't do anything wrong, so therefore, we don't have to talk about it. And I think that that's lacking. . . . That needs to be discussed if you were to have a more updated Christian education system.

Both Daniel and Randy describe Christianity's role in oppressing peoples of color and its association with Western culture, colonialism, and imperialism. For Randy, the problem with the Christian diversity statement is that it assumes that Christians themselves have done nothing wrong that needs amending; however, histories of imperialism reveal otherwise. Daniel has a slightly different critique, noting that the history of these atrocities has been swept under the rug rather than addressed. Both students agree that a relevant Christian diversity statement needs to acknowledge the role of White Christianity in an array of historical ills, ranging from imperialism and colonialism to views of the White man's burden that led to the oppression of different racial and ethnic groups.

Alice, an Asian American student at West University, also expressed confusion over the Christian diversity statement, emphasizing the Whiteness of Christianity and the multiple interpretations of Christianity: "I feel like I'm very confused by the second one in that I think it's a very common idea now that when we think of Jesus, we think of a White male. And when we think of the pioneers of Christianity, we think about colonialism and we think about White males. I think it's totally fine in the religious sense to have your beliefs about diversity come from your scripture, but . . . I feel like the Christian scripture is so tied with Whiteness." For Alice, the presumed Whiteness of Jesus makes Christian values an odd springboard for a diversity statement. From her perspective, it makes sense and is "totally fine" for Christians to derive their beliefs from their holy scripture, but she also notes that scripture is tied very closely to Whiteness. This ultimately blunts the statement's power to address the concerns of a diverse student body and makes it particularly confusing to read as a person of color.

Randy, Alice, Daniel, and Dana all recognize that there is a racialized aspect of Christianity that has led to the White racial domination of other groups. Tom, quoted at the beginning of this chapter, also described reconciliation as a White approach primarily used by White Christians to demand forgiveness from people of color. Beatrice, quoted earlier, also discussed her concerns over the language of sin and White supremacy. These students' articulation of Christianity's association with White supremacy suggests that Christianity does not hold all races equal, whether in theology or in practice, in the past or in the present. Rather, Christian discourse and practice have often supported White interests over those of people of color. Ultimately, the evangelical diversity statement's lack of a power analysis framework, or any acknowledgment of the history of systemic White supremacy in Christianity, makes it difficult for these students to accept its legitimacy.

Overall, we see that students critiqued the evangelical statement for missing a power analysis framework. When students draw on a power analysis framework to reprove the evangelical diversity statement for failing to address historical and social inequality or Christianity's own failings in creating racial oppression, they are rejecting the notion of abstract equality. Equality cannot and does not exist unless histories of Whiteness, oppression of different groups, and persistent inequality are remediated. Although not all of these students articulated a power and equity view of diversity when asked how they define diversity, their evaluations of the evangelical Christian diversity statement reveal an awareness of how evangelical Christian beliefs can prevent meaningful action and perpetuate oppression and injustice. Ultimately, a Christian university's use of religious language can reinforce inequality regimes by insisting on the abstract equality of groups and failing to address histories of oppression and ongoing injustice and exclusion.

Equality in Secular Language

Students also critically evaluated the language in the secular university's diversity statement. Specifically, they focused on the liberal language of tolerance and the diversity rationale to reveal how these ideals, just like evangelical creeds, were not neutral. Students noticed how the liberal language of the secular diversity statement was not equal to all groups but instead prioritized and centered some over others.

Tolerance Is Not Enough

LGBTQ+ students and diversity student leaders at both West University and Christ College disapproved of the term "tolerance" in the secular diversity statement. Students felt that tolerance did not go far enough; thus, setting tolerance as the goal was a problem. Rather, language like "tolerance" perpetuates inequality regimes. For example, Greg, a gay cisgender student of color in diversity leadership at West University, explained,

> The word that kind of sticks out to me is "tolerance." . . . I don't think tolerance is enough, so that I would want to switch that word to "acceptance." . . . The second statement, the first thing that I thought was sexual orientation isn't in this list. But, I did like that it said, "To love our neighbors as ourselves." That is more accepting than [what] the other statement said. . . . There are parts of this [evangelical Christian] statement that I see and that I really wish the other university statement had elements of this, especially the "love thy neighbors as ourselves" component or "living within diversity and practicing inclusion on our campus." . . . Then, this one, the [secular] diversity statement, I think, it's really hard to get the intention of, because it's very manufactured and wordy.

As a student in diversity leadership, Greg is well aware of how West University, a secular university, uses diversity discourse. Greg does not think tolerance is enough. He wants acceptance.

Amy, a White, heterosexual, cisgender woman in diversity leadership at Christ College, calls for affirmation rather than "acceptance," saying, "I was intrigued by the word 'tolerance' because to me, that feels like

'I'm tolerating you,' and that's different from 'I'm affirming you,' which is how I think about inclusivity." Greg and Amy both desire something more than tolerance, though they disagree on what that additional level of inclusivity looks like. Although Greg immediately notices that sexual orientation is missing from the Christian diversity statement, he is moved by its emphasis on loving others and living intentionally toward inclusion. These sentiments convey a depth of intention that he thinks is missing in the secular statement's "manufactured" prose and from the idea of tolerance, so much so that he tells me, "This [evangelical Christian statement] would be the diversity statement that I would go with."

Erin, a cisgender woman of color involved in diversity leadership at West University, explained that she wants more than tolerance and even more than acceptance:

> [The Christian statement] placed it very much in context of like Christ and his teachings and all of that, but they spoke about love and things like that, which is a value that—not in a Christian way—but like a value that I also embody. Whereas the secular university was more about just like tolerance and things like that. . . . I want to celebrate difference, not just tolerate it. And acceptance is patronizing. I'm not something for you to accept. I don't exist for your acceptance. I will continue living and thriving even if you don't accept me. . . . So it's just talk about being celebratory. Talk about being joyful and all those things.

Erin appreciates that the Christian diversity statement affirms loving others, a value she also holds. She describes tolerance as something akin to accepting difference, but she explains that "acceptance is patronizing" and that she does not "exist for your acceptance." In arguing against acceptance, she recognizes that there is a power imbalance between those who are doing the accepting and those who are accepted. She wants neither tolerance nor acceptance but celebration and joy of difference.

Similarly, Katie, a White cisgender woman and lesbian involved with Harbor at Christ College, expressed her displeasure over the term "tolerance" in the secular statement: "The only thing with this one [secular one] . . . I'm less comfortable with is 'fostering understanding and tolerance,' which they're good things, but I think that most places need to go one step further and have not just tolerance but equity and compassion.

And so not just 'let's all get along' but let's solve the problems that were causing us to not get along in the first place." Although Katie feels that understanding and tolerance are "good things," she emphasizes equity and compassion and the need to solve the problems that create division. To her, the language of tolerance suggests a surface-level acceptance that declines to tackle deeper problems. Notably, Katie draws on a power analysis framework in her assessment of tolerance's ills by calling for equity and problem-solving. Her understanding differs from Greg's desire for acceptance and love, Amy's call for affirmation, and Erin's wish for celebration and joy. As numerous scholars have reminded us, celebration of racial diversity in and of itself does not rectify systems and structures of racial inequality.[10] In acknowledging this, I am not attempting to downplay the importance of celebration and joy for racialized minorities but rather reiterating that these need to exist in tandem with equity.

Dana, a diversity student leader at Christ College, expressed views similar to Katie's. When she began reading the statements, she paused to exclaim, "My gosh, the first one, there's so many key words. I think of White liberalism key words, like 'tolerance,' 'open-mindedness,' 'pluralistic.'" After reading both statements and critiquing the evangelical statement, she described her displeasure with the term "tolerance": "I think the 'fostering understanding and tolerance' really bugs me in the [secular diversity statement]. . . . I don't want to live in a tolerant society. I want to live in a[n] equitable society. And like, tolerance for me is also associated with color-blindness, and so, I think that's what bugs me about the first one." Like Katie, Dana wants equity. Dana takes a power analysis framework when she describes tolerance as a part of "White liberalism" that fails to move toward equity. Moreover, she ties tolerance to color-blindness, suggesting that she understands "tolerance" as racialized. Tolerance is what White liberals seek in relationship to people of color when they omit equity from their perspective.

Brett, a nonbinary queer student involved with an LGBTQ+ organization at West University, also expressed their discomfort with the term "tolerance." When I asked why, they explained,

> First of all, I think it [tolerance] does implicitly take the voice of the majority, right, 'cause tolerance usually means tolerance of a minority. Like, I'm not tolerant of straight people, but straight people are tolerant of—

> you know, that's how the word is used, so I think using the term "tolerance" ultimately emphasizes the experience of the majority in the group's function. And when people are being intolerant, it can sometimes mean, in terms of the majority, being not accepting of minorities, but in terms of minority being intolerant, it often means being divisive in ways that are combating systemic oppression. That is also a form of technically intolerance, but I think that has every right to be in a community if it ends up benefiting those minorities and making them fit better within the whole.

Brett's comments are striking because they are the only ones that bring up a numerical understanding of diversity in their critique of the diversity statements, but they do so in a way that serves a power and equity view of diversity. Brett describes tolerance as the posture of the majority group relative to the minority group. It is the majority that tolerates the minority, rather than the minority tolerating the majority. When the majority does not accept the minority, they are considered merely intolerant, but when the minority combats oppression, they are seen as intolerant as well as divisive. Brett upholds the validity of what might be seen as the intolerance of minorities toward the majority, arguing that they are ultimately fighting for a place where they can belong.

As Brett continues, he contrasts the secular statement's emphasis on tolerance with the Christian statement's invocation of love:

> I think the [evangelical] statement is looking to foster a community that is not tolerating other views or all other views can be held, but it's seeking to reshape itself and its individual components. . . . This image of loving your neighbor as yourself—that sort of diversity statement—I'm not sure if that has any boundary end point. It is just anything that models love is like that's what they're looking for, which I think is much more than just something like tolerance. . . . I think understanding and tolerance is not an endpoint. . . . Love, whatever that means, and embodied teachings of inclusivity. Like, I don't know what that means, which means that I am pushed to do something I am not familiar with. And I think I like that. I like the imagining of a community that I haven't really seen in operation yet. I think that it's a good image to follow for a university or just in general. . . . Like, love is a radical act, I think, but I think that's a necessary component of living as a community in this world.

Like Greg, Brett was drawn to the language of love in the evangelical diversity statement. For Brett, love is about imagining a community and pushing its boundaries. Brett admits during our interview that it may be uncomfortable, but that is part of what it means to be in community. Tolerance does not bring people together into radical community in the same way as love.

Here, students critiqued tolerance from various perspectives. Some students of color, such as Greg and Erin, felt that tolerance did not go far enough, and they wanted things like love and celebration. Other students faulted tolerance for failing to move toward equity, taking a power analysis approach. Scholars like Wendy Brown and Charles W. Mills remind us that the practice of tolerance and liberalism fails because of inequalities in power and the racial situatedness of these perspectives.[11] Ultimately, these assessments suggest that tolerance does not create equality among different groups but rather favors and reinscribes the people in power—whether those are the majority or White liberals who are able to shape racial discourse.

Let us now turn to students' evaluation of the diversity rationale. Their criticisms of the diversity rationale further reveal how the secular diversity statement is skewed in favor of the privileged and the people in power.

Who Is the Diversity Rationale For?

In chapter 1, students often justified diversity as difference through the *diversity rationale*—the understanding that diversity is desirable because it allows people to learn from one another.[12] The secular diversity statement included an explicit statement of the diversity rationale. While I focus here on students' critical assessments of the diversity rationale, it should be noted that some students wholeheartedly supported the diversity rationale in the secular statement. Eric, an Asian American, heterosexual, cisgender man at West University, felt that the diversity rationale was something more people could support than a religious perspective: "Perhaps in that [evangelical] university, they believe that it can broaden and deepen educational experiences as well, but the way they've written this statement sounds like their main purpose for attempting inclusivity is . . . because Christ asks that they do so. . . . Whereas, for the former, most everyone can identify and can resonate with 'broaden and deepen educational experience,' and that I feel more readily garners genuine support for this mission statement." Eric affirms the diversity rationale because he thinks it is something more people could support than a diversity statement based on religious belief.

But a number of other students took a position opposite from Eric's, describing the diversity rationale as itself exclusive. Drawing on the perspectives of a power analysis framework and marginalized experiences, these students observed that the diversity rationale does not operate in an equal manner for all students. Take Kevin, an Asian American cisgender man at Christ College, for example:

KEVIN: So, I think the main outline of what they're talking about is kind of the same, but for this [Christian] one focuses on the religious thing, and this [secular] one focuses on education and how it's going to broaden the educational experience. But yeah, I think this second one—religious colleges, I think they foster more of an inclusion based on Christian beliefs, but this [secular] one is just inclusion to, I guess, deepen the educational experience kind of thing. 'Cause this [secular] one, if you benefit—you need other people to benefit. This one is more of a beneficial thing, but this one is more like, we're different but we're together in Christ kind of thing, so yeah, I think that's the major difference I see here.

ESTHER: Yeah. In terms of these two different purposes—one being about the educational benefits, the other one maybe about fulfilling a Christian ideal of being all together—which of those sort of purposes is more compelling?

KEVIN: Hmm. I think this [Christian] one more than this [secular] one, 'cause I feel like [for] international students or other culture students, [it] does not really help their educational experience. They would maybe not understand. Perhaps there is no need for them. But I think [the Christian one] is more inclusive in terms of even—like, this one doesn't really talk about benefits and stuff. In that case, it's more compelling.

After reflecting on the different purposes of the statements—one being educational benefits and the other for building Christian community—Kevin explains to me that he finds the evangelical statement more compelling. Although numerous studies demonstrate the benefits of diversity to different populations, Kevin wonders aloud whether international students would gain anything from exposure to other students, implicitly suggesting that the educational benefits of diversity are not aimed at them.[13] He feels that the Christian diversity statement is more inclusive because it "doesn't really talk about benefits and stuff." When I probe again, he concludes by saying, "I guess they [secular statement] are saying the right thing, but broadening and deepening educational experience seems more like it's for a benefit than for inclusion purposes." Ultimately for Kevin, the secular statement's emphasis on mutual educational benefits seems to be at odds with its stated desire to create inclusion. The language of the educational benefits of diversity turns diversity into an instrument that benefits some rather than others.

Sam, who earlier scrutinized the evangelical diversity statement for emphasizing reconciliation rather than history and change, also felt that the secular statement's focus on educational benefits could be harmful to certain populations, specifically the LGBTQ+ population:

> I worry that when [the secular statement] talk[s] about education, and they're talking about tolerance among groups. A lot of issues among my friends who are part of the LGBTQ community on campus at Christ College is that they have not been able to find safe spaces in housing. And the argument that [the] school keeps bringing back is that "If we give you a space on campus that is safe for you or we'll allow you . . . to choose your roommates based off of who is affirming and who is not, that takes away space for conversation," and that is a very harmful thing because it places all the pressure of conversation on those groups that are being marginalized. And I worry that in this [secular] statement, that's what this school is proposing, that conversation is almost being demanded by those who are being marginalized by those of the dominant group. I think that while that space should be open for conversation, you can't demand that from every person, and you have no right to.

Sam draws specifically on his LGBTQ+ friends' experiences at Christ College to explain why focusing on the educational benefits of diversity could be harmful to marginalized populations. Emphasizing education puts the onus on marginalized populations to teach others while simultaneously putting them at risk. At Christ College, this has meant putting LGBTQ+ students in unsafe housing situations in the name of educating others. Elsewhere, scholars have documented the phenomenon that Sam describes. People of color in White normative and dominant institutions experience fatigue from always needing to educate White people on the realities of racism.[14] When they do educate others, they may be met with consequential backlash.[15] By centering marginalized groups, Sam critiques the diversity rationale, noting that it puts LGBTQ+ students and other minoritized students in harm's way by making them educational instruments.

Other students focused primarily on race in the diversity rationale. Nina, a White cisgender woman and diversity student leader at Christ College, explained, "That last part—'deepen the educational experience and the scholarly environment'—just kind of stood out to me in just the way Christ College views diversity—in a way of trying to enrich the education almost in a way that it feels like they're trying to use education to enrich the experiences of the White students at the university, while not taking care of the needs of the students who are minorities." Although only the secular diversity statement specifically mentions the educational benefits of diversity, Nina ties this perspective to her own experience at Christ College. Nina feels that Christ College's emphasis on the educational benefits of diversity primarily benefits White students. Diversity becomes a way of enriching White students at the cost of racialized minority students. Unsurprisingly, scholars have shown that racial diversity must often be "sold" to White people, whether in businesses or in schools, in ways that center the benefits of diversity while commodifying people of color.[16] While Nina does not discuss how this approach puts the onus of educating their White peers on students of color, she nonetheless recognizes that the emphasis on the diversity rationale fails to take seriously the needs of minoritized students.

At West University, Kyle, a heterosexual cisgender man of color involved in diversity leadership, also felt that the secular diversity statement's emphasis on the educational benefits of diversity was aimed at White students:

> I think the way that diversity became acceptable in universities was through the argument that it was beneficial for White people. . . . So it's not about being really snobby and feeling that you're trying to avoid the peasants and stay in my castle and be fancy and stuff. It's saying, "Oh, yeah, I can chill in the castle, and I can get along with the peasants." Like, "I can go to my frat boys and be cool, but I also go to the hood and know their music and their culture," and that is accomplished through White multiculturalism, but that mobility, that cultural mobility, is still an exclusive right that other people don't get. And so I think that's necessary in order for people to maintain their privilege and power while ducking the notion of "Oh, you're racist."

Kyle explains that diversity "became acceptable" by demonstrating its benefits for White people. Indeed, scholarship corroborates this perspective. As Natasha Warikoo shows, White students at elite universities described the educational benefits of diversity, but they did not want students of color to take opportunities away from them.[17] Kyle ties the diversity rationale to discussions of multiculturalism, specifically a type of White multiculturalism, that allows a person to maintain their privilege while also having a type of "cultural mobility" that allows them to disassociate themselves from racism. This cultural mobility and separation from racism is one of the hallmark failures of diversity ideology in bringing about meaningful racial change.[18] Ultimately, the diversity rationale benefits White individuals by allowing them to dabble in different cultures and claim that they are not racist while simultaneously maintaining their positions of power.

Although many students supported the diversity rationale, the evaluations here show that students see the diversity rationale as favoring some students over others. For Sam, the diversity rationale favors heterosexual students over LGBTQ+ students, forcing LGBTQ+ students to become educational instruments at Christ College such that they are denied protections in the name of education. From Nina and Kyle's perspectives, the diversity rationale centers the experiences of White students over the protections of racialized minorities. The diversity rationale, while sounding good, does not create an environment where people receive the educational benefits of diversity equally. Rather, it benefits some over others in ways that reproduce inequality, and it turns minoritized populations into educational instruments for the benefit of those who are already privileged and powerful.

Equality in Creed and Liberalism

I began this chapter quoting an insightful discussion I had with Tom. Tom and other students realized the shortcomings of both the evangelical diversity statement and the secular diversity statement. In different ways, they recognized that both evangelical Christian and secular liberal values of diversity have a veneer of equality but ignore the real social inequalities and injustices that different groups face. The evangelical language of sin, love, and forgiveness and the statement's lack of engagement with Christianity's own history of systemic White supremacy and oppressive history meant that the evangelical diversity statement did not approach all groups equally. Student criticisms of the secular liberal values of the secular statement also focused on the statement's assumption of abstract equality. An emphasis on tolerance and the diversity rationale implicitly favors the privileged and the powerful, making minorities—whether LGBTQ+ folks or people of color—educational tools for the dominant groups. Whether creedal language or secular key words, these cultural repertoires support universities as inequality regimes.

Students also recognized that there is no neutral standpoint for diversity. Both evangelical and secular language for diversity carries historical baggage and social implications that perpetuate social inequality and injustice. Although the language may appear neutral in treating different groups equally or calling for universals—such as tolerance and love—history and continued social injustice suggest that secular and evangelical ideals and their paths to implementation are not equal for everyone. Creedal language and secular liberal language are part of how inequality regimes are perpetuated in secular and evangelical contexts, including college campuses, by promoting equality over equity. It is also important to note that either evangelical or secular language *can* promote equality and equity. Indeed, students applauded the recognition of social inequality in the secular statement, and some students at West University appreciated the challenge to cultivate love in the evangelical statement. But students also wanted more than just words and frameworks. They wanted concrete action.

Diversity statements are important because they represent what universities value.[19] Students can then draw on these values to call for change when universities fail to live up to their ideals. Diversity statements are also examples of social documents, in that they are changeable, amendable, and therefore, a space to imagine new values and ideals of diversity. Indeed, students sometimes found possibilities for improving their own school's approach to diversity through the language of the framework of the other hypothetical university's statement. Greg and Brett at West University were drawn to the language of love in the Christian diversity statement, for example, and various students at Christ College were drawn to the secular university's language of historical inequality. Students used these different frameworks of diversity to comment on their own campus's failings, imagining different possibilities that could move their universities away from inequality regimes to equity regimes.

So far, we have focused on abstract definitions and critiques of diversity. In part 2, we examine how diversity as difference, diversity as numerical representation, and diversity as equity and power operate at West University and Christ College, moving from the abstract to the limitations and tensions of these frameworks as they are experienced and lived on campus.

PART II

The Limits of Diversity

3

Equality Without Equity in Speech at West University

I arrive at West University's LGBTQ+ Center early for my interview with Ben. It is a Tuesday afternoon, and the LGBTQ+ Center is noticeably quieter than the times I have visited in the past. Fliers for recruiting LGBTQ+-identifying students for research studies, including mine, are tacked onto a wall. Offices with glass windows line one of the sides of the center, through which I see full-time staff members typing away on their computers and speaking with students.

Ben arrives not long after I have settled down at a table near some comfortable couches. His black hair is touched with some blond highlights, and both of his ears are pierced with studs. Ben is an Asian American cisgender man who identifies as gay. He is part of an LGBTQ+ student group at West University that specifically caters to Asian American LGBTQ+ students. As we discuss issues on campus, he, like other students I spoke with, mentions an event recently hosted by West University's Republican student organization:

> [Conservative speaker] recently spoke here, I think maybe like two weeks ago.[1] And his presentation is, I don't know what you would call it, was on free speech. And I do believe that protesting them is protesting against racism, sexism, homophobia, xenophobia, everything. But I also think there's nothing you can do to stop them, at least at a public university. . . . West University as a public institution is getting its money from taxpayers. The sad reality is that Trump voters also pay taxes, so in a way, they pay part of West University, and they also I guess get access to West University, and it's kind of the administration has its hands tied. . . . I am pretty, like, confident that no administrator would want [conservative speaker] here, and what you want and what you get is very different.

Ben feels that there is no way to prevent racist, sexist, or homophobic speakers from coming to the campus because West University is a public institution. Although Ben is reasonably confident that the university's administrators do not share the speaker's views, he does not see them as having a lot of options for protecting students who might be harmed by the speech. As a registered student organization, the student Republican group can plan and host events, just like any other student group on campus.

The event in question sat heavily on LGBTQ+ students' minds that semester. The weekend before the event, Rian, a nonbinary and queer student of color, told me about their concerns and frustrations over issues of speech:

> I also wish that there was more discussion about free speech versus hate speech because with the whole [Republican student group] having this [conservative speaker] come in . . . and knowing his stance on trans* students and allowing him to be here and speak about trans* identities without like even being trans* himself or like queer at that point, but calling it free speech when it's not free speech. It's literal hate speech. There needs to be more discussion with I guess the [DEI office] . . . about the safety of specific marginalized communities on campus and like also taking a stance. . . . I understand if you're in administration, you're supposed to be like neutral about some things, but there are some things where it's like, "No, you don't get to be neutral about this because if you're being neutral, you're siding with the oppressor." So, that goes to show where you stand in terms of student safety.

Rian takes a less conciliatory approach than Ben to issues of speech on campus. Rian does not think that "hate speech" counts as "free speech," and they believe administrators can and should say and do something about it. For Rian, claiming neutrality reveals the university's place in perpetuating injustice.[2]

I started my fieldwork in the fall of 2017 at West University not long after a White supremacist of Unite the Right plowed through a group of counterprotesters with his vehicle, murdering Heather Heyer and injuring counterprotesters in Charlottesville, Virginia. The night before the planned rally, Unite the Right participants marched through the University of Virginia—a public university like West University.[3] Days before the planned rally, University of Virginia's president, Teresa Sullivan, reminded the university community that the members of Unite the Right had the right to exercise their First Amendment rights. She also encouraged the university's community members to avoid the gathering and the spectacle of confrontation that the Unite the Right rally organizers wanted.[4] After the violent demonstration, West University's DEI officer released statements condemning the violence, but he also maintained West University's own obligations to uphold freedom of speech.

Issues of speech repeatedly arose during my time conducting fieldwork at West University. Diversity student leaders described an array of incidents that occurred on campus: antisemitic and White supremacist comments posted in public spaces, a blackface fraternity party, the use of the N-word in a dorm birthday party, Black Lives Matter protests, protests of the Trump presidency, and more. Students told me that the event with a popular conservative speaker sponsored by Republican students sold out within the hour. Some students were planning to protest, while others planned a healing space. In the month prior to the event, the university's DEI office held a panel on free speech and released an informative guide on free speech on campus. In this context, students found themselves grappling with how to reconcile the good of diversity with the Pandora's box of free speech.

In this chapter, I focus on issues of speech and dialogue to highlight the tensions between *diversity as difference*—including diversity as differences in perspectives—and *diversity as power and equity*. Prioritizing diversity as difference over diversity as power via an absolutist approach to free speech is one way that West University reproduces inequality on campus. This approach, which suggests that speech should not and cannot be censored, rests on a legal interpretation of the First Amendment that highlights the university's role as a public institution.[5] US courts have narrowly defined when speech is not protected, and hate speech is not one of these categories.[6] An alternative interpretation—known as the "realist" position—puts more stock in the Fourteenth Amendment's Equal Protection Clause, which, when applied to public education, emphasizes equal access to education.[7]

West University's commitment to free speech has earned the campus a "greenlight" ranking from the Foundation for Individual Rights in Education (FIRE), which is given when a "college or university's policies do not seriously imperil speech."[8] West University also consistently ranked within the top 20 percent of colleges for free speech according to FIRE's standards.[9] The DEI office at West University plays an active role in promoting the university's absolutist free-speech perspective by releasing educational material upholding the university's commitment to the First Amendment. In fliers, pamphlets, and statements to students, the DEI office explains why the university cannot legally censor speech, even speech that some administrators and students may disagree with. Rather than censoring speech, students can use their own speech to express disagreement. This, too, is diversity—at least within the diversity as difference frame.

Students at West University struggled to understand, critiqued, and expressed discomfort and dissatisfaction with the university's legal absolutist approach to speech. Diversity student leaders, in particular, were stuck between a rock and a hard place. Some student leaders—particularly those who worked with the DEI office—recognized and reluctantly accepted the university's constraints as a public institution and the legal consequences of restricting speech. These students tried to balance equality *and* equity in speech by creating avenues for groups affected by speech to host alternative events while also allowing incendiary speakers to speak. Other student leaders held unwaveringly to a power analysis approach to diversity, recognizing that speech has humanizing and dehumanizing consequences. In their view, the access and ability to speak represent more than individual acts; they are the very result of social history and inequality. These students took a realist approach to speech. Unlike those with an absolutist approach to speech who believe in few restraints on speech, those with a realist approach argue that speech that intimidates and prevents the full civic participation of individuals, especially those belonging to marginalized groups, should be limited.[10]

Universities have grappled with how to maintain everyone's right to speech and nondiscrimination laws throughout US history, but they are now doing so within a publicly stated commitment to diversity and inclusivity.[11] For students, it is confusing for a university to invest in a LGBTQ+ student center while simultaneously allowing a known trans*phobic speaker to promote trans*phobic views on the campus.[12] Similarly, students found it inconsistent for a university to value racial diversity but then fail to punish a fraternity for hosting a blackface party.[13] The lack of alignment in purported values and action, especially when it came to issues of speech, is why some students question university diversity policies and vehemently argue that the university should be doing more to promote inclusion and equity.

Student Body Concerns Regarding Speech at West University

Throughout my interviews, it became clear that students at West University were concerned about the invitations of right-wing speakers to their campus. This was particularly so for LGBTQ+ students, who worried that extending a welcome to right-wing speakers whom the Republican student organization sponsored would cause harm not only to their community but also to other marginalized groups.[14] A minority of Asian Americans also questioned the supposed free-speech benefits of bringing these speakers to campus. When students objected to the presence of speakers who might target marginalized communities or spread bigoted ideals, student narratives reflected a power analysis understanding of diversity. They centered groups that were historically and remain socially disadvantaged in challenging speakers whose words they felt demeaned, dehumanized, and could incite violence against groups.

Aaron, a trans* biracial student at West University, described his concern over diversity and speech:

> I think that people can sort of twist the word [diversity] to make it mean the things that it doesn't mean. I don't like it when people say we need to include Nazis and White supremacists because "diversity." I do believe that we should listen to a lot of different viewpoints. But I also believe that . . . if you let those people take over, they're kind of just gonna stamp on everyone else's viewpoint, and it's gonna make the whole thing sort of collapse. So, I think that diversity in its real meaning is not harmful. But I think when people are sort of like, "You have to listen to my toxic viewpoints because 'diversity,' 'cause I'm making it more diverse," it's like, "No. You're trying to make us less diverse. You need to go away." So, I think you need to protect diversity.

Aaron rejects the idea that a university's commitment to diversity includes a free-speech absolutism in which all viewpoints are permitted.

Speech, he argues, should be regulated based on the consequences of the ideas espoused:

> I think in order for us to really live up to our First Amendment right to free speech, we have to be intolerant of certain viewpoints. We have to drive them out. . . . These White supremacists Nazi extremist people, they don't want free speech for everyone. They actively try to silence people of color, people with disabilities, LGBT people, women, all these groups. . . . I think that we need to look at the consequences of viewpoints acted out to determine how good they are. Like, for example, these Nazi extremist groups—we look at how they would want to act out these opinions, these viewpoints that they hold. It would result in the mass killing of millions of innocent people, billions of innocent people globally. So we can say that this viewpoint: not as good.

Aaron takes a power analysis approach to speech. From Aaron's perspective, the value of diversity needs to be protected from those who would use the term "diversity" to argue for the inclusion of dangerous ideas. He rejects the idea that people who espouse White supremacist views can claim inclusion through abstract equality, instead favoring equity and inclusion for marginalized groups.

Jacqueline, a biracial Asian American, bisexual, cisgender woman involved with AAW and other cultural organizations at West University, also spoke about her concern regarding free speech:

> Free speech I think doesn't apply when right-wing speakers are saying things like, "Oh, I think Jewish people should be dead," basically. Like, if they're basically neo-Nazi and if your speech at some point is actively like harming others or like actively saying, "Oh, it's like my opinion, but my opinion is that these people should not be alive or that these people are explicitly inferior" kind of thing, I think that kind of speech should not be protected exactly. . . . I don't think it's worth the resources to hold them [speaker events] there [on campus] . . . because you would have to like hold extra security too, because you're like, "Oh no, people are going to attack the speaker." . . . But in this case, like there's a reason why people want to protest this speaker, and it's because they literally think that women should only be in the kitchen or because they think Hitler

> was right kind of thing. It's like you don't need that here. There are other, more important things that you could host on campus instead.

Jacqueline takes a realist approach to speech, arguing that speech that actively denigrates the dignity, safety, and the lives of different groups should not be protected and allowed on campus. Jacqueline's description of the material cost to the university in hosting controversial speakers is also notable. Security for speakers can indeed be costly. The security that West University hired for the Republican student organization's event cost several thousands of dollars.[15] In some cases, universities have spent hundreds of thousands of tax dollars on ensuring the safety of conservative speakers and university property from protesters or violence that may erupt between different groups. For example, UC Berkeley spent $600,000 on an event hosting Ben Shapiro in 2017 and over $800,000 for Milo Yiannopoulos's canceled Free Speech Week.[16] Jacqueline feels that the university could put its resources to better use than expending it on security for speakers whose speech she feels should not be protected.

Sol, a gender-nonconforming student of color who identifies as pansexual and is involved in LGBTQ+ organizations at West University, felt similarly. When they reflected on the diversity statement from the hypothetical secular university presented in chapter 2, which included a commitment to ensuring freedom of expression dialogue, they noted, "I know a hot topic today is freedom of speech and how taking the example of [UC] Berkeley, how Milo Yiannopoulos . . . was going to specifically attack undocumented and queer and trans* people and release their names. . . . Berkeley was just going to let him speak and even though he's very much a White supremacist and all that. So if the university allows that stuff to go on, that really just attacks the populations that they're supposed to protect, then the diversity statement doesn't mean anything if they're not leading up to what they're saying." Sol sees a disconnect between a university's stated commitment to diversity and allowing speakers like Milo Yiannopoulos to come to their campus and target students from marginalized backgrounds. The lack of action to protect marginalized populations on campus leads Sol to believe that university statements about diversity are nothing but hot air. Sol's comments suggest that they endorse a power and equity approach to diversity in which the point of diversity is to ensure that marginalized populations can attend college without experiencing denigrating speech directed at them.

Willow, a cisgender woman of color who identifies as bisexual and pansexual and is part of an LGBTQ+ organization at West University, expressed ambivalence in describing the events at UC Berkeley:

> Well, I think UC Berkeley experienced a little bit of this with some alt-right people [who] came to campus to talk about their side. It's important to give everybody an equal platform because, you know, there's like First Amendment rights. Everyone has a right to talk. In that case, I feel like if you're going to be inclusive toward them, it's going to be hard because they're stomping on other people. So, it's hard to determine where is the line that you draw, if you should include everybody to give them a space to talk or when that becomes toxic to other groups. So, it's like gauging the balance between those two things. I'm still kind of like, *ugh*, but between both sides, like, should they have spoken on the college campus and caused riots and violence and talked down to other groups? Or like, do they have First Amendment rights that allow them to do that, and they should be able to talk and we should somewhat listen to their opinion at least?

Willow, in contrast to Aaron, Jacqueline, and Sol, is not sure how universities should manage speakers. She recognizes the absolutist and legal approach to speech, but she is also conflicted when speech "stomps" on other people. She does not know how and where to draw the line of inclusion for speakers when their speech has the potential to erupt in violence and "talk down" other groups.

As these students' comments show, campus controversies about the limits of free speech directly affect marginalized students' feelings of inclusion and safety on campus. Students, to varying degrees and using different language, expressed apprehension over how different groups—whether Jewish people, people of color, LGBTQ+ people, or others—might be denigrated or even outrightly attacked. In centering marginalized populations, students implicitly took a power analysis approach to diversity, yet the students' opinions about how universities should manage speech that could potentially harm marginalized groups were not unanimous. Even the students who agreed that universities should not allow hate speech on campus disagreed as to why. Aaron mentioned the need to protect diversity because of the consequences of speech, Jacqueline cited dehumanization and resource allocation, and Sol noted the hypocrisy of developing diversity statements and then ignoring them. Willow, on the other hand, struggled with the absolutist approach to speech and how to be inclusive of all perspectives, even those that put down others.

These students were not employed in diversity leadership positions at West University; rather, their views represent a "lay person's" perspective on how the university engages issues of speech. Let us turn now to how West University's employed diversity student leaders managed issues of speech and dialogue across difference. How do diversity leaders manage *diversity as difference*—difference that includes social identities as well as diversity in perspectives—with their own desires to see *diversity as equity and power*?

Responding to the Legal Framework of Speech on West University

West University's DEI office includes a team of legal scholars and lawyers. As such, when student leaders who served on the DEI office's diversity board described upholding free speech, they often did so relative to a legal framework of speech that prioritized an absolutist approach to speech.[17] This approach recognized West University's status as a public institution beholden to the First Amendment and stressed the legal ramifications that West University could face if it chose to censor speech. With public universities subjected to legal constraints regarding speech and growing resistance to hate speech among college students, diversity student leaders must negotiate and mediate these conflicts between the institution, its legal pressures, and the student body.[18]

Victoria, a student of color who identifies as a cisgender, heterosexual woman, and I had a lengthy exchange regarding how the DEI office approaches issues of speech. She described this legal approach:

> [The DEI officer] pretty much said that as a public institution, they have to allow for free speech. And he's saying that even hurtful speech—you know, it's very kind of unsatisfying answer—but even hurtful speech counts as freedom of speech. And that he can't say, "Don't say that," to

> students, but he can obviously say he takes a position against that, he doesn't agree with that, etcetera. But he cannot silence this group of people is what he was trying to allude to, because of their freedom of speech. . . . He brought up an aspect of the law saying that the reason for freedom of speech is to protect speech that people may not like. In fact, it's to protect, for example, speech that [the] government may not like, right? . . . However, it kind of poses a problem on campuses when, like what we've been talking about, students are attacked by these comments.

In representing the views of the DEI office, Victoria emphasizes the legal impetus of free speech. Her understanding, based on advice from the head diversity officer, is that the university cannot legally prevent people from speaking. Both the DEI officer and students can take positions on the views expressed, but they cannot legally stop speech they may disagree with.

Victoria explains how the DEI office has tried to create alternatives since they cannot ban speech and to help students who are disturbed by the presence of hateful speech on campus to express themselves:

> What we have done also is open a fund. So, say these students want to raise awareness on these issues and stuff. They have a fund through which they can access money. They apply for it and everything. They access money, and they can have their own events. . . . So, there was an event [on illegal immigration] that was really hurtful. . . . It was hosted by the [Republican student organization]. . . . The use of the term "illegal" is also dated. It's hurtful. It kind of makes people who are undocumented feel as if their very presence is not legal, and you know, most people are under the understanding that no human should feel like they are illegal. . . . We couldn't take the event down because of freedom of speech. . . . But what we did do was open this fund for students to access, and what they did was they hosted an event in which a lot of students who were undocumented were able to speak and say, "Hey this is my experience," and kind of talk about their trials and tribulations of being undocumented. . . . So, in that sense, we didn't shut down someone else's event, but instead, we used resources to uplift our own motivations. . . . So, that's an example of what we've done to compensate that discrepancy that we can't shut down another event.

Rather than preventing an event, the DEI office provides funding for student organizations to hold alternative events where counternarratives can be shared. Student groups apply to the fund, and then Victoria and other members of the diversity board select which projects merit grants. By providing resources for marginalized students to hold separate events, the DEI office tries to create an avenue through which an understanding of diversity as power and equity may operate in tandem with diversity as difference—especially the diversity of perspectives.

When I asked Victoria how she felt about this alternative and the issues of free speech at West University, she emphasized standing with the legal framework but still feeling dissatisfied:

> I mean, he [the DEI officer] himself . . . admits to it, and I kind of agree that it's a very unsatisfying answer because you want something to be done. You want these people not to be able to say hurtful things on a campus that is supposed to be conducive to student growth; it's supposed to be conducive to us feeling safe. You know, he agreed that it's kind of unsatisfying, and I personally agree as well that it was unsatisfying, but I too have to put myself in the position of the law and have to put myself in the position of freedom of speech, and I, although it's an unsatisfying answer, I do agree that to an extent, we can't completely shut down events just because we don't agree with them.

Victoria sided with the legal framework, even as she found it lacking. Instead of banning hateful speech, Victoria looks to the creativity of other diversity leaders and the student body in lifting alternative voices. She continued, "But I do, on the other hand, think it's really important to find other ways—more innovative ways—to address—I call it a discrepancy—just to address this unsatisfaction with not being able to absolutely shut down events or inflammatory instances of student speech. And that's where I come in too. I need to put on and think and come up with those ways myself. And it's not an individual duty, but it's kind of like we should strive to brainstorm." In emphasizing that it is not an individual duty to address the "discrepancy" she perceives in speech but rather a structural and communal problem, Victoria implicitly embraces the tenets of diversity as power and equity. Providing funding for those who may be affected by such an event to host their own may be one way to rectify historical processes that reproduce inequality.[19]

Quinn, a gay student of color who identifies as a cisgender man, also described the difficulties of managing free speech:

> I think a big issue was, like, protesting on campus because students were still very, like, aggravated by the election [of Donald Trump] and still processing that, and so we had to kinda like confront . . . the boundaries of protesting and then also the boundaries of having speakers on campus, especially speakers that may inadvertently cause harm onto students and bring out hate speech and understanding the repercussions of hate speech. . . . We really wanted to address this issue and, like, have students be able to know that the [DEI] office, like, does have to protect the right to free speech but also does advise for students to use their right to protest and to really, like, use their voice and to come to the office if they have any issues.

Quinn's comments present the DEI office as a resource available to all students. The DEI office will not prevent speakers from speaking, but it will also encourage students to use their right of speech to protest whatever is being said.

After describing the DEI office's stance, Quinn reflected on how his work with the diversity board changed his own perspectives on speech:

> I think it made me think about diversity in a more understanding way, in a more broad way, because when it came to the [DEI] office, I was very much just, like, you know, like social movements and we need to protest and things like that, and then I realized, well, there are kind of repercussions to these sorts of things, and West University has to, like, really defend themselves in certain times and really stand up for all students. Like, just because one student feels some way doesn't mean that another student doesn't feel another way and that we have to equally represent our students. And we can't choose sides, and we have to be as neutral as possible and things of that nature, and I think I gained more of a neutral perspective about diversity.

Both Quinn and Victoria espoused an absolutist approach to free speech in their comments to me. Neither student started off with that position but rather developed it through exposure to the DEI office's legal rhetoric.[20] A legal framework treats speech through a perspective of abstract equality in which everyone, regardless of background, should have the right to speak, even if their words are ugly or horrific. Quinn calls this being "equal" and "neutral" to everyone's perspectives.[21] Because the university's position is that it cannot legally prevent a speaker from speaking on the basis of the content of their speech, the DEI office tries to lift the voices of those who may be targeted or harmed by the speech. In this way, the DEI office maintains its commitment to the abstract equality of diversity as difference while also attempting to promote equity by providing alternative avenues and resources for students who disagree with speakers.

These student diversity leaders who sat on the campus's diversity board frequently found themselves in positions where they had to articulate not only how the university should respond to an incident but why. They found themselves explaining why the university could not ban speech that other members of the campus community found offensive. Their descriptions invoked legalistic protocols and bureaucratic processes, rather than power or equity. Greg, a gay diversity leader of color, spoke with ambivalence as he described the operations of the diversity board to me:

> A lot of things happen to go unaddressed, even by board members. I know that one of the board members brought up a lot of incidences of antisemitism on this campus, and in my opinion, we failed to recognize them adequately. It's just troubling, and you have to balance, obviously. We have to balance, I think, how we address all issues. . . . There's a specific [event] that I think that there was a group that had an open [gallery], . . . and I think people would come write on it, and someone did end up writing something antisemitic on it, and this person that was on the [diversity] board pointed it out to us, and there was virtually no written response to this person. I didn't respond either. I would take ownership of that; but that's frustrating. I can understand how that's frustrating to that person, because they are representing students on this campus, and if they are telling us that this is a problematic statement towards the students on campus, then we all need to mobilize and get behind them.

Greg describes the diversity board's struggles to "balance" the concerns of students while also "representing" them. He feels the board failed to respond to this incident due to board members' own political stances toward Israel. Greg explained to me that he is very much on the side of Palestine in the Israel-Palestine conflict, but he also feels that the board ought to have responded to the incident.[22]

When I asked Greg how this could be improved in the future, he relied on protocols:

> I think the board would benefit from some kind of protocol in terms of these events. If someone is raising [a] concern, we . . . respond as a statement. But even as a board, there was no statement [on these] issues, which is frustrating. But it's also seeing how long it takes a statement to get through the board is also frustrating, and it's also, is this the best response we can do? If we're supposed to be representing students and we release a statement, . . . there's a degree of disconnect between the statement and the students, and that's what's already felt with an administrator releasing a statement.

Although Greg sees the usefulness of protocols with regard to bringing everyone on the diversity board to the same page, he also questions the utility of statements, recognizing that they leave students feeling disconnected and dissatisfied. Like Sol, Greg questions what diversity statements actually do for the lived experiences of students. Working within the constraints of the university and as a diversity board member, he is torn between the usefulness of bureaucratic protocols that would verbally condemn actions and the need for concrete action in creating a more equitable and inclusive environment on campus.

Victoria, Quinn, and Greg converge in their shared view that one way to address hate-speech incidents on campus is through more speech. In other words, while the DEI office cannot ban speech, it can sponsor events and release statements. Countering speech with more speech emphasizes every person's right to expression. This form of abstract equality, which views all speakers as being equally endowed with freedom of speech, embodies diversity as difference. Some student leaders, however, rejected this perspective in favor of an approach to speech based on the power and equity diversity framework.

Unequal versus Equitable Participatory Conditions of Speech

While the student leaders in the preceding section described their struggles with the process of managing issues of speech on campus within the legal and bureaucratic processes of the university, other student leaders criticized these policies as inequitable. These students focused on the conditions of speech and the social inequality of speakers and groups themselves. In doing so, they argued against the university's approach to abstract equality. They characterized it as power blind, not only toward the content of speech but also toward the groups hosting speakers and the speakers themselves.

Tessa, a White, queer, cisgender woman who is part of the diversity board and a facilitator for intergroup dialogue at West University, described true free speech as a matter of equity:

> I think that a lot of times in conversations about free speech, people neglect to examine institutional influences on free speech—just like the fact that if a trans*phobic speaker comes to campus, what they say is supporting a lot of laws that are already in place. It is also supporting a lot of violence that's already taking place. Allowing anyone to have a certain platform is not free speech. Because that's equality, not equity. I think free speech is about equity. I think oftentimes university debates don't look at that because they just look at like explicit barriers to speech and not like if a trans* rights activist wants to come and speak, to what extent are they putting themselves at risk. It's easier for some people to speak freely than others, and I think that that should be paid attention to.

Quinn's and Tessa's responses to issues of free speech reveal different approaches to equality and equity in speech. Quinn, channeling the university's legal position, focuses on the university's need to be equal toward all speakers. This means allowing speakers whose words may target and harm marginalized populations and countering the harm by encouraging students to use their own capacities of speech to respond. This is a form of abstract equality that undergirds valuing diversity as difference. Tessa, in contrast, focuses on equity by discussing access and barriers to speaking. Tessa illustrates her concern over equity by comparing the barriers a trans*phobic speaker would be likely to encounter versus those of a trans* rights speaker. The trans*phobic speaker will promote cisgender perspectives that support the existing status quo, while a trans* rights speaker faces more risk as a member of a marginalized community that often encounters threats and acts of violence.[23] Tessa recognizes that speakers come to speech with different privileges that lend them real differences with regard to possible repercussions for voicing their perspectives. For Tessa, free speech can only exist when the *inequitable conditions* of speech are addressed.

Similarly, Kyle, a student of color who identifies as a cisgender, heterosexual man and is also part of the diversity board, spoke with frustration over issues of speech: "If you don't have a framework of power, privilege, oppression, . . . you'll think that your experience is representative of everyone else, and you'll think that we're on equal playing fields, and you'll think that people have the same—we talk about this freedom of speech and the marketplace of ideas, but not all speech is equal speech. Not all speech is received equally. Some speech gets heralded and respected more than other forms of speech." Kyle actively rejects the metaphor of a marketplace of ideas—a common metaphor used in defending free speech—in favor of a power and equity approach to speech.[24] From his perspective, free speech is not equal because the marketplace is not fair or equal. Some speech receives more attention and respect than others due to the inequitable *norms* that govern speech and its evaluation.

Kyle specifically identified the type of speech likely to succeed in the marketplace as speech that conforms to a form of White masculinity. He reflected on this after reading the diversity statements presented in chapter 2:

> I get really irked by the "We are committing to ensuring freedom of expression dialogue in a respectful and civil manner." I think this notion of respectful and civil very much so centers Whiteness, specifically White masculinity, what it means to be respectful, what it means to be civil. . . . I'm not a big fan of saying an argument is invalid because it wasn't expressed in a respectable way. If you scream, "Black Lives Matter," I'm not gonna say you're wrong because you screamed it and I didn't like that you screamed it. So that's a big crux. And especially freedom of expression—you have freedom of speech and all those issues, and you get to this almost false dichotomy of free speech and hate speech that, again, kind of

> centers constitutional, legal rhetoric over historical happenings and the moral impetus that we have as human beings who are responsible to one another.

Kyle rejects both the idea that speech delivered uncivilly is invalid and the absolutist perspective of speech. He feels that the legal perspective of speech has created a "false dichotomy" between "free speech" and "hate speech" that centers the legal rhetoric of the First Amendment over the "moral impetus" for human beings to be "responsible to one another."

Kyle went on to describe this moral impetus through the example of a free-speech event he attended:

> I just went to a whole panel debate on free speech, and there was this conservative guy there, and he had this really smug argument where he said, "If you want to attack a certain sector of speech and call it hate speech, that undermines your own confidence in your speech, because speech is about competing ideals that are tested and dismissed and rejected, and the best ones win." . . . And he was saying . . . rejecting hate speech, . . . you can't do that without delegitimizing the speech that you want to accept or the speech that you produce. And I was like, . . . it's not about the speech itself. . . . When people don't like the speech, it's not about, "I don't like that word," right? . . . It's not just about the words, but it's about, one, the ideas connected to the words, which you cannot separate words from, and two, the prospect of and the remembrance of what things were like when those words were acceptable, when those words were the norm. So, then he's talking about this constant testing of ideas, . . . and I'm like, these ideas have already been tested, and the reason that we don't like them, . . . the same reasons that we say we don't like racism anymore, the reasons we don't like homophobia anymore, the reasons we don't like antisemitism anymore is the same reason that people are targeting these things that we call hate speech. It's the same reason that people want to get rid of this from the vocabulary. So, they've already been tested. . . . And that's why it's so important to stress the moral imperative.

Kyle argues that the framing of speech as an exchange of ideas in which ideas are tested against one another, with the best surviving, fails to recognize that some words were already found wanting on *moral grounds*.

Like Aaron above, Kyle argues that there is a moral component to evaluating speech. Aaron describes this as evaluating speech through its consequences, while Kyle describes this as recognizing the moral responsibility humans have to one another and the moral history of speech itself.

Erin, a cisgender woman of color who facilitates intergroup dialogues, similarly rejected the idea that speech could be treated in a neutral manner where everyone was treated equally. For her, facilitators played an important role in transforming the conditions of speech in dialogue spaces:

> [In my position] what we do is intergroup dialogue. So, dialogue, the way that we define it, is this ebb and flow of information, and it's more about finding common ground than trying to convince anyone. And it's about making sure everyone feels heard while also understanding how people's lived experiences and the way that those lived experiences impact the way that they move through the world may mean that they may feel entitled to take up more space while someone is consistently pushed to the background. Like, for example, . . . the men speak a lot [*laughs*]. . . . It's on the duty of the facilitator to be like, "Hey, I'm noticing that there are some folks who aren't speaking so much. Can everyone just self-reflect on how they feel they've participated?" And take a step back and take a step forward. . . . The facilitator walks the line between neutral—well, actually, no, I don't think we're neutral. I think that we want everyone to be heard, and that means telling some folks to take a step back, which isn't neutral per se, 'cause neutral means staying out of it, and that's not what we do.

Erin recognizes that people come into dialogue with different lived experiences that are anchored within different privileges. These privileges mean that some people can speak more and take up more space. While at first Erin says facilitators are "neutral," she immediately corrects herself: facilitators are not neutral because they play an active role in drawing some voices forward while telling others to step back. While Erin speaks about the importance of "making sure everyone feels heard," then, she also situates this process within historical and social legacies that enable and silence individuals. A facilitator's role requires them to be cognizant of these differences to create an inclusive environment for equitable dialogue.

Tessa's, Kyle's, and Erin's comments critique the idea of equality embedded in diversity as difference to examine the participatory conditions of speech. They do not assume a place of equality among speakers. Instead, they take a power analysis approach to diversity and evaluating speakers. Tessa, Kyle, and Erin recognize that participants come into speech under positions of social stratification. This means that some speakers have more access and privilege. Saying that everyone has the freedom to speak overshadows unequal conditions of access and privilege in speech. For Tessa, this access and privilege mean that speakers who benefit from the status quo do not need to fear for their safety, as they are reproducing the "norm." For Kyle, this access and privilege mean that some voices are taken more seriously than others, based on whether the message conforms with the conventions of White respectability. Erin alludes to how men take up more space in dialogue and the need for them to step back for other voices to be heard. All three reject the idea that people come to, and can engage in, speech equally. By approaching issues of speech through a power analysis frame, they recognize that speakers themselves—whether students or orators—come to the table suspended in histories of continuing social inequalities. This shapes access, ability to speak, and the ability to be heard.

Creating an equitable environment for speakers with different power and privileges, simultaneously trying to be as inclusive as possible, is not easy. Student diversity leaders recognized the tensions that came with trying to pull off this balancing act. Wesley and Sarah each described this in the context of trying to facilitate dialogue between political conservatives and socially disadvantaged and marginalized people.[25] Wesley, a biracial student who identifies as queer and a cisgender man, explains,

> We've talked a lot about issues of is it the responsibility of marginalized people to educate their oppressors, you know, 'cause that's kind of what dialogue is for? . . . Is it even possible to find common ground with people who are bigoted? Like, who's expending more emotional labor? And one of the issues we had is that people who identified as more conservative would not come to our events, so it would be kind of more of an echo chamber, because, like, when you're having dialogues about social justice, who's going to come out, right? It's people who are like pretty liberal or

> progressive. So, we had a lot of problems outreaching to [conservative students], you know. That's a continual thing we're always trying to do is outreach to conservative groups to have them there. Then, like, what's the safety of that for marginalized people? They [conservative groups] feel uncomfortable, . . . like, roll your eyes, but, like, they feel uncomfortable, right? Like, they literally do. So we have to do something to alleviate that. It becomes very complicated.

Wesley describes the unequal power conditions of dialogue in which marginalized groups must expend more emotional labor and put themselves at risk to "educate their oppressors." Indeed, studies on racial dialogue show that students of color and White students have different emotional responses to racial dialogue.[26] In avoiding feelings of guilt or trying to exonerate themselves, students of color may feel a rising sense of frustration and anger toward White students who deny their experiences.[27] Students of color may also experience fatigue in their efforts to educate White students about structural racism.[28] At the same time, Wesley observes that self-selection may mean that only students who come out to their dialogues are those who identify as "pretty liberal or progressive."

Wesley notes in his comments that, when conservative students do attend dialogue sessions, their discomfort itself becomes a topic that has to be addressed. Some surveys bear out Wesley's observation: conservative students *do* feel less comfortable than liberal students when it comes to sharing their views on campus.[29] At the same time, regardless of political views, there are racial differences where Black students also feel less comfortable than White students.[30] These studies suggest that how one engages in speech is not simply a matter of political perspectives and campus climate but also a matter of the social location by which students enter speech. As Wesley observes, ensuring marginalized groups' safety while also trying to be inclusive to students and groups whose views may actively suggest that others are less than human, criminals, gender confused, and such is a complicated matter.

Sarah, a biracial, cisgender, heterosexual woman who facilitates intergroup dialogue, also described this tension:

> Sometimes I felt like people were just putting [dialogue] events on for ourselves and for like other people who already cared about those

> things to come speak. And that's fine too. But that's not the intent, you know. And so, and then there was a lot of backlash because some of us in the group wanted to invite—deliberately reach out to conservative groups like [Republican student organization] and that kind of thing and schedule it. Because a couple of them came to one of our dialogues, but they left early on because they didn't feel like welcomed, basically. And so, then our idea was instead of having it open to everyone, just have a dialogue between them and us [leaders]. We thought that would be like fostering a productive relationship. But then, there were some other . . . leaders who were like, "No, like, we don't want to talk to them," which is funny because the whole point is to learn how to, like, dialogue and that kind of thing.

As Sarah's comments indicate, even the student facilitators could not agree on how to incorporate conservative student groups or if that was even desirable. She found her peer facilitators' reluctance to engage conservative students ironic to the stated goals of intergroup dialogue. The leaders discussed several alternatives, but they did not reach consensus.

Sarah's and Wesley's comments reveal the tensions and difficulties of creating equitable and inclusive conditions for speech. As Erin notes, in these smaller dialogue sessions, facilitators may be able to draw out students from less privileged backgrounds while asking the more privileged to reflect on their own engagement. Yet, these intergroup dialogues have their own issues, such as self-selection and the feel of an echo chamber, which student leaders, such as Sarah and Wesley, critiqued as unfortunate realities.[31] Given that their intergroup dialogue topics often related to social justice, they felt that conservative students typically either did not attend or left early because they felt uncomfortable.[32] This raises two questions for facilitators: Should they be actively seeking out these groups to participate, or are they trying to promote a space for the marginalized to be heard without being put down? And if these groups are actively sought, how do facilitators manage the power differentials of marginalized populations and voices that may actively denigrate marginalized groups? Students were ultimately divided on these questions, with no clear solutions.

The Tensions Between Equality and Equity in Speech

Student narratives reveal the tensions between diversity as difference and diversity as power and equity in the context of speech at West University, a public institution. Because the university adopted a legalistic, absolutist approach to free speech, it treated all groups' speech equally, regardless of content, effectively enshrining diversity as difference. In contrast, a diversity as power and equity framework recognizes that student groups, speakers, and students are not equal. Rather, they come to speech with different social characteristics that lend some greater and some lesser ability to speak and be heard.

Diversity as difference in speech is manifested through an absolutist approach to speech in which all people have, in the abstract, equal freedom to speak their perspectives. This absolutist perspective suggests that speakers and speech should not be curbed, with legal recourse if these rights are violated.[33] The DEI office at West University played an active role in promoting diversity as difference through its absolutist approach to speech. The office released educational material, held a panel on the importance of free speech, and taught students about the legal repercussions of curbing speech on campus. At the same time, the DEI office at West University attempted to balance diversity as difference and diversity as power and equity by providing resources for those students who might be affected by hurtful speech to speak through counternarratives and alternative events. Rather than prohibit speakers, they encouraged students to hold their own events and engage in counterspeech. This is exemplified in the alternative events held by students who opposed the right-wing orator and the Republican student group's event on immigrants.

The sociologists Wendy Leo Moore and Joyce Bell argue that the call for counterspeech in the face of hate speech is an "abstract-liberal, color-blind approach [that] decontextualizes racist speech from the historical and contemporary reality of structural racism that informs speech acts and symbols used in these displays."[34] Students like Aaron and Kyle recognized the moral texture of these words. Speech has systemic histories and systemic repercussions that the abstract liberal and color-blind approach to speech does not consider. These inequalities do not disappear simply by encouraging students to engage in counterspeech. Further, by focusing on the right to speak, the university does not recognize how social inequality also shapes the participatory conditions of speech for different speakers and groups. These social inequalities do not go away when students or invited speakers enter a university. This decontextualized approach to speech and speaker thus allows contemporary forms of exclusion and inequality to persist on college campuses.

The struggle to create equitable environments for speech plays out in unresolvable ways on contemporary campuses, particularly at public universities. The education and legal scholar Liliana Garces and colleagues argue that the absolutist frame and the threat of legal action create a repressive environment in which universities' commitments to creating inclusive and equitable environments are subsumed under the need to uphold free speech.[35] The legal scholar Brian Soucek argues that universities are caught in a "double liability dilemma," in which they are liable for curbing speech but also liable for failing to do so when it denies another person's access to education. Courts, however, have favored speech over equal access to education on university campuses.[36] This has set universities up for failure in creating equitable environments against the impetus of speech and reinforces the university as an inequality regime.

Administrators at West University have attempted to thread this needle by educating students about the legal basis of the absolutist approach, while simultaneously creating space for students to engage in counterspeech and host alternative events and producing condemnatory statements. The university also offers intergroup dialogue, but as we saw, facilitators were divided in how to make those spaces equitable and inclusive. Diversity student leaders' experiences reveal an impasse on how to address speech and uplift marginalized people. They envisioned policies that enshrined equity, but they questioned whether it would be possible to achieve this while operating under the university's constraints. Without addressing either the moral nature of speech or the social inequality that shapes speakers and conditions of speech, the university's attempt to balance equality and equity ultimately falls short.

4

Equality Without Inclusion for LGBTQ+ Students at Christ College

Josh agrees to meet with me at one of the popular meeting places at Christ College. Conversations from busy tables fill the air, and an expresso machine constantly belches over the chatter. I am grateful to find a table for our interview in the bustling lounge. Josh approaches me tentatively—neither of us is sure if we have found the right person until we introduce ourselves. Josh, a White cisgender man who identifies as gay, is tall and thin. He wears a navy fleece sweater over skinny jeans, and round glasses sit neatly atop the bridge of his nose. Josh folds up his glasses and places them on the table as we speak.

> I feel like Christ College has a really kind of conflicting [stance] on queer and trans* students. Professors are generally really accepting. I've rarely met a professor that I'm like, "Oh they're probably not affirming," but administration I would say is pretty trans*phobic and homophobic—not like the people itself but like the policies and maybe even the highest-up administration probably has conflicts with queer issues. And it's in the policy statement, like the lifestyle expectations at Christ College, that they have traditional views on marriage and stuff. So, like, from a policy perspective, I would say Christ College is a pretty homophobic and trans*phobic institution, but in practice, it's less so. I can't really speak on being trans*, but I have lots of friends who are, and it's definitely hard to navigate that, especially with living, where you end up in the dorms. And that's such an important aspect of college that there's not a lot of protections for that.

Josh's words encapsulate key areas of concern for LGBTQ+ students at Christ College: administration and policy, housing, and treatment in the classroom by peers and professors. Josh describes Christ College's approach to LGBTQ+ students as one that is "conflicted," in which Christ College's policies are homophobic and trans*phobic, but he also feels that people on campus vary in their acceptance of LGBTQ+ students.

Tina arrives thirty minutes late for our interview, admitting that she nearly forgot about our meeting. Tina is a biracial cisgender woman in diversity leadership who identifies as gay. Wearing a chunky black sweater, she tells me she tries to dress androgynously. Although she identifies as gay, she is not part of Harbor, the LGBTQ+ student organization at Christ College. She does, however, subscribe to Harbor's email list. Tina feels that Christ College should not and cannot stand behind its religious faith to exclude LGBTQ+ students while purporting to be diverse:

> If you're also saying you're a Christian institution and not everyone at that institution has to be Christian, then something needs to change, because if you're welcoming people of all religious backgrounds, then you have to acknowledge that people have differing opinions on gay issues, and by invalidating those, I think it becomes a human rights issue in that not everyone is being treated equally because they are being discriminated against because of their sexuality. So, I think Christian campuses, if you're going to state that you're an institution open to everyone, that you can't then turn that around when students come to this campus and have issues when it comes to the treatment of LGBTQ+ [students] and throw the religion in their face when you said you were open to everyone.

Tina sees hypocrisy and inconsistency in Christ College's representation of itself as "open to everyone" when it simultaneously uses religion to justify its exclusionary practices toward LGBTQ+ students. Combined, Josh's and Tina's comments hint at some of the tensions evident at Christ College over diversity as it relates to gender identity, sexual orientation, and evangelical Christianity.

Across the students in my study, nearly one-fourth included religion in their definition of diversity. Religious identity and beliefs are a type of diversity that students recognized. Nearly twice that number, however, defined diversity through race and LGBTQ+ identities. Christ College has an affiliation with an evangelical Christian denomination, but the school does not require students to be Christian to attend. Christ College also purports to value diversity, even having a high administrative position and office dedicated to issues of diversity, equity, and inclusion. Religious colleges face several types of diversity conundrums, including how to manage religious diversity, but here, I focus on the particular set of tensions between religious identity and diversity, equity, and inclusion for LGBTQ+ students at Christ College.

As a private college, Christ College has arguably more freedom in defining its policies than do public universities, which must abide by federal and state regulations. Private religious colleges that receive federal funds are beholden to Title IX, which protects students from discrimination on the basis of sex; however, religious colleges and private K–12 schools have been able to apply for Title IX exemptions since 1975. From 1975 to 2016, 285 schools have received exemptions to Title IX, and not a single request for exemption was denied.[1] In these requests, religious schools discuss their theological beliefs about gender that prevent them from adhering to Title IX.[2] Religious schools have argued that Title IX violates their freedom to practice their religion and that Title IX brings religion under the regulatory purview of the government, which is prohibited under the church and state divide.[3] The Obama and Biden administrations expanded federal interpretations of Title IX to include prohibiting discrimination on the basis of gender identity and sexual orientation.[4] While Christ College does not have a Title IX exemption, it does maintain policies and statements that disavow same-sex relations and university practices that maintain a cisgender binary. Christ College's Board of Trustees has also drawn on the language of religious freedom to maintain its opposition to same-sex relationships and resist proposed changes to university policies.

Although private religious universities sometimes argue that their freedom of religion allows them to exclude accommodations or services for LGBTQ+ people, few students found this argument persuasive.[5] Rather, students felt that principles of Christian love compelled the university to be as inclusive as possible to LGBTQ+ students. As we saw earlier, students at Christ College often critiqued the language of love for creating a veneer of equality and preventing meaningful change. Here, students argued the opposite, articulating a view of Christian love based on equity and inclusion. For them, love triumphed over the idea of freedom of religion because Christian love is not about diversity as difference but about creating a more equitable and inclusive world.

In this chapter, I show how Christ College's approach to LGBTQ+ inclusion solidifies the university's role as an inequality regime. Christ College granted official status to Harbor, the LGBTQ+ student organization, after years of denying it access to university resources. This was important, as other research has shown that having access to officially recognized student organizations is important to minoritized students' sense of inclusion.[6] At the same time, LGBTQ+ students understood that Christ College's stance on sexuality, housing arrangements, and mixed experiences within the classroom effectively ostracized them from the university community. Their status as an official group set them on the same footing as other registered student organizations, but the remaining areas of exclusion suggest that LGBTQ+ students have not been incorporated into the university's larger efforts for diversity, inclusion, and equity.

At Christ College, LGBTQ+ inclusion takes the form of a student-run organization, rather than a broader university effort to change its structure and culture. This is a diversity as difference strategy. In taking this approach, Christ College continues to deny the full inclusion of LGBTQ+ students while also suggesting that there is indeed space for LGBTQ+ students on the campus. When LGBTQ+ students and their allies sought organizational changes, they were rebuffed by university administrators, who cited the diversity rationale, donors, and Christ College's denomination. Walking this tightrope, in which the university recognizes a student organization but refuses to make deeper organizational changes, allows Christ College to center its material and relational concerns with some of its donors and denomination to the detriment of LGBTQ+ students.

Exclusion of LGBTQ+ Students

LGBTQ+ students described three different ways they were not included at Christ College. First, they recognized that Christ College excluded them through its statement on sexuality. Second, Christ College maintained cisgender binary housing practices. Finally, LGBTQ+ students worried about experiencing discrimination in the classroom environment and reported mixed experiences with their professors. Therefore, while LGBTQ+ students are allowed to attend Christ College and Christ College purports to value diversity, LGBTQ+ students felt that Christ College's practice of diversity did not include them.

Katie, a White cisgender woman and lesbian, pointed to Christ College's statement on sexuality as one of the areas where LGBTQ+ students were clearly excluded from the campus:

> One, the outright things, the statement on human sexuality outright excludes us. And then when you enter, you have to sign a lifestyle agreement, which says we won't drink, we won't smoke, we won't whatever, and one of those things we will not do is "homosexual behavior." This isn't defined. No one even knows what "homosexual behavior" is. Is it me eating a sandwich? Maybe. . . . Every day I'm experiencing the fact that the human statement on sexuality is a thing, . . . that I signed an agreement to not engage in "homosexual behavior" and stuff like that, but I personally have not been called a slur or been told I should not be there or anything.

By placing sexuality in the context of marriage between a cisgender woman and man, Christ College reflects the dominant view of marriage and sex among evangelical Christians.[7] Students are required to abide by certain lifestyle expectations, which include abstaining from alcohol and illicit drugs as well as "premarital, extramarital, or homosexual activities." Even though Katie has not personally experienced harassment on campus, her very presence on the campus was dependent on her willingness to sign a statement that directly contradicts her sexuality.

LGBTQ+ students experienced exclusion most acutely in Christ College's housing arrangements. Indeed, LGBTQ+ students sometimes saw housing issues as the biggest challenge LGBTQ+ students faced at Christ College. Avery, a White nonbinary student, noted, "I think a big [challenge] is for trans* students living with people of their opposite gender and being forced to live there and being misgendered a lot. That's a big thing."

Craig, a White, gay trans*man, shared his dormitory experience during his first year as a student at Christ College:

> When I was living [in the dormitories] my first quarter, I was assigned to a random roommate, . . . and during orientation week, my roommate told me I was going to hell. . . . As I came out and more girls on my floor found out, like, I was trans*, . . . I would not get invited to floor events. And at one point, my roommate came to me and was like, "You know, people on the floor aren't comfortable with you being here." It was very, like, an alienating experience. Like, I was very much not a part of my floor. And it was hard enough having to live on a woman's floor in the first place.

At Christ College, housing is organized around cisgender identities, making it impossible for trans* and nonbinary students to find housing around their gender identities. To find safe housing environments, LGBTQ+ students rely on networks and relationships within Harbor to find roommates in the dormitories. Craig now lives with Genesis, another member of Harbor.

Even being cisgender in the dorms could be difficult for students who are not heterosexual. Josh, a White, gay, cisgender man, explained,

> Let's say I'm assigned to a new roommate, and I'm concerned how they'll treat me or how they'll think of me. Mostly I'm just worried that I'll make them feel uncomfortable just 'cause—I don't know—they'll think that I'll be into them or something like that, especially in living situations. That can be sort of uncomfortable. . . . I'm a gay man. I'm cisgender, so people at least recognize I conform to my gender norms. For a trans* [student], I would imagine that that experience is a lot more difficult because I think the general population of straight people are more used to gay men than they are to trans* people.

When Josh articulates the possibility of making his roommates uncomfortable and speculates that housing experiences are even worse for trans* students, he is describing how Christ College's policies exclude students on the basis of gender and sexuality. Cisgender binary housing suggests that there is no room for people who identify otherwise. The sociologist J. E. Sumerau and colleagues call this the "cisgendering of reality"—how religious beliefs and religious organizational practices demarcate cisgender identities as the only legitimate gender identities.[8]

Many cisgendered organizations, like Christ College, are also heterosexualized organizations in which heterosexual norms pattern practices.[9] In Christian organizations, gender and sexuality are often tightly linked.

Students also shared mixed experiences in the classroom, including fears of discrimination from faculty members and other students. Christ College requires that its faculty and staff adhere to a statement of faith and lifestyle expectations that include refraining from sexual behaviors outside of marriage and same-sex relationships. Students, unlike faculty and staff, do not need to identify as Christian to attend the college, but they must agree to lifestyle expectations regarding same-sex relationships. This meant that students could not expect to have any openly LGBTQ+ faculty on campus, but it also presented the possibility of differences in religious outlooks between students and faculty. LGBTQ+ students shared a perception that Christ College faculty, especially those teaching required religion classes, may not be affirming; this perception was a cause of fear and anxiety.

Genesis, a White lesbian student who uses she/her and they/them pronouns, notes how these concerns were ubiquitous whenever it was time to enroll in courses:

> We have a group chat on Snapchat for a lot of the recurring Harbor members, . . . and every time around class enrollment: "Is this professor affirming? Is this professor affirming?" . . . We have [core religion classes], and it's especially hard with those professors, because as a theology major, they're more likely to be extremely conservative, and since reconciliation is a very big thing for Christ College, like, a lot of the hot topics often come up, and so yeah, that's gonna always be really tricky, I think, not knowing what professors are or aren't unless you, like, ask an upperclassman. Yeah, that's stressful.

Rae, a biracial student who uses she/her and they/them pronouns, also described concerns over faculty:

> I definitely think one of the more prominent problems that I hear about a lot are when people are approaching other students asking, you know, "Is this teacher affirming" or "Is this advisor affirming?" And I think it is definitely a big problem that people are scared of being discriminated

> against by their teachers when really . . . there should be a lot of respect in that relationship. And I also think that, you know, making sure that all students are educated about being respectful and being a good ally is super important because some people completely misunderstand what it's like and what it even means to be an LGBTQ person.

The fact that Christ College requires core classes on Christianity, even as it does not have faith-based admission requirements, is a cause of anxiety among LGBTQ+ students. They consider these faculty more conservative than faculty in other departments, and they do not trust these faculty members to approach difficult topics, such as gender and sexuality, in a sensitive manner. Since the creation of Harbor, it has provided LGBTQ+ students with a whisper network that helps them avoid certain faculty members and identify sympathetic instructors. Yet, even after students receive advice from Harbor members, they may experience chilly classroom climates.

Josh, quoted at the beginning of this chapter, did not have negative experiences with faculty members, whom he felt were generally affirming and accepting. But other students reported more varied experiences among students and peers in the classroom. For example, Chelsey, a queer cisgender woman of color, described her experience and a friend's experience in the classroom:

> I have said that I am queer, or in a class discussion, I've brought up something related to queer and trans* issues. It was never shot down by a professor, but it was by, like, a student who disagreed or just didn't want to participate in the conversation because they fundamentally disagreed with the idea of queerness. . . . I have a friend who's in a women's history course, and in that class, most of the students are women, and I think there are only a few male-identifying people, and then there are a lot of trans* people in that class, and there is one student in that class who is very openly conservative Christian. . . . He has expressed really problematic opinions, but the professor believes that all opinions are valid, all opinions should have a space on the floor when there's an open discussion. I know that's important, but I also think that it's important to make way for queer and trans* students in that area. If it is harmful, then that should be where there is a line, where it's like, "No, that shouldn't be al-

> lowed," and I feel like right now, that line doesn't really exist. Like, "We're all here, so we have an equal experience," but we don't because it seems to be more normal to be straight and White than it is to be a person of color, to be trans* and queer.

While Chelsey's comments regarding queer and trans* issues were never "shot down" by the professor leading the class, other students voiced their disagreement. Chelsey's friend, meanwhile, encountered a situation where a faculty member encouraged a conservative student to express harmful opinions on the theory that "all opinions are valid." Chelsey rejects the approach to abstract equality that she perceives in the professor's actions. For Chelsey, phrases like "all opinions are valid" and "we're all here, so we have an equal experience" do not consider how different groups experience privilege and marginalization. Instead, Chelsey draws on a power and equity view of diversity to argue that faculty need to make more space for queer and trans* students in the classroom. For Chelsey, this means that faculty members ought to take a more active role in facilitating discussions and taking stances.

Genesis also described an experience with a faculty member that ultimately led to an apology from the professor:

> I'm lucky in that I haven't had a professor say anything like flamboyantly homophobic to me yet. I had a professor say something that was pretty trans*phobic to me . . . It's very hard when you're a student because obviously there's a power dynamic where the professor is in charge of your grades. . . . What I did was I just tried to be like, "Hey, that's something offensive. . . . You should refrain from saying that in the future." And she just got like defensive . . . but half an hour later called me back up to her desk and was like, "Hey, I realize what you said was correct. . . . That was not right of me to say, and I'm sorry if I looked like a total jerk. I will not say that again, and thank you for educating me." So, I think these sorts of things can be dealt with in a good way.

Although Genesis's confrontation with their professor ended well, allowing her to conclude that these conflicts "can be dealt with in a good way," the possibility that LGBTQ+ students might be discriminated against by faculty creates a sense of anxiety for LGBTQ+ students.

Together, Christ College's policies against same-sex relations, cisgender binary housing, and the classroom environment create a sense of exclusion for LGBTQ+ students. University statements against same-sex relations and lifestyle statements posture the university as disaffirming, even as it recognizes Harbor as a student organization. Housing is organized around cisgender and heterosexual norms. This cisgendering of reality and heterosexual norms at Christ College mean that, outside of Harbor, there is no space for trans* and genderqueer students and for those who are not heterosexual on campus. Students could not expect to encounter openly LGBTQ+ faculty, and they feared a chilly classroom environment. From living arrangements to the classroom environment to the broader university policies, LGBTQ+ students inhabited the realities of exclusion on multiple levels, even while the university purported to value diversity and reconciliation and recognized their student organization.

The Love Critique of Freedom of Religion

One way religious colleges and organizations deflect change and maintain their exclusionary policies toward LGBTQ+ students is to invoke the idea of religious freedom.[10] Although the success in arguing for religious freedom over inclusion varies depending on institutional factors, such as a university's ranking, wealth, and broader secular or religious ethos, freedom of religion is a common refrain.[11] Freedom of religion in relationship to sexuality continues to be litigated among courts across different institutions, ranging from universities to medical care.[12] In chapter 3, students at West University struggled with balancing their university's legal arguments for freedom of speech with their desire for an inclusive environment. At Christ College, however, most of the students rejected the university's legalistic logic. Students felt that love trumped any argument to discriminate as a form of religious practice and freedom. For these students, Christian love is not based on equality but rather on equity and inclusion. Practicing love means recognizing the needs and full humanity of LGBTQ+ students so that they may thrive on campus.

Students felt that Christian colleges were failing to live up to their Christian mission of loving others when they excluded people on the basis of their sexual orientation. Consider John's statements:

> I think everyone should be accommodated regardless of anything. I feel like it really goes back to religious universities not fully understanding the message that they're trying to send with being a Christian university, missing the whole aspect of inclusivity regardless of someone's background or sexual orientation or how they view themselves or how they wished to be viewed. Even more so, religious university than not so, I feel like they should be even more called to be inclusive to those groups of people, 'cause if you're not, it's almost like being hypocritical about the message of love and inclusivity. 'Cause then I guess you're saying, "I'm going to love everyone except you." . . . I feel like Christian universities have even more of a responsibility to meet up to that standard than public universities because it's not a matter of laws at that point. It's a matter of moral obligation and calling, and if you don't want to follow through with that, I guess you should change the message you're putting out about love and inclusivity.

John, a biracial Asian American who identifies as a cisgender man and heterosexual, speaks of the moral obligation of Christian universities to carry out their message of love. He contrasts this with public universities, which may have more legal oversight and consequences for discriminatory practices against LGBTQ+ individuals. In his opinion, the inclusion of LGBTQ+ students is not about meeting legal requirements but instead about the moral responsibility of Christians to love all people, which means recognizing the LGBTQ+ community and bringing changes for them for their full inclusion on campus.

Beatrice, a biracial diversity student leader who identifies as heterosexual and a cisgender woman, described her qualms with the university's decision to use religious freedom to limit its inclusion of LGBTQ+ students:

> BEATRICE: I think that with Christian universities, they can fall on this crutch of "homosexuality is a sin" and all that, but there are so many other things that are a sin in the Bible that are not acknowledged that we do all the time, so why is it this specific group of people you're choosing to ostracize and demonize in a lot of cases? So I think that making the LGBTQ+ community feel welcome is the best thing, especially if you're preaching the Christian message

of accepting and loving everyone as God would. So to [say], "We're going to love everyone except you guys," like, "you can't come here," that's a lot of the hypocrisy that turned me away from Christianity in general.

ESTHER: What do you think of the "that's my freedom of religion" sort of argument?

BEATRICE: Every single time I hear that argument, I think you're doing religion wrong. . . . What I've read of Jesus and God, I don't think he would be okay with you throwing hate speech at people in the name of God or Bible thumping or bringing out scripture you don't fully understand based on the way you're trying to interpret it. Freedom of religion is great, but I would say just check your facts first, and maybe try to do it in a way that's not so hateful.

In chapter 2, we saw that some students objected to the language of sin in a hypothetical Christian diversity statement, arguing that the language of sin imposed abstract equality in the way it deflected from issues of equity and justice. Here, Beatrice repeats these sentiments when she describes Christian universities as hypocritical in singling out sexuality, all the while preaching love and practicing exclusion. Beatrice, like John, feels that excluding LGBTQ+ students is failing to live up to the Christian message of love. She does not find arguments for exclusion based on the freedom of religion compelling.

Nina, a White cisgender woman who serves in diversity student leadership at Christ College, described the exclusion of LGBTQ+ students in relationship to the university's policies: "[University policy] prohibits both sex on campus—premarital sex and specifically mentions same-sex intercourse in the code of conduct as being prohibited as separate from the premarital sex thing. I just think for a university that is trying to put on a face of diversity and inclusion, that is just so absurd to have that in the code of conduct. And I don't know, it just seems very hypocritical and discriminatory." Nina finds it "absurd" and "hypocritical" for a university that is trying to promote diversity and inclusion to prohibit same-sex relationships. Notably, Nina stresses the importance of marginalized students' right to their education. She does not think "freedom of religion" should be used to exclude students when it creates a hostile educational environment. She explained,

> I think that the idea of religious freedom is questionable when that religious freedom means the discrimination of other people and their right to a safe and comfortable learning and living environment. There's always the arguments that are thrown around that are always like, "Go to a different university if you don't agree with it," and that kind of thing, but that is not always necessarily what is best for those individuals' education, you know, if there are other things about the education of schools like Christ College that are really attractive or beneficial for them. It just seems unfair to impose that when it so deeply infringes on another person's identity.

Nina does not find prioritizing religious freedom over inclusion compelling. Nor does she feel that telling LGBTQ+ students to go somewhere else is helpful when their education should be centered.

It should be noted that several students at Christ College offered different interpretations of Christ College's responsibilities to its students and its values. For example, David, an Asian American, heterosexual, cisgender man, felt that the private nature of a Christian college overruled the demands of LGBTQ+ students:

> If the university is religious, it's a private university, I think it is freedom of religion. It is a private institution. They can do whatever they want pretty much. That's the reason they are private, and . . . they have their own set of core values they believe in, and I think it would be wrong for these students to think it's a lot of discrimination. I feel like if somebody made clear that this was their intention and if they don't want to accommodate for that, they shouldn't have to do that, because—obviously, it's going to be hindering if you are one of those people [who feels discriminated]—but I don't know. It's private institutions. They were founded upon a certain ideology, so yeah.

David is adamant that private institutions have the freedom to run their organizations as they like, based on their own ideologies. David does recognize the difficulties LGBTQ+ students may face, but he maintains that private organizations founded on religious beliefs have the freedom to exercise those ideologies, even if they are discriminatory to certain groups.

Ian, another Asian American, heterosexual, cisgender man, struck a more strident tone, suggesting that the university had already gone "too far" in incorporating LGBTQ+ students into what he had understood to be a Christian environment:

> Lately, people have been moving to make pangender bathrooms, if you will, one bathroom with one stall for you. That's what they've been asking for, but now they're arguing that all bathrooms should be the same, and I think that's asking for too much. . . . From a religious perspective, what they're [LGBTQ+ students and their allies are] doing is wrong. . . . If they want, say like, a girl who identifies as a guy wants to live in a guy's dorm—you just can't really do that. I feel like in cases like this, you choose to come to a religious university, you have to abide by their rules. . . . I think as Christians, we should accommodate to a certain extent this particular people group, LGBTQ, . . . but if they try to go too far, it becomes unreasonable.

Ian claims that universities should "accommodate to a certain extent" the needs of LGBTQ+ students, but his other comments make clear that this is an approach to accommodation that represents tolerance, at best. Instead of invoking the Christian ideal of love, Ian indicates that LGBTQ+ students have tried to "go too far" and that they ought to follow the university's rules. Ian makes clear his preference that religious ideologies should trump inclusion.

Both David and Ian identify as Christians, but neither invokes the ideal of love. Nor does either one of them explain the theological reasons why LGBTQ+ students, in particular, should be excluded.[13] David's and Ian's comments more closely reflect a logic of rights that undergirds arguments *for* and *against* religious freedom. When used in support of religious freedom, this logic of rights argues that people and privately owned organizations or businesses have the right to practice their religion without governmental interference. Neither thinks that religious organizations should be compelled to do something outside their religious beliefs. Students like Nina also discuss rights, but they focus on the rights of LGBTQ+ folks and other groups to be free from discrimination.[14] LGBTQ+ student allies recognize the right of LGBTQ+ students to attend a school free from discriminatory conditions, but rather than frame their argument exclusively in terms of rights, they argue against freedom of religion by calling Christians to more fully embody and practice Christ-like love. For them, love trumps rights.

Seeking Organizational Changes

At the time of my interviews, Harbor members were actively working with administrators to communicate their needs. In this way, Harbor members were like the LGBTQ+ students at other religious universities who develop activist identities to bring about change on their campuses.[15] The LGBTQ+ students at Christ College did not necessarily see themselves as pathbreakers but instead recognized that their ability to seek institutional changes rested on the prior labor of students of color. Indeed, it is possible that LGBTQ+ students felt empowered to seek changes precisely because of the success of student activists of color, whose work had brought about significant organizational changes at Christ College, including the hiring of a DEI officer.

Reese, a gay student of color who uses he/him and they/them pronouns, told me a bit about this history:

> They [Christ College] just created a new [DEI administrator] position. . . . We've been in conversation with her too, and pretty much her role is to provide inclusion and stuff at an institutional level. So that position again was suggested by students who came before me here, including my cousin, who just graduated. Like, they had a group that was trying to fight for liberation of Black and Brown people. They were like, "We need institutional changes," so they started getting the ball rolling, and the students involved in that are the reason why we have that position now. And so, Harbor came up to [the DEI officer] and said, "There's also these issues too."

The students' labor produced tangible results, including the creation of a DEI office on campus. A high-level administrator who worked at Christ College for over thirty years confirmed these students' sense of agency, telling me that these student activists met with the university's president and were invited to participate in the search for the DEI officer.

With the new DEI office and officer in place, LGBTQ+ student leaders sought to bring about additional organizational changes that focused on gender and sexual orientation in addition to race. Their efforts included discussions with the DEI officer, housing administrators, and even the university president. Katie provided a succinct summary of Harbor's different approaches:

> So, we're trying to get the statement on human sexuality—it's on Christ College's website—we're trying to get that changed, so that it's less homophobic and makes LGBTQ students feel more welcomed here. We're also working with the housing people to try to get the housing application changed so that there's a way for LGBTQ students not to be paired with a homophobic roommate. And we're also setting up an event for spring that will allow dialogue between faculty and students to talk about how to be more equal and inclusive in the classrooms with regards to LGBTQ issues, topics, because just about every LGBTQ student you talk to on campus will have at least one experience in a classroom where they experience a microaggression or a topic just wasn't handled very well, or they felt flat-out unsafe, or topics were just avoided when they should have been talked about. So, we're trying to reduce that number of experiences people have by working with faculty.

Katie's comments reveal Harbor's multipronged approach. The group is attempting to pressure the university not only on language—for instance, the statement on human sexuality—but also on issues of material concern to LGBTQ+ students, including inclusive housing and classroom environments.

Genesis described working with the DEI officer on housing and other issues:

> So, one of the ideas that we brainstormed was . . . the roommate match form, like where you fill out a little bit about you, it's very much like, "What's your music taste? . . . How messy do you like or how neat do you like your room? What time do you get up?" . . . That's not a hill to die on. Feeling safe with someone, that's—I mean that might be something that straight people don't have to think about, but for me, that's a huge thing. Am I going to be accepted and respected by my roommate? . . . We

> brought up to [the DEI officer] the possibility of having a . . . "Are you, like, accepting of queer identities?" and just like one little question that you can click or not click on the form. And then possibly even of a second one, "Do you need a queer-friendly roommate?" And then another thing that we brought up was the counseling center at Christ College is entirely affirming, . . . and it's like that's sad that people just don't know. That should be common knowledge for our people. So we were talking to her about the possibility of adding in just a bullet point . . . on the counseling [web]page that it is affirming and just kind of brainstorming ideas with her on how to make Harbor's resources more known.

Being able to bring their concerns to high-level administrative officers was important to Harbor members because it suggested the possibility of enacting concrete change. Harbor students recognized that even seemingly modest changes, such as adding questions on the housing form and information on the counseling website, could prevent a lot of anxiety and protect LGBTQ+ students from harmful environments.

The language of Christ College's statement on human sexuality was a sticking point for the college's LGBTQ+ students. They adamantly wanted it changed, if not eliminated entirely. Reese discussed the statement on sexuality and their desire to bring changes so that LGBTQ+ students would feel safe:

> So they have a statement on human sexuality, and it's *agh*. . . . The statement on human sexuality is one of the big first or one of the only things that you're able to find regarding queer issues, so it's kind of like scary to read right before you go to the school, 'cause it's like very homophobic language. And so one thing we want to do is . . . just scrap the whole thing and change it completely, but right now, we know that the only realistic thing we can do is to just change the kind of language they use. . . . If we at least change the language, like, hopefully that will lead to change, because language holds a lot of meaning for people. So if you change the language, that might change people's lives, you know, in terms of how they see things, just to make it seem more like a human issue.

In Reese's telling, Christ College's statement of sexuality has outsize importance for incoming LGBTQ+ students because it is one of the first things they learn about the school. Indeed, at the time I was writing this book, the statement on sexuality was the first Google search result for a query on Christ College. Reese's ultimate goal is to get rid of the statement entirely, but they recognize that updating the language may be the best they can do for now. Even if they could not effect all the changes they wanted, even modest changes would make Christ College more inclusive toward LGBTQ+ students.

Obstacles to Change

Administrators at Christ College were skilled at deflecting LGBTQ+ students' demands for change. Students reported that the university primarily relied on two strategies to block their efforts. First, administrators centered the diversity rationale. When LGBTQ+ students brought their needs to different administrators, at least some of them framed the LGBTQ+ students' struggles as a learning experience for both LGBTQ+ and homophobic or trans*phobic students, rather than something that needed to be fixed. Second, administrators invoked the needs and desires of university donors as well as the university's affiliation with a conservative evangelical denomination. According to LGBTQ+ students, administrators pointed to these donors and the college's religious affiliation as the primary obstacle to creating inclusive environments at Christ College.

Tom, a White, gay, cisgender man, reflected on issues of housing over his three years at Christ College:

> I guess, like, right now, we need protections in place in our non-discrimination agreement, and we need resources so that queer and trans* students who are living in the dorms know that they are safe. We've had lots and lots of incidents where students have had virulently homophobic, trans*phobic roommates and have had to literally switch dorms to get out of that dangerous situation. And oftentimes, upper administration doesn't understand that there's, like, a gravity there. I've been told, like, "Oh, it's a learning experience," as if any students coming to Christ College have never experienced homophobia before. . . . Trans* students need to have protections and resources.

Tom observes that administrators construe the challenges that LGBTQ+ students may face in the dormitories as "learning experiences," failing to recognize that experiences of homophobia and trans*phobia are not learning experiences for queer and trans* students but rather issues of safety. The diversity rationale suggests that diversity is important because it provides educational benefits.[16] Critics of the diversity rationale argue that the diversity rationale centers the learning of dominant groups.[17] The idea of educational benefits in diversity has trickled into housing on campus. Housing administrators and residential advisers sometimes perceive discriminatory experiences, like microaggressions, as learning experiences. In doing so, they tend to be more sympathetic toward perpetrators rather than consider how they could ameliorate the harm done to students experiencing microaggressions or blatant racism, sexism, homophobia, trans*phobia, and ableism. They assume that perpetrators are ignorant of their errors and can learn, rather than centering the needs of those who were wronged.[18]

Reese similarly noted,

> Like, "What if my roommate is homophobic?" or even me and two other leaders [at Harbor], we've had experiences where our housing situation, we didn't feel safe, and we had to move at the end of the first quarter. . . . Like, it was only a fast process for us because we were able to get connected. My cousin helped me, and then the other leaders got the Harbor leaders to help them, but not everyone has that access or will want to approach people, and sometimes the people who work in the residence life are like, "Oh, but this is a growing opportunity for both people to just learn how to reconcile," but then it's not our job to do that. Our physical safety should be first.

As Reese's comments reveal, one of Harbor's roles is to help LGBTQ+ students move to safer environments when housing administrators dismiss the gravity of their concerns.

Genesis suggested that at least some university administrators are more willing to take their concerns seriously once Harbor is involved: "Prior, when [the housing administrator] had known that it was an issue of me feeling discriminated against, she had been like, 'Oh, well, I think you guys can probably just talk through this. I think it'll be like—it's just, like, a communication issue.' And so I asked for a one-on-one with her, and I described the issue, and she immediately took my side and was like, . . . 'I understand. Thank you for involving Harbor in this. We're gonna speed up this process. We don't want you feeling unsafe.'"

When Christ College administrators construe experiences of discrimination as learning experiences for both LGBTQ+ students and cisgender heterosexual students, they center the learning experiences of cisgender and heterosexual individuals, who enter these relationships with more privilege.[19] Queer and trans* students who live in cisgendered housing spaces at a university that does not offer alternatives may be harassed and outed, which can subsequently shape their physical and mental health and educational outcomes.[20] Treating their experiences as "an opportunity for growth" does not recognize the differences in advantages and disadvantages between LGBTQ+ students and heterosexual and cisgender people. Nor does interpreting LGBTQ+ individuals' experiences through the diversity rationale recognize the detrimental consequences for LGBTQ+ students living in unsafe housing conditions. Rather, administrators, who draw on diversity rationale rhetoric, deprioritize the safety and health of LGBTQ+ individuals and turn LGBTQ+ students into object lessons. By drawing on the idea of educational benefits in the diversity rationale to inform housing policies and practices, the university acts as an inequality regime that reinscribes cisgender binary and heterosexual norms.

Administrators responded differently when leaders of Harbor intervened; however, as Reese notes, not everyone has the access or the ability to approach administrators. Therefore, some students may simply be stuck in unhealthy and dangerous housing situations because they lack advocates. In our conversations, students conveyed to me that administrators should center the safety of students in their housing situations without having to have Harbor arbitrate. This would mean centering equity and inclusion in housing to prioritize student safety over the theoretical educational benefits of exposure to different views.

In addition to responding to student concerns through the rhetoric of "learning opportunities," students told me that Christ College administrators would cite the college's relationship with donors and the denomination for changes that could not be implemented. Craig illustrated this in recounting a meeting he and other members of Harbor had with the president of Christ College and other administrators:

> We go, and we have meetings with different administration and kind of talk about what we'd like to see and what we need, like, bridge the gap between the students who want to see certain issues resolved but don't really have the access to leadership or administration. . . . We're always meeting with the diversity officer, the president of the university, the president of housing, just trying to get different balls rolling. . . . The first time we met with him [the president of the university], which was the last time we met with him, we came in, and we were like, "These are the things we want to do," and he was kinda able to say, "All right. Here are the people you should be talking to," which was kind of tough at first 'cause it felt like, "Oh, like, we kinda wanted to hit that top guy first and get that kind of support." But because of our different donors, it's really hard for him to be in support or help us directly, so we're having to talk to a lot more people in slightly different positions.

Although Craig and other leaders were hoping to gain the president's support, the president referred them to other administrators and pointed to the university's relationship with its donors as a challenge to enacting change. Craig described this relationship:

> I think because they [Christ College] are affiliated with [evangelical Christian denomination] . . . and a lot of our donors are very conservative, which is what administration will always point to when they can't do things. It's really difficult to kind of tie the LGBT issues into that and keeping everyone, like, in quotes, "happy." . . . They tend to go to first is thinking about the funding for the school rather than the health and safety of a group of their students. . . . When we try to get something done, the president of the university or other administration will be like, "Oh, we can't do that because our donors or our funding source wouldn't appreciate that." . . . The donors are primarily Christian or all Christian.

When I asked another student why she thinks diversity at Christ College does not include LGBTQ+ identities, Felicia offered a similar explanation to Craig's: "Because it's a Christian campus, they're probably afraid of the backlash they get from more conservative members of alumni, where they get their money. So if they had classes, more open, loud support for the LGBTQ community, they might lose a lot of funding, and I understand that, but it's also like, is it worth the funding if there are people who are really unhappy on your campus?" Craig and Felicia both recognize how those who have money also have power in influencing the university's policies. Even though donors may be alumni, they are no longer students on the campus and therefore distant from the experiences of those who are currently enrolled. This distance means that they influence university policy without having any knowledge of how students are affected or needing to experience the consequences.

Diversity student leaders concurred. Tina explained how Christ College's affiliation made it difficult to truly include LGBTQ+ students:

> I think something I saw a lot last year was a greater push for acceptance and support for gay students on campus, which at a Christian university supported by [affiliated evangelical denomination] is not something that they're affirming of, and so that can be tricky. It can be hard to deal with that on this campus when your university isn't even affirming of different identities, so I think as an institution, on an administration and faculty level, there's a lot of work to be done in diversifying the population, which again is tricky when everyone on staff has to identify as a Christian, but also just having more opportunities on campus to get involved, and I think a lot of that too comes from funding.

While it is difficult to verify students' sense that donor resistance is the ultimate barrier to change, it is undeniably the case that undergraduate enrollment in colleges and universities has been declining for over a decade.[21] Full-time enrollment in CCCU universities has dropped slightly from 2012 to 2017, and Christian colleges have been struggling financially.[22] In a context of declining tuition money and increased operating expenses, institutions like Christ College often find themselves increasingly beholden to donors. It is not always the case, however, that donor relations create barriers to inclusion, even at Christian colleges. Jonathan Coley's study of LGBTQ+ activism on conservative Christian colleges has highlighted how donor pressure can also lead to inclusive policies for LGBTQ+ students.[23]

Unfortunately, such pressure does not appear to be the case at Christ College. Since my interviews with LGBTQ+ students at Christ College, the Board of Trustees reaffirmed Christ College's statement regarding human sexuality. In the months leading to the board's decision, faculty members and the student government called for the removal of the statement and a communal recognition of the ways Christ College failed to love its LGBTQ+ students. Despite these statements from the faculty and the student government, the Board of Trustees chose to reaffirm Christ College's view of heterosexuality and cisgender binary identities. Indeed, when Christ College's Board of Trustees voted to maintain the statement on sexuality, it directly alluded to the college's relationship with its denomination, suggesting that its affiliation was significant to the decision the board made. The decision to maintain the statement on sexuality continues the process of diversity as difference and the university as an inequality regime. Harbor stays as a recognized student organization and broader changes to the university are deflected.

Equality Without Equity and Inclusion

At the time that I conducted my interviews, it was clear that LGBTQ+ students felt a degree of comfort coming to Christ College because of the existence and official recognition of Harbor. Even though they knew Christ College upholds heterosexual and cisgender binary identities as the norm, Harbor's existence, and particularly its official status as a recognized student organization, suggested a safe space at a university with hostile policy statements and housing arrangements. Indeed, many students pointed to Harbor as one of the reasons they felt they could enroll in Christ College despite its policies.

The university's decision to recognize Harbor reflects a strategy of diversity as difference. This strategy reproduces inequality and unsafe conditions for LGBTQ+ students and relegates LGBTQ+ inclusion to a student interest group, like a chess club or intramural basketball club. LGBTQ+ students described Christ College's statement on sexuality, housing policies, and concerns over the classroom environment as areas where they remained excluded. Studies show that LGBTQ+ students, compared to their cisgender and heterosexual counterparts, experience less satisfaction in college, have more negative mental health outcomes, and perform less well in their academics.[24] Even as campuses purport to value diversity, it is not enough to have affinity groups where students have a space on campus to meet with others like them. When Christ College promotes inclusion and equality through student organizations but does not instantiate university-wide changes, it is acting as an inequality regime. It has chosen a distorted version of the diversity rationale and relationships with its donors and denomination over its LGBTQ+ students.

At a time when college enrollment is shrinking and Christian universities are struggling financially, Christ College is met with the conundrum of protecting its institutional survival while also expanding equity and inclusion for LGBTQ+ students. The university is faced with difficult questions about how to instantiate diversity, equity, and inclusion under these conditions and constraints. For LGBTQ+ students and their advocates, the answer is relatively easy. Equity and inclusion are more important than money and the relationship the university has shared with a denomination since its founding. Actively opposing the full inclusion of LGBTQ+ students to please donors or the denomination, while using Harbor to reassure prospective LGBTQ+ students that they will be welcome, allows the university to reap material benefits at too high a human cost. Other, more conservative students, faculty, and staff assert that freedom of religion outweighs issues of sexuality and gender identity; they prioritize institutional survival and Christian identity.

Since I completed my fieldwork at Christ College in 2018, concerned students, faculty and staff, and alumni have continued to challenge Christ College's policies and statements on gender identity and sexual orientation. Harbor students and leaders continue to lead these efforts, now joined by LGBTQ+ allies across the university. Opposition to their work persists, but students have not grown weary of calling for equity, inclusion, and a truer ideal of love.

5

Asian Americans and the Limits of Representation

I wait for Joyce in the quad near one of the residential halls. The dining hall nestled at the bottom of the residential hall is not busy, and students flit in and out. It is a holiday, so West University feels quieter, missing its usual frenetic energy of students walking, jogging, skateboarding, or longboarding across the campus. Joyce texts me, and I look up to see her standing in an oversized West University homecoming sweater outside the hall. Joyce lets me into the residential hall, and we go up several flights of stairs to find a study room to meet in. During our interview, Joyce and I laugh over some Hong Kong television dramas we have both watched and speak some broken Cantonese to each other.

During her four years at West University, Joyce planned one of AAW's large cultural festivals to learn more about her family's history and how it related to Asian Americans' broader history in the United States. Joyce, a heterosexual cisgender woman, wants to work in the entertainment industry and increase the representation of Asian Americans in the industry. When I ask Joyce if she thinks Asian Americans are included in the term "diversity" when she hears it at West University, she tells me,

> I think we're included in that there are so many different Asian American groups here. We're not just Chinese people. We're not just Korean people. We're so many different kinds of Asians, and we all have a niche to go to, like AAW. There's also the Vietnamese Student Association, there's [the] Korean American Association, there's different ways people can be diverse within Asian Americans.[1] And it's not just West University has the rep[utation], like, you see a lot of Asians, but there's also a lot of White people around and a lot of African Americans and Hispanic people too.

Joyce points to the diversity of Asian ethnic groups and the variety of student organizations in responding to the open-ended question. Joyce recognizes that West University is known for having a large Asian

American population and emphasizes the recognizable diversity not only among Asian ethnic groups but also across racial groups. For Joyce, Asian Americans are part of the racial diversity at West University.

At Christ College, where Asian Americans make up a minority, I pose the same question to Kevin, an Asian American cisgender man. The child of Christian missionaries who worked in China, Kevin tells me about trying to figure out his identity in China as someone who is not ethnically Chinese and is trilingual and then experiencing culture shock when he first started attending Christ College. He explains, "I thought I would fit perfectly here because I've attended international school [in China] for like twelve years, . . . but I realized that the way they think is kind of different than international Americans." Throughout our discussions of diversity, he sometimes wonders about the experience of international students as someone who has lived in another country for most of his life. When we discuss diversity and inclusion of Asian students, Kevin considers Christ College's composition:

KEVIN: I think that most Asian students do [think they are included], but I think Christ College itself is a White-based school. So it's diverse in some sense, but [the] majority of people are White population. There's—I don't know if it's diverse diverse, but yeah, I guess there are people from other countries, so it's pretty diverse.

ESTHER: So when you said you don't know if it's "diverse diverse," what would be an example of—

KEVIN: Diverse diverse?

ESTHER: Yeah.

KEVIN: I guess, first of all, diverse diverse [*laughs*] would be more like, there are not certain populations that [are] exceeding [in] number, so I guess [a] good balance of race and culture or color. So I think that's what "diverse" means.

Kevin indicates that he thinks Asian Americans probably consider themselves part of the racial diversity on campus, but he raises the issue of Christ College's composition and questions whether it is truly diverse when the majority of students are White. He clarifies that true racial diversity and inclusion are when no group exceeds another in proportion.

In contrast to Joyce and Kevin, Jason feels that Asian Americans are not included in diversity programs. Jason, an Asian American, heterosexual, cisgender man, explains, "I don't think it [diversity] does necessarily [include Asian Americans] . . . because Asians and Asian Americans are overrepresented in higher education, so a lot of times, diversity is focused on Hispanic groups or African American groups. So it's very—it's focused on those underrepresented minorities, so Asian Americans, Asians, we're in that awkward middle group where we're minorities, but we're also seen everywhere in education." Joyce's, Kevin's, and Jason's comments reflect how Asian Americans at both West University and Christ College draw on numerical representation and the university's racial composition to make sense of whether the concept of diversity applies to the Asian Americans on their campuses.

In this chapter, I examine the centrality of numerical representation for the way students perceive diversity, equity, and inclusion. As we saw in chapter 1, students often draw on numerical representation in considering the diversity of a space. Studies on campus climate suggest that numerical representation is an important part of diverse learning environments, including establishing inclusion for racial minorities and other minority groups.[2] Numerical representation is vital for the comfort of minority students as well as for driving institutional changes.[3] Numerical representation, then, is not only a key part of how students conceptualize diversity but also an important part of how scholars and advocates conceive of campus climate and inclusion.

There are nonetheless several complexities in thinking through the relationship between numerical representation and racial diversity. An overreliance on quantifying diversity overshadows the ways inequality can persist beneath the numbers and divorces inequality from people's lived experiences.[4] Metrics that treat a group's greater numerical representation as an index to inclusion might suggest that a society that has numerically incorporated minoritized populations into historically exclusive institutions, like higher education, has moved beyond structural racism, thus leading to color-blind racist perspectives. When people draw on color-blind racist ideology, they explain away racial inequality, distance themselves from overt acts of racism, and ultimately maintain the systemic racial status quo.[5] Numerical approaches to diversity and color-blind racist ideologies therefore go hand in hand, as they deflect attention away from the persistence of structural inequality.

What is unclear is how students of color interpret their numerical representation and role in racial diversity when their community becomes the numeric majority or the largest group in a compositional plurality. These perceptions are important because they allow us to see how numerical interpretations of diversity are connected to people's lived experiences and different social identities. In turn, these perceptions can reinforce or mitigate inequality. Perceptions—even if empirically inaccurate or based on false premises—can have objective realities.[6] This is because perceptions, in part, shape social reality. Students' interpretations and perceptions of numbers are therefore an integral part of how universities operate as inequality regimes.

This chapter primarily compares the experiences of Asian Americans at West University, where they are the largest numerical racial population, with their counterparts at Christ College, where they remain a numeric minority, to examine the limits of numerical representation for diversity, equity, and inclusion. At the same time, we will occasionally hear from other student populations who consider diversity through numeric metrics or provide a contrasting perspective that allows us to perceive the limits of numerical representation for race and other social identities more fully.[7]

As we will see, Asian Americans at West University feel that their large population size, the diversity of Asian ethnicities, and the variety of Asian student organizations are ample evidence that they are represented in the university's racial diversity. Across state borders, Asian Americans at Christ College are ambivalent. They discuss their inclusion in numerical terms, but their low numbers leave them equivocating about how the university's numerical racial diversity affects their belonging. In contrast, a minority of Asian Americans on both campuses think of inclusion and diversity through diversity programs. In their view, diversity programs do not, and should not, apply to Asian Americans. For these students, the model minority myth—whether they themselves espouse it or they feel that the people in power believe it—removes any need to incorporate Asian Americans into diversity programs. Finally, a minority of students pointed to their lack of representation in student leadership. Their reasons for this lack of representation tell us how a reliance on the model minority myth and other racialized views of Asian Americans perpetuate racist cultural ideas.

These interpretations reveal how people's understandings of diversity as something that can be quantified contributes to the university's status as an inequality regime by reinforcing color-blind racist ideology and reproducing racist racial hierarchies. When Asian Americans rely on their numerical representation to consider whether they are represented in their university's racial diversity, their understandings of racial diversity reflect a color-blind racist ideology that overlooks other forms of racial inequality.[8] This color-blind approach incorporates a belief in abstract equality, in which representation indicates inclusion. When other Asian Americans (and/or university administrators) draw on the model minority myth to explain why they should be excluded from diversity programs, they are invoking an understanding of diversity that reflects a racist racial hierarchy. In this telling, Asian American students suggest that diversity is about uplifting other racial groups that have flawed cultural values in need of remediation. Ultimately, these diverging interpretations of numeric representation and inclusion have the same result of perpetuating racial inequality.

Numerical Representation, Visibility, and Inclusion

The majority of Asian Americans at both universities discussed their inclusion in diversity by focusing on their numerical representation in their campus's racial diversity. As the largest population on West University, Asian Americans pointed to their size as evidence for what makes their campus diverse and why they are part of West University's racial diversity. They also sometimes connected this to student organizations for different racial and ethnic groups, which suggests that the university welcomes many different groups. Meanwhile, Asian Americans and other racial minorities at Christ College interpreted their low numerical representation with ambivalence as to whether they were part of the campus community.

At West University, the majority of the Asian Americans I interviewed felt that their numerical visibility on campus provided obvious evidence that they were included in the term "diversity." Consider Diana's comments: "I think we're pretty included in that term [diversity]. I feel like there are just so many Asian Americans here that not including us is almost impossible . . . compared to some other groups on campus that are pretty underrepresented. I think that we're pretty included." Iris, an Asian American, heterosexual, cisgender woman, felt the same as Diana: "I think they're pretty included because Asian Americans take up a large portion of the student body and because it includes all sorts of Asian ethnicities. So, I think when I hear the word 'diverse,' I definitely would include Asian Americans in that."

Caleb, an Asian American, heterosexual, cisgender man who recently graduated from West University, discussed the inclusion of Asian Americans in reference not only to their relative share of the student population but also to the diversity of Asian ethnic groups. He explained, "I think they're hugely included in it. . . . I feel like this university is very highly composed of Asian Americans and not just Asian Americans but the very different Asians within that Asian American, like Vietnamese, Japanese, and even the smaller ones, like the Thai and Cambodian. And everyone has their different experiences." For these students, the large presence of Asian Americans and the diversity of Asian ethnic groups on campus meant that Asian Americans contributed to the campus's racial diversity. Their numbers and representation provided ample evidence that they were part of the diversity on campus.

Asian American students also pointed to the broad range of student organizations as evidence that the university incorporated them into its student body. Madelyn, an Asian American, heterosexual, cisgender woman, explained, "There's a huge Asian population, and that's great, but there's also diversity amongst Asian American population, where . . . it's like Southeast Asia[n], pan-Asian, just like any of those ethnicities. . . . There's so many orgs on campus that you can name anything. There's one for the Cambodian students, . . . Hong Kong [students]." From Madelyn's perspective, the sheer number of student organizations that cater to different Asian ethnic identities demonstrates Asian Americans' inclusion in the university's diversity efforts.

For students of color attending predominantly White institutions, student organizations are an important part of establishing a healthy campus climate.[9] While providing safe spaces, student organizations also help students acclimate to their campuses and develop a stronger sense of identity and other civic skills, such as leadership.[10] Students interpret the existence of many student groups coalescing around racial and ethnic identities as evidence of an inclusive university by suggesting that there is a place for everyone. As we saw earlier, universities try to establish equality and inclusion by recognizing student organizations, and students look to student organizations to find community. Student organizations operate as a sign of abstract equality, as different groups can form their own student organizations on campus. When Asian American students point to the existence of these student organizations as evidence for their inclusion on campus, they are reflecting an understanding of diversity as difference.

At Christ College, students also mentioned numerical representation, but their narratives revealed greater ambivalence and variability about what their low numbers say about their inclusion in the campus community. The majority of the students mentioned that they are a small part of the student population. For example, David, a heterosexual cisgender man, explained, "I think we're actually rather small at this school. For Koreans, in general, it's hard to come by another Korean for me. For Asians, as well, you don't see a lot of Asians." The emphasis on the rarity of these encounters and the "small" population suggests that David would feel a greater sense of belonging if the campus had more Asian students.

Helena, a cisgender woman who identifies as bisexual and who worked in diversity student leadership at Christ College, described her feelings of community in numerical terms:

> I think Asian Americans are about 11 point something [percent of Christ College's population]. It's pretty noticeable that if you count ten people, one of them is Asian. If you count nine, you're the Asian. I think I'm fine with it. It used to be less than that last year, which was fine, because I can look at somebody in the room and be like, "I know your name. I know a little bit about you." It's kind of this understanding that at least I have this family, so I really liked it. . . . So yeah, it's a nice small community.

Helena describes her experiences of inclusion through numeric terms, to the point that she can recite the percentage of Asian Americans on campus. Like David, she acknowledges the small size of this population, but she interprets this through a positive lens, in that it has allowed her to know most of the other Asian Americans on the campus. She describes these other Asian American students as a "family" and a "nice small community." Unlike David, she does not perceive any problems with the low representation of Asian Americans.

When I asked Ian, an Asian American student at Christ College, if he felt that Asian Americans were included in diversity when he hears the term, he began by thinking numerically: "Like a percentage? . . . I feel like the diversity isn't that great. Maybe like 10 percent diverse, including African Americans, Hispanics, Asians, because I think Christ College was categorized as a primarily White institution, so I don't imagine there would be too much diversity." Like other students, Ian thinks about racial diversity and inclusion of Asian Americans through numerical metrics. Although the overall percentage of racial minorities at Christ College is much higher than what Ian perceives, it is nonetheless notable that he describes the inclusion of Asian Americans and other racial groups through their quantity. Ultimately, Ian's focus on numeric racial diversity leads him to conclude that there is not much racial diversity at Christ College; he calls it a "primarily White institution."

Other racialized minority groups at Christ College also discussed diversity and inclusion through quantifiable metrics. When I asked Oscar, a Hispanic student employed in diversity leadership, if he felt that Hispanic students were included in the term "diversity" when he heard it on campus, he said, "I think we're kind of low [in numbers]. I don't think there's that many Hispanics or . . . they are kind of out there somewhere. There's not much. I think the most we counted was around fifty [Hispanic students]." Oscar, like the Asian American students I interviewed, considers racial diversity and inclusion through numeric metrics. Although Hispanic students make up around 16 percent of the student body at Christ College, Oscar perceives this number to be much lower than that, based on visual cues and encounters with Hispanic students across the campus.

These students at West University and Christ College primarily understood their racial or ethnic group's inclusion in the campus community through numerical representation and visible cues relative to the university's racial composition. Students at West University felt they were included in their university's racial diversity because they were numerically represented and had racial and ethnic-oriented student organizations. Even at Christ College, where Asian American students make up a smaller percentage of the student population, students nonetheless considered the question of their inclusion on campus in numerical terms. When students emphasize numerical representation in describing their level of inclusion on campus, they are implicitly assenting to a colorblind racist ideology that some scholars argue is endemic to thin understandings of racial diversity.[11] None of the students described systemic inequality on their campus or how racial systems shape the representation of students on campus. Numerical representation allows students to count diversity without engaging in more difficult questions about *why* or *how* their university's racial composition looks the way it does.

It is important to note that several LGBTQ+ students also drew on numerical representation to make sense of their inclusion on campus. In other words, while Asian Americans and some other racialized minorities drew on numerical representation to understand *racial diversity*, my study shows that some LGBTQ+ students adopted the approach for understanding diversity in gender identity and sexuality as well. When I asked whether the term "diversity" applied to LGBTQ+ students at Christ College, Rain, a student of color who identifies as bisexual and nonbinary, began by questioning this numerically: "Like the amounts? . . . It's slowly growing. . . . In my five years here, it has grown so much. There's been so many more people of different races and ethnicities and religions and stuff like that from when I was a freshman. That's for sure. Everybody's getting a little bit more open too. Although this is a Christian campus, there's other people who go to this campus. And the LGBTQ [community], that's become bigger, but it's not like giant. I mean, I want to say about twenty kids here are like that." Similarly, Queena, a White queer student at West University, felt that LGBTQ+ students are included in the term, drawing on their visibility:

> I feel like it [diversity] includes them a whole lot. I've just been so surprised coming here and seeing all kinds of different people, and it's like . . . [*laughs*] you know, people have gaydar, and it's like, I can kind of tell when I see someone. I'm like, "Oh, yeah, they're definitely in the LGBT community." And I feel like I didn't really have that back at home. There weren't really a lot of LGBT people. So, I feel like here, it's really cool that I can, like, see them out there and actively living. . . . It's really cool.

Rain and Queena both use numeric and visual cues to consider the levels of diversity and LGBTQ+ inclusion on Christ College's and West University's campuses. They use numeric metrics to consider the growing population, and visual cues allow them to feel a sense of belonging.

Other LGBTQ+ students sometimes questioned their inclusion in the term "diversity," noting that "diversity" usually referred to race or ethnicity. For many of them, this distinction largely derived from the apparent visibility of racial identities in contrast to LGBTQ+ identities. For example, Fred, a White, gay, cisgender man at West University, explained,

> I think the first thing that comes to mind when I think [of] diversity is, like, racial and ethnic diversity. I think that's just instinctual, but I do think it does include queer and trans* students depending on who's talking. . . . I just think people normally—the default when someone says "diversity" is racial diversity, and then normally they would specify if they are talking about sexual orientation or gender diversity. . . . I think also that one is just less readily apparent, like visually. You can't really tell as much whether there's sexual orientation diversity or gender identity diversity.

For Fred, racial and ethnic diversity are "instinctual" forms of diversity, while other types of diversity, such as gender identity and sexual orientation, are usually named. He considers that gender identity and sexuality may not be as visible as race, thus making gender and sexuality less "readily apparent" in visual measurements of diversity. In this way, Fred echoes a critique of visual diversity that other scholars have noted. Other types of diversity, such as class diversity, may not be as easily identifiable and thus quantifiable as racial and ethnic diversity.[12] The lack of visibility means that people may have to specify diversity in sexual orientation or gender identity in a way that they do not for racial diversity.

Taylor, a White, nonbinary, and asexual student who attends Christ College, agreed with Fred, noting how racial identities had greater visibility in comparison to LGBTQ+ identities: "Like, you might look at me and be like, 'This person is queer,' or maybe not. You might just be, 'This person is straight,' and all of that, but you can't really look at a person of color and be like, 'Oh, that person is White.' I mean there are exceptions, but for the most part." Although they recognize that there are racial ambiguities, Taylor feels that there is a difference in how sexuality is visibly perceived and how race is visibly perceived. Therefore, while LGBTQ+ students could sometimes identify LGBTQ+ individuals on the basis of visual cues, such as their attire, they were divided over to what extent visual cues allowed them to assess the levels of diversity or their inclusion on campus. Nonetheless, their comments highlight how social identities that can be categorized quickly, based on appearance, are important for the way students assess diversity and inclusion. Overall, the majority of the LGBTQ+ students I interviewed did not focus on numerical representation, quantitative measures, or visible cues to discuss their inclusion on campus. Instead, students pointed to different parts of the university's organizational structure and culture to make sense of their inclusion.

The sociologist W. Carson Byrd argues that the ascendancy of quantifying diversity is dangerous and eclipses other important metrics of diversity, equity, and inclusion.[13] When students rely on numerical representation relative to their campus's racial composition to assess their campus's level of inclusion, they are taking diversity at face value. Emphasizing numerical representation as an index for inclusion, however, fails to consider how numerical representation on campus may be the result of unequal social structures that privilege access to higher education for some while disadvantaging others. Focusing on numerical representation also obscures how power and resources among racial groups may remain unjustly distributed despite greater numerical representation and how numerical representation itself may be culturally interpreted in inequitable ways. We turn to these cultural interpretations next.

Model Minorities and the Exclusion of Asian Americans from Diversity

A minority of Asian American students on both university campuses felt that the language of diversity did *not* include them. These Asian American students felt that they were overrepresented in higher education and similar to White students. For them, "diversity" referred to programs for racialized minority groups that lacked the cultural values or skills that would allow them to succeed in higher education. Although students ranged in their awareness and use of the term "model minority," their belief that Asian Americans did not "need" diversity programs reflects key assumptions of the model minority myth. When these students describe their exclusion from racial diversity programs as the result of cultural differences, they are evincing an understanding of diversity that perpetuates racist racial hierarchies through racial triangulation.

Aiden, an Asian American, heterosexual, cisgender man at West University, felt that Asians were not, and should not, be included in diversity programming because of their "culture":

> I feel like diversity doesn't really include Asians . . . in the same sense that diversity doesn't include Caucasians, 'cause Caucasians are doing well in Western society. Well, so are Asian Americans in West University. So, I feel like diversity is more directed towards other groups, like Hispanics, Blacks, Native Americans, like those groups. . . . Asian American culture is about pushing for higher education and, like, really emphasizing more education for your kids and, you know, having a better life, but that's not really reflected in Hispanic culture or Black culture as much. . . . Should it be the case that Asians shouldn't be included [in diversity]? Yes, for the culture reasons, because we push for education.

When asked an open-ended question about whether Asian Americans are included in diversity, Aiden answers differently than the students who described diversity through the numbers of different racial groups and student organizations at West University. Those students took an abstract equality approach to understanding diversity and inclusion, emphasizing diversity as difference. Aiden, in contrast, argues that Asian Americans should not be included in discussions of diversity in higher education because they are "doing well." Although Aiden does not explicitly talk about diversity as *diversity programs*, his discussion of diversity and inclusion suggests that diversity is about programs for racial groups who are underrepresented in higher education due to their cultural values.

Asian Americans at Christ College also felt they were excluded from the university's definition of diversity for cultural reasons. Jason, a heterosexual cisgender man whom we met at the beginning of the chapter, acknowledged that Asian Americans are a minority at Christ College, but he nonetheless felt that Asian Americans were excluded from diversity initiatives because they are overrepresented in higher education. When I asked why he thought Asian Americans were not included in diversity, Jason, like Aiden at West University, called on culture to provide an explanation: "Probably cultural aspects. . . . I can only speak with certainty my own perspective is that culturally, when I think about Koreans and historically, since Korea had been such a poor country up until the 1980s, . . . you have this huge cultural significance in finding success and [the] path to that success has to be hard work, education, and if you don't do well in school, then you're considered someone who is weighing down on your family, and that's a huge aspect of I want to say Asian culture in general—very family centered, very community centered." Rather than understanding South Korea's transformation as being a result of economic policies and development, Jason asserts that the country escaped financial difficulties through a culture of hard work and valuing one's family and education. For Jason, these cultural values have directly produced the overrepresentation of Asian Americans in higher education, a numerical fact that removes any need to include them in campus diversity initiatives. Like Aiden, Jason appears to understand diversity primarily in relation to programs for certain racialized minorities of which Asians have no part.

Many Americans, including Asian Americans, understand the overrepresentation of Asian Americans in higher education through the model minority myth—the idea that despite being a racial minority, Asian Americans have gained success and, in some outcomes, even surpassed White people through exceptional cultural values that emphasize hard work and education.[14] The model minority myth places the success or failure of a racial or ethnic group on its culture rather than on historical and contemporary forms of advantage and disadvantage. Although these students did not name the model minority myth, their reliance on cultural explanations for why Asian Americans are excluded from diversity reflects key assumptions associated with it.

When students suggest that Asian Americans, alone among racialized minority groups, do not need assistance in succeeding at an institution that has historically excluded them, they are engaging in racial triangulation. The political scientist Claire J. Kim argues that racial triangulation occurs when people valorize Asian Americans' culture, such that they are seen as superior to Black people (and other racialized minorities), while also being constructed as foreigners to White American society.[15] Asian Americans actively participate in this racial triangulation when they express and act on anti-Black sentiments while also trying to obtain the material benefits of those who are racialized as White.[16] When Asian American students emphasize their cultural uniqueness and set themselves outside of diversity, they engage in a process of racial triangulation in which they no longer understand diversity in terms of abstract equality but rather through a racist racial hierarchy. In other words, while color-blind approaches to racial diversity suggest that abstract equality can be achieved through simple representation (either numerically or through the existence of an organizational space for different racial groups), racial triangulation leads to racial hierarchical approaches that designate "diversity" as a stopgap solution for "problematic" racial groups with deficient cultural values.

Notably, when Asian American students discussed their exclusion from diversity programs, they implicitly drew on aspects of a power analysis frame of diversity—a framework that Asian Americans did not draw on in their articulation of diversity, as shown in chapter 1. The power analysis framework recognizes inequality and the need to fix inequality through interventions. What is interesting is that these students are exhibiting an implicit understanding that diversity is about policies and programs aimed at improving educational outcomes for racialized minorities. Moreover, they recognize that other racialized minorities have poorer educational outcomes than do Asian Americans writ large.[17] But instead of understanding these differences in attainment in relation to historical or ongoing forms of structural discrimination and different immigration patterns, these Asian American students interpret them in relation to cultural values. In asserting that Asian Americans are excluded from diversity programs to support racialized minorities because of their cultural values, these students' statements reproduce racist ideas.

While the students quoted previously in this section implicitly invoked the model minority myth to argue that Asian Americans *should* be excluded from diversity, other Asian American students explicitly pointed to the model minority myth to explain why diversity programs *excluded them*. For example, Orlando, an Asian American, heterosexual, cisgender man from West University, explained, "I feel like diversity in colleges,

. . . it excludes people of European, like, White descent and Asians. So, by diversity, they are talking about people who are not that represented on campus, such as people of Hispanic or African descent. Basically, diversity does not include Asians." When I asked him why he thought Asian students were not included even though they are still a minority group, Orlando responded by pointing to the model minority myth:

> Why do I think Asians aren't? Okay, that's kind of harder. I feel like how Asians are portrayed as a model minority and the purpose of portraying Asians as a model minority is to discredit discrimination against other ethnic groups, so in that sense, by placing Asians as a model minority is to turn people of Asian descent against people of other minority descents. So, in a sense, "Oh you're Asian. You're probably smart already," stuff like that. It sounds like a positive thing, but it's more like a backhanded compliment in a sort of way. Like, as an Asian individual, it discredits your own achievements just because of your descent. So, I feel like Asians are not that included because of that: "Oh they're already good at everything. We don't need to show them."

Like Aiden and Jason, Orlando thinks Asian Americans are excluded from campus diversity initiatives, which he understands as programs designed to support underrepresented minority groups. But in contrast to their views, Orlando does not see this as positive or appropriate. Rather, Orlando recognizes the power of the model minority myth and criticizes it for the way it discredits discrimination. He does this even as he evaluates the model minority myth for the damage it levels on individuals, rather than a structural perspective; that is, he complains that the model minority myth takes away from individual achievements by attributing it to one's descent. Orlando's sense is that administrators may actively promote the model minority myth when they develop diversity programs that exclude Asian Americans.

At Christ College, Peter, a heterosexual cisgender man, also pointed to the model minority myth. When asked why he thought Asian Americans were not included in diversity, Peter responded, "I think again it goes back to the idea of being the model minority, and I think when we talk about diversity, we often think of more of the underprivileged ethnic minorities and accommodating to their needs, which is completely necessary and relevant and important. But because that tends to be the goal and focus, I think maybe Asian Americans sort of fall outside a little. Like, 'You all are fine. You seem to figure it out, so we're not going to focus [on you] too much.'" Like Orlando, Peter suggests that the exclusion of Asian Americans from diversity programs has to do with administrators perceiving Asian Americans' positive outcomes as an artifact of "being the model minority." He also understands diversity as something connected to equity, as something that should improve the life outcomes of racial minorities. Although he would like Asian Americans to be included in diversity programs and discussions, he tells me that he thinks about "checking [his] own privilege, . . . learning to just step back a little bit, look at the deeper issues." Because he perceives that Asian Americans are largely doing well, he would prefer that universities focus their resources on other racialized minority groups.[18]

Overall, students like Peter and Orlando observed that Asian Americans were excluded from diversity programs because an imagined *other* perceives them through the model minority myth. They were seen as successful or "already good at everything" and having "figure[d] it out." There is some evidence for Peter's and Orlando's perception that university administrators may indeed perceive Asian Americans through the model minority myth.[19] Sharon Lee argues that Asian Americans have been "de-minoritized" on campus—no longer seen as minorities—due to their overrepresentation (on some campuses), the model minority myth, and legacies of "yellow peril."[20] The term "yellow peril" comes from White Americans' xenophobic response to a growing Chinese immigrant population and immigration from other Asian countries during the late nineteenth century.[21] During this period, US legislators passed restrictive immigration laws, including the Chinese Exclusion Act of 1882 and the Asiatic Barred Zone Act of 1917, with the goal of ending immigration from Asian countries. When tied with the legacies of "yellow peril," the model minority myth suggests that the overrepresentation of Asian Americans presents a threat to higher education.[22] Indeed, on some campuses, Asian Americans are not considered minorities; Asian Americans are sometimes excluded from definitions of underrepresented racial minorities among funding agencies.[23] To the extent that Asian Americans are excluded from diversity programs on the basis of their overrepresentation, the model minority myth, and "yellow peril" fears, university policies and administrators may be complicit in the racial triangulation process that suggests that Asian Americans are somehow exceptional. Regardless of who is claiming the model minority myth, when Asian Americans are seen as exemplary and excluded, who and what counts as a racially diverse population reflect a racial hierarchy.

Students also articulate an unsettling relationship between White people and Asian Americans that may be indicative of shifting racial alliances and stratification. The same students who excluded Asian Americans from their understanding of diversity typically did so by alluding to Asian Americans' similarity to White students. As demographics indicate that the United States will no longer be a majority White nation by 2050, researchers theorize how racial stratification and inequality might look in the future.[24] Moving beyond a Black–White binary for considering racial stratification, some scholars have integrated Hispanic groups and Asian Americans to develop a triracial system. For example, the sociologist Eduardo Bonilla-Silva argues that certain Asian ethnic groups and lighter-skinned Hispanic groups will form an "honorary White" grouping that sits between White people and Black people.[25] While the White group largely retains its homogeneity, the Black group extends to include darker-skinned Hispanic groups and certain Asian American groups, becoming the "collective Black." "Honorary Whites" provide a buffer between White people and the "collective Black" in such a way that White people remain in power. Such a triracial system fits well with the process of racial triangulation that elevates Asian Americans toward the privileges associated with Whiteness while maintaining their foreignness as neither White nor Black.[26] When Asian American students perceive themselves as culturally distinct yet similar to White people in their exclusion from diversity, they actively engage in restructuring race on their campuses in ways that may produce a triracial system and perpetuate racist racial hierarchies.

Students here articulated their exclusion in ways that suggest an implicit understanding of diversity as something that promotes equity—that is, a power analysis frame of diversity. However, their understanding of how that equity might be achieved—by filling a cultural deficit—carries cultural baggage that hurts racial equity in the long run. Whether Asian Americans claim distinct cultural values or whether others perceive them as the model minority, the model minority myth ultimately does no one any favors—even if marshaled in the name of equity. When equity stands on the dubious foundation of the model minority myth, movements toward equity will only reinforce racial hierarchies that maintain White racial dominance, anti-Blackness, and cultural essentialist views about racial groups.

Representation in Student Government Leadership at West University

Several students noted a tension in the extent to which Asian Americans are truly included on their campus: while Asian Americans make up a sizable portion of the student body at West University, they are underrepresented in student government. Unlike the Asian American students who pointed to the size of their population as a sign of inclusion, these more critical students recognized a disconnect between their overall representation on campus and their underrepresentation in positions of student leadership. Darren, a heterosexual cisgender man, explained, "I feel like we're fortunate here that Asian Americans have a pretty large representation, being that we make up a solid amount of the student body. Except my only concern is that while we do make up a large percentage of the student body, most of the governing is still done by Caucasians." When I asked Darren to speculate on why this might be the case, he focused on Asian students' personal upbringing and how other students view them on campus: "I feel like that could just be a difference in upbringing. At least for me, my high school, while it was a lot of Asian dominated, most of the student government was Caucasian. So, I feel like that might kind of translate over into college. But you could also say it's a personality difference in that Asians are regarded as more reserved and not as outspoken, and so that may translate into people [not] wanting to run for student government offices."

Orlando, who felt that Asian Americans were excluded from diversity because of the model minority myth, also voiced issues regarding representation and leadership positions: "I feel like because Asians take up a big portion of the student demographics at West University, like, even though we're a minority, it doesn't feel like it. So I feel like, regarding discrimination, I guess it's limited to student government positions, where most people—even though I think Asian Americans take up one-third of West University's population and Whites take up one-third, so it's kind of equal—but regarding student government, people of European descent still take up most of the spots." When I asked Orlando why he thinks there are so few Asian Americans in student government, he responded, "This is a little bit of generalizing, but I feel like for people of Asian heritage, it's just in general, we have different priorities to people of different ethnicities. It's not so much about the race; it's about how we're raised. So, I feel like a lot of Asians just feel like student government is a vain popularity contest and there isn't much of a point in partaking, but it's just disproportionate. There are still Asians on the student government. I just feel like it's more of our culture." Orlando and Darren both sense that there is something odd about the demographics of West University's student government, given its distance from the demographics of the student body as a whole. When asked to explain the relative absence of Asian Americans from student government, both speak of individual differences and differences in upbringing. Darren speaks of personality differences, while Orlando suggests that many Asian Americans read a desire to run for student government as a sign of vanity; but both also describe elements of culture. Orlando speaks of culture directly, suggesting that Asian American culture lends to less involvement in student government. Darren mentions how Asian Americans are culturally regarded as reserved and quiet, transitioning uneasily between individual personality and outside perceptions.

Numerous studies show that Asian Americans are underrepresented in leadership positions in various sectors of US society.[27] Scholars have dubbed this the "bamboo ceiling," where Asian Americans have excelled but the top echelons remain unobtainable.[28] Some scholars and commentators have attributed the underrepresentation of Asian Americans in leadership positions to cultural differences, which might work in different ways. Asian Americans might, for instance, internalize cultural values that do not fit Western views of leadership and therefore be evaluated as ineffective leaders by Western power brokers.[29] When Asian Americans do not view themselves as leaders, they may also evaluate Asian Americans in leadership negatively.[30] In contrast, some scholars reject the notion of an essentialist Asian American leadership style as Orientalist and as ignoring how Asian Americans are racialized in ways that depend on constructing the East as inferior to the West.[31] The idea of "Asian American leadership" is itself a social construct that reveals how dominant ideas of leadership are White-centric.[32] In other words, if our ideal leader looks like a White, heterosexual, cisgender man, that is not by accident but by racialized and gendered design.[33]

The view of Asian Americans as lacking in leadership skills is the result of the racialization of Asian Americans through racial triangulation and the model minority myth. Proponents of the model minority myth suggests that Asian Americans are culturally superior to other communities of color and contend that all one needs is the "right" cultural values to get ahead. Instead of engaging in social activism or vying for positions of power, the "right" kind of minority achieves the American dream through hard work and education. This model not only valorizes Asian Americans relative to Black people and other communities of color but also constructs them as apolitical outsiders, forever apart from US civil society.[34] Asian Americans' status as political and civic outsiders can further be encapsulated in their racialization as "perpetual foreigners." They are unique (and therefore foreign) in their cultural values yet also outsiders who are excluded from the echelons of power.

Indeed, as we move to discussing Asian American representation and disadvantages outside of West University's walls, Orlando's comments gesture toward the idea of Asian Americans as "perpetual foreigners": "But other than that [lack of representation in student leadership], . . . people of Asian descent have good standing at West University. I feel like I still have a lot of opportunities because of strength in numbers, but I feel like after college, for Asian Americans, it's a lot different, because, from my experience, being someone of Asian descent is inherently a disadvantage in society beyond college." When I asked why he feels this way, Orlando pointed to how Asian Americans are seen as "perpetual foreigners": "In short, Asians are perpetual foreigners where it's 'cause historically, there weren't that many Asians here, but now recently, in the last few decades, there's been a huge influx of Asian immigrants, and these immigrants have children. So Asians don't fit the stereotypical American picture. So I feel like, just because of how you look, especially in some industries, maybe not like tech, . . . it's a disadvantage, say, like interviews, they won't admit it, but I feel like they would prefer someone who looks more stereotypically American in a sense that Asians are perpetual foreigners." In contexts where there are many Asian Americans, such as at West University, Orlando attributes Asian American underrepresentation in leadership to different priorities and culture, but in contexts where there is no "strength in numbers," Orlando described Asian Americans as "perpetual foreigners." From Orlando's perspective, then, Asian Americans' representation in leadership shifts depending on their numeric context. Where there are many Asian Americans, leadership may come down to an individual's choices or priorities, while in spaces where Asian Americans are numeric minorities, their lack of representation is because they are not White. For Orlando, being a "perpetual foreigner" is connected to the racial composition of a context, which can shape an Asian American's ability to become a leader or obtain success.

Darren and Orlando observe a tension between their campus overrepresentation, on the one hand, and their underrepresentation in positions of power, on the other hand. Their ability to recognize their overrepresentation in the student body and underrepresentation relative to positions of power both inside and outside the university allows them insight into how their campus's approach to racial diversity may not be equitable. But even with this insight, Darren's and Orlando's explanations for their lack of representation in student government reflect cultural beliefs endemic to the model minority myth and legacies of racial triangulation that exclude Asian Americans from positions of power. Their explanations of their underrepresentation challenge neither the racist ideas in the model minority myth nor the process of racial triangulation that has left Asian Americans excluded from positions of power.

It is important to note that students of color in diversity leadership were sometimes divided over what their role in leadership meant for their racial or ethnic group. Take Greg's reflections on his identities while serving in diversity leadership at West University: "I'm the only South Asian person on that [diversity] board that I feel like, 'Oh, I'm the token person that is here to talk about these issues.' It's hard, and there's different levels. I'm a South Asian student that grew up in the US. There's South Asian students that—I don't know if I'm supposed to speak for them, but my presence on that panel is supposed to be representative of their experiences, as well, and that's just not the case." As a South Asian student born in the United States, Greg recognizes that he cannot speak for all South Asians, but he finds himself in the difficult position of representing South Asians as the sole South Asian American on the diversity board. This raises difficult questions for him in how he ought to engage and represent South Asians.

Contrast Greg's concerns with Oscar's reflections on being one of three Hispanics in student diversity leadership at Christ College:

> Being an ethnic minority working in a coordinator position has been—is like a big boost. I have friends who say the same things: "It's good to have [a] Hispanic working in leadership here in the university, 'cause we don't really see that." The ones I know, there's like only three of us. . . . I have a Hispanic friend. We talked about it, but she was encouraged, said it was good to have people. 'Cause we're also taking cross-cultural psychology class, and we have the same class. So we talk about diversity and want more Hispanics or Latinos involved in leadership around campus.

Although Oscar does not reflect on whether he can speak for all Hispanics or Latinos at Christ College, his presence alone in leadership has received affirmation from other Hispanics and Latinos on campus. His presence is an encouragement to other Hispanics and Latinos when the leadership at Christ College is predominantly White.

When racialized minorities obtain leadership positions, they are met with ongoing conflicts. Oscar's comments remind us that many people take inspiration from having people who look like you or are from your racial or ethnic group in leadership. This is worthwhile, but Greg's comments remind us of the very real difficulty of representation, especially if one is a token in leadership. Even if a person of color breaks any kind of racial ceiling to obtain a position of power, they must contend with the difficulties of representing their heterogeneous group and managing different expectations and hopes among their coethnics and the broader inequitable racial structure. Representation matters to students, but inequitable racial structures and racist understandings of culture shape who is represented and how.

The Pitfalls of Numerical Representation

In chapter 1, we saw that students defined diversity through numerical representation and metrics. In this chapter, we have interrogated what numerical representation means for students' understanding of diversity, inclusion, and equity. Scholars find that numerical representation or compositional diversity is important for the inclusion of minoritized groups.[35] Here, we see the ambivalent ways numerical representation matters to students and the consequences of these perceptions for their assessment of equity and inclusion.

Numerical representation and metrics are part of the way universities operate as inequality regimes because these numbers do not exist without interpretation. When students rely on numerical representation to assert that their presence constitutes diversity, their discussions of numerical representation and inclusion reflect the color-blind "equalizing" or flattening part of diversity. Quantifiable approaches to diversity can thus support the view of *diversity as difference*. This understanding of diversity works through numerical representation and visual cues, rather than in any deeper structural way or in relationship to inequality. An approach to diversity and inclusion understood as numeric representation or visual cues overshadows other social identities that may not be easily visible or quantifiable.[36] It also elides structures of inequality that shape representation and experiences of inequality and exclusion that exist beneath the numbers.[37] When students interpret the presence of minoritized groups as a straightforward marker of inclusion, they are acceding to one way that the university works as an inequality regime.

A minority of Asian Americans in my sample at both West University and Christ College felt that the university's language of diversity and diversity programs did not apply to them. These students also drew on numerical representation, but they made sense of their numerical representation through the model minority myth. Some students drew on cultural arguments endemic to the model minority myth to assert that there was no need to include them in diversity programs because of Asian cultural values. These types of beliefs—even when wrong and in the minority—matter. Leading up to the end of race-based affirmation action, some Asian Americans, such as Chinese Americans, called for the end of affirmative action on cultural arguments. These cultural arguments upheld values supposedly specific to Chinese students and denigrated those of Black and Hispanic groups.[38]

Notably, when Asian American students described why they were or should be excluded from campus diversity programs, they sometimes did so in a way that reflected a *power analysis* understanding of diversity. They saw diversity programs as means to improve access for underrepresented groups or other racial minorities; however, this understanding of diversity produces a racist racial hierarchy through racial triangulation. This was evident when students suggested that Asian American students are already similar to White students in education; in their account, it is Black students or Hispanic students who need help from universities because they do not value hard work or education. Even as these students understand diversity through an equity framework, they are still relying on racist cultural essentialist narratives.

Ultimately, Asian Americans' appeal to numerical representation to understand their relationship to campus inclusion and racial diversity reflects *different* understandings of inclusion with *similar* racial equity results. One narrative reflects the flattening, color-blind approach to diversity that does not acknowledge systemic inequality, thus leaving racial inequality and racist structures intact. The other narratives reflect a reliance on the model minority myth and racial triangulation. Neither the color-blind perspective of racial diversity nor the model minority myth challenges racist racial structures. Numerical representation and numeric metrics more broadly can perpetuate universities' role as inequality regimes through color-blind interpretations or cultural essentialist explanations.

PART III

Diversity Challenges and Futures

6

LGBTQ+ Students

In part 2 of this book, we examined the limitations of diversity as difference and numeric representation as paths to inclusion and equity. In part 3, we move away from these limitations to consider how LGBTQ+ students and Asian American students work toward equity regimes and the challenges they face in creating equity and inclusion for themselves. We begin with LGBTQ+ students in this chapter and turn to Asian Americans in chapter 7.

Chelsey, a queer, cisgender woman of color, has short, dark hair that she tosses frequently to the side. Chelsey told me that she thought she would be closeted forever—that is, until she met other LGBTQ+ students at Christ College. Her friendships with members of Harbor gave her the social support to come out about her sexuality. Chelsey told me about how she imagines diversity and equity on campus for LGBTQ+ individuals: "Like, what equity would look like, what it would look like to have diverse communities and openly accepting communities, and I think that what it would look like is that it would just feel really normal. Like, there's an otherness that comes with being a person of color or being trans* or being queer that is still prevalent even in the queer community. Like, even in openly accepting communities, there's a sense of otherness that I feel like if a community was completely accepting, that would just—that wouldn't exist. That wouldn't be there." Chelsey describes equity in relationship to inclusion. She imagines equity in a diverse community as one where belonging is not dependent on dominant identity markers.

Across state borders at West University, I met with Sol, a student of color who identifies as nonbinary and pansexual. Sol's short, dark hair is dyed slightly green, and on the day I met them, they were wearing a Star Wars–themed T-shirt over green khaki pants. When I asked Sol about inclusion, Sol said, "There is a queer community here, and when you get involved, you meet so many people. They're my chosen family or, like, all the queer people I've met here. And there's definitely that community, but to [be] truly inclusive, it can't just be that community. It needs to be on a deeper institutional level too." Sol, like Chelsey, recognizes that true inclusion means something more than feeling safe within one's chosen family. True inclusion requires institutional change. Sol told me about their ideal vision of diversity:

> It would be that we're all just celebrating, like truly seen as equals, and White supremacy is abolished. . . . All these institutions—education, justice system, and all that—are still very rooted in all these isms and phobias—so in an ideal world, all these institutions would be ridden of their oppression, and every community would be truly served and feel safe and protected, 'cause I feel true diversity isn't just like a population. I mean, you could say that the United States is a very diverse population, but to reach diversity, that would have to include making sure that this population feels safe and represented, which is not the case as long as White supremacy and all this stuff is still active in all these institutions and society.

For Sol, a truly diverse community is one in which institutions and systems are emancipated from systemic forms of exclusion and oppression. Chelsey agreed, imagining what it would be like if the normalcy she seeks were embedded in the system:

> It functions as a part of the system. It's not something that's separate. It's fundamentally linked into our institutions that we have, like in government, and even at universities and schools, race isn't a separate issue. Diversity isn't a separate issue. Queerness isn't a separate issue. It's linked and a part of the system, and there's a normalcy to it. . . . I feel like if we ever get to a point where . . . we've been surprised by hate because we've gotten so accustomed to love and acceptance, then that will show that we've accepted that diversity works and that diversity has become a part of our system.

Both Chelsey and Sol draw on a power analysis frame of diversity to imagine what equity and inclusion might look like for their communities. They envision a world of belonging where cultural norms are oriented around love and acceptance, a just world where institutions and broader systems are unfettered from patterns of injustice.

This chapter examines how LGBTQ+ students at West University and Christ College imagine and engage in future building to create equity regimes. For the students at West University, I focus on student advocacy and experiences of organizational change; at Christ College, on how LGBTQ+ students are expanding and challenging religious beliefs. At both universities, students imagine cultural norms that do not depend on cisnormativity and heteronormativity. The last section looks at how LGBTQ+ students recognize the challenges of creating intersectional equity within their own communities and across their universities at large. LGBTQ+ students confront current challenges and imagine futures for themselves by dreaming up new possibilities for diversity, equity, and inclusion, both within and beyond their communities.

Organizational Changes and Challenges at West University

West University is known for being one of the friendliest LGBTQ+ campuses in the United States. Despite this, LGBTQ+ students described their inclusion within the university's structure as incomplete. I focus on two areas where students identified organizational change that fell short of true inclusion: student identification cards and gender-inclusive bathrooms.[1] While both examples indicate West University's willingness to change its structure and policies for LGBTQ+ students, the uneven implementation left students feeling unsure of the university's commitment to diversity.

At West University, students can use either their legal names or their chosen names on their university identification cards. This is especially important to trans* students, who may go by a different name than their legal name. For trans* and nonbinary students, being able to identify as they see themselves is important for their sense of belonging and can affect their mental health.[2] When I started my fieldwork, West University had just started allowing students to change their names on their student identification cards.

Ben, an Asian American, gay, cisgender student at West University, spoke about how he had waited for this policy change throughout his entire time at West University:

> For a concrete example I can give is on our IDs. . . . It was just recently that you were allowed to change the front of yours to a preferred name, and that took like four years to do. And like, it sounds like a really easy thing to do, right? It's not like we're changing legal paperwork. We're just changing maybe one line of code or something or printing job, but it took them four years. It's done behind closed doors, and I will never know the process, but I have to be happy that it was at least done.

Ben's comments suggest an awareness that even changes that appear simple require many conversations and layers of coordination between different administrators and offices at the university. It took several years for the change to be made. Ben described how he feels about the process of change: "I think in my freshman year, I would have been like, 'Yeah, they could have done a lot more,' but for me right now, the change in pace that West University is going through I think is at an acceptable level. . . . It takes time, and there's always the bureaucratic thing; there's always red tape." Ben no longer feels impatient with the university, and, at least in his comments to me, he does not question the process or seek transparency on why it took so long. Instead, he is satisfied that West University is making an "acceptable level" of change to incorporate LGBTQ+ students on campus.

Dani, a queer student of color who uses he/him and they/them pronouns, expressed more frustration with the university's approach to policy change. As a leader of a LGBTQ+ coalition that works with various LGBTQ+ student organizations, Dani encountered various stakeholders' resistance to changing the policy:

> [*Sighs*] At some form, I would say that diversity on this campus does include tokenism especially in how they portray the campus as . . . being quote unquote "diverse." And seeing how the administration, how the campus, how different institutions take people of color but also most importantly queer people and how they co-opt the work. So, like, an example would be . . . [one of the LGBT groups has] been working on trying to get rid of the dead names off of the [identification] cards, but they're still facing retaliation against that from [the university police] because they want to put the dead names on the back—I think in gold lettering— . . . Infuriating! Why do they even need to have it in the first place,

> especially gold! And then, how some of the student government is taking some credit of doing that work.

Unlike Ben, who expressed satisfaction with the changes at West University, Dani felt the process was riddled with conflict and found the results far from satisfactory. The policy allowed students to have their dead names removed from the front of the cards but still required that their legal names appeared on the back and in a different color. Dani also resented that various groups tried to take credit for LGBTQ+ students' efforts.

Even after the university nominally changed its policy regarding student identification cards, it continued to rely on forms and databases that referred to students by their legal names. As a first-year student, Aaron was part of the first cohort of LGBTQ+ students who could use his chosen name on his identification card throughout his entire tenure at West University. Aaron, a trans* student with disabilities, spoke of his experience using his identification card:

> I am registered through [the student disability center]. . . . I get special food, . . . but the problem was the form didn't have anything for my preferred name. So everything was under my legal name. And then I tried to get in touch with the dietitian who runs the program, and she was like, "Who are you? I don't know who this is. Who's Aaron? We don't have an Aaron listed in the system." And I was like, "Oh, that's because you have my legal name because you didn't ask for my preferred name." And I also had trouble—they keep a directory in there for all the people that have access to the gluten-free food, and they took my [identification] card, and they just looked at the front of it, and they were like, "You're not on this list." And I was like, "Yes, I am. Turn it over, look at my legal name, and then look at the list again." So, it's been a little tricky.

Aaron's experience reveals that West University's system has failed to incorporate students' preferred names across the campus's administrative units. A charitable interpretation is that the policy is new; hiccups are perhaps to be expected. At the same time, Aaron's specific experience reveals a telling lack of sensitivity to intersectionality on the university's part. As Aaron put it later in our conversation, "I just felt like the system was set up for trans* or disabled. It wasn't set up for trans* and disabled." Too often, institutional diversity initiatives focus on one salient social feature, rather than intersecting ones.[3] LGBTQ+ individuals frequently experience other intersecting forms of oppression, such that their gender identities and sexuality intersect with race, class, and other social locations that shape their disadvantage.[4] When the identification system is set up on a single axis, students who sit at different disadvantaged intersections struggle to access the university's resources.

At the time of this writing, West University no longer requires students' legal names to be listed on the back of their identification cards. West University's website describes that this change was made, in part, through the advocacy work of different LGBTQ+ student organizations. A perusal of West University's resources suggests that the university is continually changing how it incorporates students' names, such as providing diplomas with students' lived names. These changes suggest that university administrators are actively listening to LGBTQ+ students and amending their policies to move the university more toward an equity regime.

LGBTQ+ students also told me that the university's approach to gender-inclusive bathrooms fell short of their needs. Jay, a student of color who identifies as nonbinary, trans*, and queer, found many of the university's supposedly LGBTQ+-friendly policies "performative" rather than supportive:

> I know that West University is one of the most friendly LGBT campuses and one of the top trans*-friendly campuses. . . . I feel very lucky to be here and to have certain resources that we have, but I know we can do better. And a lot of the resources West University presents feels performative and not to the best of their ability. . . . I'm nonbinary, . . . so I try to seek out gender-inclusive bathrooms around campus. And we have a lot, but not enough. . . . I have a couple of classes where there are no gender-inclusive bathrooms in that building, so I have to walk five minutes to the next building and miss fifteen minutes of my class, just so I can use the bathroom for two minutes, and then I'm missing out on my education, which is why I'm going here. So, yeah, we're one of the top trans*-friendly campuses in the nation, but it's like a very low bar, I think, to even reach.

To Jay, the university's efforts feel more like a staged performance than a sincere attempt to create inclusion and equity. Jay continued, "And even if there are [gender-inclusive bathrooms], they are very poorly taken care of. . . . And even where the menstrual hygienic products go, they still have written, 'Place your feminine hygiene products here,' and I'm like, 'You don't even—' so, yes, they transformed a single-stalled bathroom and put a sign on it that says 'gender inclusive,' but they're not actually catering to the community they're supposed to be helping." Jay points out the logical inconsistency of providing a gender-neutral restroom that uses cisgendered language to describe menstrual products. Jay interprets the university's failure to provide convenient gender-inclusive bathrooms and to remove gendered language from the bathrooms' signs as evidence of its limited commitment to full inclusion. West University is willing to issue policy statements and designate a handful of gender-inclusive bathrooms, but these actions fall far short of the sorts of changes needed to transform its cisnormativity.

Rian, a queer, nonbinary student of color, also brought up the university's lack of gender-inclusive bathrooms. When I asked them whether the university's approach to diversity included their identities, first they laughed before they explained,

> They claim diversity in the sense that, "Oh, we have gender-neutral bathrooms" . . . [*sighs*]. Like, you can't say that it's diverse and, like, we have gender-neutral bathrooms when it takes me like thirty minutes to find one. They should literally be in every building. The one in [building A] literally has a sign that says, . . . "The open gender-neutral bathroom is in [building B]." So, if I have to leave from lecture, I have to walk all the way to, like, [building B] just to go to the bathroom. . . . And at the same time, I know some people who are like, "Oh, well, just, like, you pass for like a girl, so just, like, go to the women's restroom." I'm like, "Yeah, I understand that, but also, like, I'm not comfortable going there," and when I do go there, I'm just like, "This is not, like, the space that I want to be in."

Rian, like Jay, emphasizes how difficult it is to access the campus's limited supply of gender-inclusive bathrooms. While the existence of gender-inclusive bathrooms might suggest an openness to the presence of trans* and nonbinary students on campus, the reality of their placement makes them inaccessible. Forcing students to choose between leaving a lecture to access a distant bathroom or using one nearby at risk to their mental health and physical safety does not represent true inclusion.[5] Since conducting my interviews, West University has released an updated map of gender-inclusive restrooms. Even so, the majority of campus buildings still lack even a single gender-inclusive bathroom.

The lack of gender-inclusive bathrooms can also be a problem in housing on campus. Jordan, a biracial, queer, trans* and gender-nonconforming student, explained,

> Queer trans* folks, especially queer trans* folks of color, are more impacted [financially] and have more difficulty just getting to college and being able to pay for college. For example, even our LGBTQ+ housing, which is meant to be a safe space for queer trans* folks, a lot of folks can't afford that space because we're more expensive, . . . because most classic residential halls have common restrooms, and the LGBTQ+ housing rooms don't. Each room has an individual restroom, and that is just an issue. . . . A lot of the freshmen that I interact with coming in are like, "I can't afford it." And that's why they can't access that space.

Although LGBTQ+ housing only differs from "classic" housing with regard to its bathroom configuration—en suite bathrooms compared to gendered bathrooms shared by a floor—this difference nonetheless makes the rooms inaccessible because it increases the cost of student housing. When trans* students navigate gendered housing, they face potential harassment and must strategize how and when to use bathrooms for their own safety.[6] In our conversation, Jordan observed that the university could solve this problem by designating even some of the bathrooms in traditional dorms as gender inclusive, thereby lowering housing costs and creating safer living conditions for LGBTQ+ students.

A conversation with Dani helped me understand why LGBTQ+ students are in separate housing in the first place. In short, the university created the separate housing option to address "unsafe conditions in terms of housing, because of how trans*phobic people are." Dani explained,

> That's why LGBTQ+ housing has to be located in [one type of dormitory] compared to [classic dormitories], because the bathrooms are really gendered. It's either male, female. . . . The overall residential government institution behind our housing—they're really slow, or they're not really up to times—and when we try to propose, "Oh, let's make the bathrooms gender neutral," they're like, "No, that isn't how it is. Look at the doors, those are clearly men and women. . . . No, just make them go to the respective bathroom." And I'm like, "What if they don't have a respective bathroom?" . . . But over multiple times, the [residential] life—the higher-ups—they're like, "No, we can't do that." And I just want to tape a sign on the door and be like, "Gender neutral."

Dani's narrative describes a type of administrative violence in housing that LGBTQ+ students at Christ College also experienced.[7] The trans* scholar and activist Z Nicolazzo and colleagues argue this violence occurs when "trans* oppression is embedded throughout administrative policies and practices."[8] Since my interviews, the university now provides gender-inclusive housing for students who request it without requiring them to live in LGBTQ+ housing.

Students' experiences with the university's changes to its identification cards and gender-inclusive restrooms suggest that creating equity regimes is a work in progress. West University made some changes—indeed laudable ones—but the changes were incompletely institutionalized. Students continued to seek changes to move the university away from an inequality regime. West University has heard their demands and has made more changes, but the work toward transforming the university continues.

Changing Culture at Christ College

In chapter 4, we saw how LGBTQ+ students tried to bring organizational changes to Christ College by focusing on the college's statement on sexuality and housing. Here, we focus on how LGBTQ+ students lean into Christ College's emphasis on racial reconciliation in hopes of expanding reconciliation to include themselves. Christ College has a Center for Racial Reconciliation and hosts talks with famous evangelical speakers and seminars on racial reconciliation.[9] The premises of racial reconciliation call for interpersonal healing among people of different races, the unity of religious faith over racial identity, and individual and relational responses to racial discrimination.[10] Although practitioners of racial reconciliation often focus on individual change, racial reconciliation historically had a systemic edge—one where ministers and theologians understood racial inequality not only through individuals and interactions but also via institutions and systems.[11] The contemporary limiting of racial reconciliation discourse to individuals and interactions is largely the result of White evangelicals' emphasis on color-blindness over race consciousness.[12]

LGBTQ+ students drew two conclusions from Christ College's emphasis on racial reconciliation. First, by centering the university's diversity efforts on race, the approach excluded other identities that might otherwise be considered part of diversity as well as those identities that might intersect. At the same time, the approach provided a potential discursive resource to expand reconciliation to include the LGBTQ+ community and move the university toward an equity regime.

Genesis, who uses feminine and nonbinary pronouns and identifies as lesbian, shared their conflicting opinions on the university's approach to diversity in our conversation: "When I hear 'diversity' at Christ College, it's usually . . . tied up with the word 'reconciliation,' and that is almost entirely always used for race, which I think is an absolutely incredible, excellent thing. We have the [Center for Racial Reconciliation], and that's all incredible. I'm so glad that Christ College has that. LGBT not as much." Genesis affirms the importance of racial diversity and the push for racial reconciliation at Christ College, asserting that it is "an absolutely incredible, excellent thing," but they note that LGBT identities are not included in this definition of diversity. Genesis went on to describe working with the DEI officer at Christ College and closed on a hopeful note that diversity and reconciliation will eventually expand to LGBT identities: "I have hopes for the future that eventually they [DEI officer and the university] will start to work in the term 'reconciliation' with LGBT people as well. Right now, it is almost entirely used for race. But I have hopes. I think we are moving in the right direction, just very, very slowly and on the backs of the Harbor leaders and our allies in faculty and staff who are willing to help us. It's a slow march, but we'll get there."

When I asked Josh, a White, gay, cisgender man, about the possibilities of expanding racial reconciliation to LGBTQ+ students, he exclaimed,

> Oh yeah, 100 percent. I think that needs to be another term in Christ College's vocabulary is "LGBTQI+" or "queer reconciliation"—something like that. That is definitely what is missing, and it's almost awkward. It's like, how do you talk about diversity without talking about being LGBT? How do you talk about racial issues without—it would be like, to me, talking about race without talking about being a woman or something like that? Because that's like a completely new layer to the whole story. So you can't talk about just one leg of diversity. I think you have to talk about the whole picture, or you're not talking about diversity.

For Josh, diversity and reconciliation are not just about race but also about the different social parts that make a person. Without using the term "intersectionality," Josh implicitly recognizes that race cannot be separated from other social identities. Josh believes that including LGBTQ+ identities in reconciliation discourse at Christ College would create a fuller understanding of diversity.

While Josh and Genesis argued for the expansion of reconciliation discourse, Felicia, a White cisgender woman who identifies as bisexual, had mixed feelings about reconciliation:

> I think racial reconciliation comes from a really good place, but I also think, in a lot of ways, using the word "reconciliation" is a way for White people to assert themselves into the equation of race. Like, yeah, "We want to make amends with you. We want to make amends for our actions by supporting you and, like, being inclusive," when in reality, the way [to] reconciliating [is] not just apologize but actually do something, like actively changing a system that is inherently flawed and that kind of thing. So, in some ways, I kind of resent reconciliation because . . . I don't think it's the best way to go about bringing in an all-inclusive community.

Felicia's view of the limits of a reconciliation approach to inclusion is based on a power and equity understanding of diversity that differs from the relationally centered approach to racial reconciliation often promoted by White evangelicals. She explained how this is connected to her view of LGBTQ+ reconciliation:

> I think it [LGBTQ+ reconciliation] would be something similar to what I said about diversity. It's not like apologizing but fostering a community. . . . Harbor is called Harbor as if it's a safe place, and I mean, that's great, and having a safe place is great, but having a safe place shouldn't be necessary. So, having a community where there can be an LGBTQ club for students to relate to one another so they can have "Oh, there's people who are really similar to me" but also not a place that needs to be, like, where they go when they feel discriminated against.

Without a power and equity approach to reconciliation, Felicia argues that true LGBTQ+ inclusion is not possible. Felicia wants a type of reconciliation that changes the system. This approach would translate into a campus that no longer needs safe spaces for LGBTQ+ students. Rather, organizations like Harbor could simply function like other student organizations, where students can meet over similar identities and interests. Felicia's ideal world is one where systemic changes have created a place of belonging.

When Tom, a White, gay, cisgender man, and I discussed reconciliation, he described his dissatisfaction with it, saying, "It's easy to throw it around and make you feel good when you say it, and any word like that is easy to become a buzzword." Later on, when I asked him about the difference between true reconciliation and "buzzword" reconciliation for LGBTQ+ students at Christ College, he responded, "It [true LGBTQ+ reconciliation] would be a Christian university acknowledging that being gay is not a sin, and that feels like a lot to ask, but I feel like that's literally not that much to ask. And like, acknowledging that it's possible to be trans* and that it's not a sin to be trans*. Really, like, basic kind of stuff would be what reconciliation would look like." I asked him, "What do you think buzzword reconciliation would look like for the queer and trans* community?" He replied, "It would look a little bit like it does now. Like, queer students satiated with not being attacked and queer students doing all the work. Like, Harbor does all the work instead of the institution stepping in and putting resources forward. Basically, what it looks like right now. We're really good at buzzword reconciliation as far as queer students." Like Felicia, Tom wants to see organizational changes that prioritize LGBTQ+ students. What is more, he wants the university to initiate those changes without prodding from Harbor. As we saw earlier, Harbor has often stepped in to help students move out of dangerous housing situations and advocated for LGBTQ+ students in meetings with high-ranking administrators. Tom imagines a campus where these actions are no longer needed. Instead, Christ College, as an equity regime, would change its theological positions on sexuality and gender and support LGBTQ+ students out of its own volition.

Even though Christ College continued to exclude LGBTQ+ students through its statement on sexuality, students hoped for cultural and structural changes through expanding reconciliation narratives. The students quoted in this section criticized racial reconciliation discourse for lacking a systemic edge, but they also saw possibilities of expanding it to include LGBTQ+ students. Racial reconciliation acts as a cultural resource and an important part of Christ College's values and theology. Students perceived how expanding reconciliation, implemented with organizational changes, could move the university toward greater equity and inclusion.

Challenging Cisnormative and Heteronormative Culture on Campus

Organizations are gendered and heterosexualized in that they perpetuate inequality in gender and sexuality.[13] Students' commentary on organizational changes earlier in this chapter and in chapter 4 show that they recognize that supposedly inclusive policies would remain hollow if the university did not address cisgender normative and heteronormative understandings of gender and sexuality. To transform their universities from inequality regimes to equity regimes, shifts in cultural understandings and norms around gender and sexuality must also occur on the community level.

Brett, a nonbinary and queer student, described this disconnect between policy and community well:

> When we are talking about diversity, a lot of times [we] are talking about sexuality and gender diversity. And I think in some parts that gets incor-

> porated into structure, right? Like, a lot of TAs [teaching assistants] are trained to ask about people's pronouns, and you know, these fiery op-eds come into the [university newspaper], and now we are one of the only campuses that lets you change your name on your identification card, or you know, we have all these maps of these gender-inclusive bathrooms. Whether this gets incorporated into the structure of West University as a community, I don't know.

Brett names many of the policy changes discussed earlier: identification cards, gender-inclusive restrooms, and even the fact that teaching assistants and instructors ask students for their pronouns. Brett, however, questions whether these changes have truly been incorporated into West University's community values. Here, Brett differentiates between the university's organization and community norms and values. The university can make these organizational changes, but unless transformational change occurs across the university community, the efforts will still fall short of inclusion. For Brett, inclusion must also be lived out in community values and norms.

Willow, a student of color who identifies as a cisgender woman and as pansexual, also discussed the university's community norms:

> I think people are still kind of uncomfortable with those who identify as trans*. I think that people who identify as genderqueer often feel ignored, and . . . people just assume their PGPs [personal gender pronouns], and that could be really hurtful. Some professors are trying to be really conscious and ask you for PGPs on the first day, which is great. I think a lot of STEM professors don't really know about that, so that could be difficult. [I] think the biggest struggle is that some people don't know. They don't know what PGPs are. They don't know what bisexual is, and heteronormativity is just everywhere. People are like, "Oh yeah, if you look girly, then you must be straight, right?" . . . So, if we could increase queer visibility around campus and talking about the things that maybe people don't know about, like what asexuality is, what genderqueer is, people would be more aware.

Although Willow acknowledges that some professors consciously ask students for their gender pronouns, she identifies a lack of understanding around gender identities and sexuality in general. Like Brett, she feels that this understanding is missing from the broader university community. For Willow, the way to combat heteronormativity and ignorance is to better educate students, faculty, and administrators on the different aspects of gender identity and sexuality. Once the university community is more aware of these concepts and identities, she argues, it will be more inclusive to LGBTQ+ students.

When faculty and instructors do not ask for gender pronouns, it becomes more difficult for LGBTQ+ students to share their pronouns. Julian, a queer student of color who uses nonbinary pronouns, explained, "If you identify with certain pronouns in a classroom and it's mostly full of people who aren't LGBTQ, like, how do you navigate that without—you know, the burden is put on the person to kind of out themselves in order to be comfortable. But you know, it's like, people should be able to make each other comfortable, rather than . . . one designated person to put all the energy into making their own comfort a priority." Julian's comments suggest that, at least at West University, it is unusual for one to announce their gender pronouns outside of queer spaces. This places a burden on the student to "out themselves in order to be comfortable." In Julian's perspective, the onus to create a gender-inclusive space should not fall on one person but should be a shared value in the university community.

Similarly, Jay described their experience being misgendered in the classroom:

> It stresses me out a lot when your teachers are blatantly homophobic or even casually homophobic, trans*phobic. . . . I'm queer and trans*, so being queer is hard, . . . but being trans* for me is one of the harder things, because it's how other people perceive me. . . . Like, going through a class where my TA and my professor and all my classmates misgender me is very draining. . . . And he picks on me a lot because he thinks I have "astute observations," he says, which is nice. He's nice, but he also calls me a girl: "Look at her. She knows what she's talking about. Everyone else follow." I don't feel comfortable enough to stand up in the middle of my history class and be like, "By the way, I'm trans*." Even though I have a trans* button on my backpack, it's a different thing to verbally confront everyone. . . . Not only am I trans*, but I'm nonbinary, so even if they

> do accept trans* people, explaining to them that there's more than two genders is a harder concept for most people to get, so that's a hurdle I've had to go through. . . . It's daunting to . . . walk into this room and have everyone treat me like something I'm not for like an hour or two, and this is for . . . weeks and then for the rest of the year, and it adds up.

Echoing Julian's concerns, Jay does not feel comfortable standing up and correcting their TA and classmates every time someone misgenders them. This leaves Jay in a difficult position, in which they are continuously misgendered even while trying to engage in their learning environment. This leaves Jay feeling fatigued. The day of our interview, Jay missed class to give themselves mental and emotional respite. Jay's comments reflect the emotional and physical toll trans* and nonbinary people experience in a cisgender binary world.[14]

Gender binary, cisnormative, and heteronormative thinking is also prevalent and institutionalized at Christ College. Despite this, students I spoke with described how they and other members of the university community challenge cisnormative and heteronormative thinking. Sam, a White cisgender man in diversity leadership, described trying to create an inclusive environment for LGBTQ+ students during the worship services he helps plan and host:

> It's difficult because in, like, from what I understand about our school's position on LGBTQ+ identity, they are not completely affirming, and [that] is what I have experienced from talking to close friends and faculty. And so, it makes it hard knowing what we can say as an on-campus worship service and what we can't. The simple way we try to engage with it is to not use anthropomorphic imagery or . . . removing pronouns [when referring to God] as much as possible. . . . It's tied to those two things of just making sure when we're talking about God, we aren't making it into a male God, and we aren't speaking about relationships as if they are one specific normative type and not putting people in binaries.

Sam acknowledges the tensions between Christ College's stance on LGBTQ+ students and its attempt to be inclusive of them as members of the student body. University policies prevent Sam from openly supporting LGBTQ+ students during worship services. To get around the university's policies, he uses more inclusive language about God and resists heteronormative and binary ways of talking about relationships.

Reese, a gay student of color who is part of Harbor, takes a more confrontational approach. When speaking with Christians, Reese argues for queer identities and acceptance:

> One thing I always say to Christians that they kind of all get angry about is like, "If we're made in the image of God, then that means God embodies all these things that we are too. So if my identity is in Christ, that means my queerness is in Christ, because God is gay." . . . If God is real, then God is not a human. Then that means that all these things came from God. So celebrating your queerness, your racial identity, your whatever is . . . celebrating your queerness is I guess celebrating your love for God because it came from God.

Sam and Reese are both attempting to change Christ College community's language around God and views of gender and sexuality. While Sam is trying to do so without garnering censure from university authorities, Reese pushes members of the campus community to rethink their theological assumptions. Indeed, Harbor has hosted events about being queer and Christian. Reese told me that he was invested in discussing theological reasons to support LGBTQ+ identities when he identified as a Christian. These efforts to change not only how people view sexuality but also how they view the gender of God are important because Christians' views of God shapes their attitudes toward same-sex relationships and support for various social issues.[15] These attitudinal shifts therefore hold the power not only to make Christ College more inclusive to LGBTQ+ students but also to create broader social change beyond Christ College's walls.

LGBTQ+ students at Christ College also recounted how student leaders sought to make housing more inclusive for them. Craig, who identifies as a trans*man, explained how his residential adviser (RA) worked to ensure he felt included and comfortable in his current housing arrangements:

> Like, the current floor group I'm on and have been on since halfway through last year has been really affirming, even though I do have to be

> on a women's floor still. The people I'm living with now are very affirming and intentional and reaffirming my gender and not only just using, like, my correct pronouns is the bare minimum but kind of, like, almost sometimes going out of their way to use masculinizing terms, that kind of thing. And my RA this year made the floor gender neutral in words and terms because that's something that she can do as the RA that the administration can't really veto.

Even if LGBTQ+ students and their allies cannot force the university to implement policy changes, student leaders at Christ College are working to create a more inclusive environment within their spheres of influence. Even though there are no gender-inclusive housing options and students must live in housing organized according to a cisgender binary, Craig's residential adviser made executive decisions regarding Craig's floor, thus creating a safe space that circumvented the university's broader policies.

Avery, a White nonbinary student at Christ College, also described how the current dormitory leadership appears to be more aware of gender identity and pronouns than the previous year's:

> At the beginning of the year, . . . the whole dorm met together, and the RAs and the [student leadership in ministry], like the leader people on the floors and within the dorm as a whole, got up and introduced themselves and said a little bit about themselves. And they didn't do this last year, but this year they all said their pronouns, and everyone was cisgendered, but they still did that even though there was not necessarily anyone who was part—who is trans* or nonbinary who is driving that but just showing that they recognized that nonbinary and trans* people exists and it's important to know people's pronouns and you can't always just assume.

Avery's and Craig's stories are significant because they show how student leaders—even those who are not part of the LGBTQ+ community—are taking the initiative to make housing safer and more inclusive even though the university's administrators are willfully inactive.

Mike, a White, heterosexual, cisgender man who was one of the ministry leaders Avery referred to, explained how he became more aware of gender identity and pronouns and began to incorporate it in his ministry position:

> I just had a completely binary thought system until about two years ago. . . . I just never thought anything beyond that, and anything else was super weird to me. So I would totally say I wouldn't know what I think or believe about a lot of gender identity kind of stuff. But I think my development and my growth is exploring and really being open with the understanding that "Hey, I'm straight, and that gives me a lot of privilege, but there's a lot else out there, and I want to have a compassionate sympathy." So that practically looks like changing the way I speak, and this is like a hard one even. So I send emails using gender-inclusive language, that being a really big one, just 'cause I think it's an act of hospitality. It's an act of making people feel safe, or like, naming my pronouns before I speak in front of certain groups and audiences would be another practical touch point.

Mike acknowledges having held a binary system of thinking about gender until he was challenged to learn more about gender identity and his own privileges. Now he tries to use gender-inclusive language and identifies his pronouns at meetings to create a hospitable and safe environment for LGBTQ+ students. Mike's and other student leaders' efforts were not lost on LGBTQ+ students, who appreciated the changes they made to expand community at Christ College.

Even if students at Christ College could not change their university's policies, LGBTQ+ students and their allies are trying to change cultural assumptions and language about gender and sexuality. Students in leadership positions advocate for using gender-neutral language in places of worship and in housing. While Christ College remains an inequality regime in its approach to diversity and exclusion of LGBTQ+ students, students are able to push the university toward greater equity and inclusion by changing community norms and values.

LGBTQ+ Intersectionality

At both campuses, LGBTQ+ students called for the need for their university to recognize the effects of intersectionality and different social locations of privilege within the LGBTQ+ community. Intersectionality recognizes that social inequality is shaped by multiple social axes that work in tandem rather than existing on a single axis.[16] Within these different matrices, people's social locations can reflect positions of privilege and disadvantage.[17] As inequality regimes generate inequality along multiple lines of intersecting social difference, creating equity regimes requires attention to intersectionality.

The students I spoke with at West University were aware of how different groups were privileged within the LGBTQ+ population. Jordan, a biracial, trans*, queer, and nonbinary student, explained,

> I think when it comes to diversity, it applies more to the LG part of the acronym, and the BTQ [part] is not seen as strongly, or the visibility is just lacking. . . . Like, for example, in the diverse spaces that I am in, I notice that a lot of the diversity or the representation it presents are, like—and not to be critical—but a lot of them are, like, cis gay guys and often White cis gay guys. And of course, they are a part of the community, but when you're not seeing trans* representation, when you're not seeing bi folks, it makes you think like, "Oh, is this just the one part of the community that they see as, like, being diverse, and they just kind of forget that the rest of us exists."

Jordan recognizes that "White cis gay guys" are usually privileged in spaces devoted to thinking about diversity and LGBTQ+ students. Their visibility comes at the cost of making trans* and bisexual individuals invisible. Jordan wants to see better representation of different queer identities.

Julian, a queer and genderqueer student of color, also noted the need for West University's community to better recognize different types of queer identity and intersectionality: "I think it should include LGBTQ+ students and beyond just those letters—LGBTQ+. There's, like, more identities than just that, and identities are fluid. And in addition to that, recognizing the intersections between being a person of color and being queer, trans*, or you know . . . as an international queer trans* person and all these other identities that intersect with queerness. Like, it's all very unique and different in its own way. And it's important to recognize that." Intersectionality means that LGBTQ+ individuals do not experience inequality solely on the basis of their gender identity and/or sexuality but that their experiences of inequality also encompass other forms of social difference and stratification. By discussing the intersectionalities that exist within the LGBTQ+ community, Julian hopes West University can recognize the diversity of LGBTQ+ experiences and support them in their diversity.

While Jordan and Julian noted the need for both student groups and university policies to acknowledge intersectional identities, Kristy, a bisexual student who uses she/her pronouns and is currently working through her gender identity, described intersectionality in relationship to learning:

> Diversity is kind of marketed, but then it's not supported in the fact that queer and trans* students—especially queer and trans* students who are at intersections of disability and mental health divergence and anything other than . . . White cis male neurotypical—we're not really supported in our learning. . . . I don't think [West University] really supports different ways of existing and learning unless it gets them recognition. . . . It's a very mixed population, and queer and trans* students, because they live at so many different intersections, are especially included in that but, yeah, not supported.

Kristy's comments specifically address the lack of educational support for LGBTQ+ students on West University's campus. Kristy notes how educational norms center White neurotypical cisgender men to the exclusion of LGBTQ+ students and other minoritized groups that may learn differently. This is important because studies show that LGBTQ+ students' educational success on colleges requires institutional-level support and attention to intersectionality.[18]

Aaron, a biracial trans*man, echoes Kristy's perception of a lack of educational support at West University:

> So, there's this tutoring program on campus called Advance, and they have a specific branch of Advance that's for underrepresented students.[19] And so, I was like, "Oh, underrepresented. It doesn't get much more underrepresented than trans*." But what they meant by underrepresented was people who are people of color, people who are low income, which is fine. I think that those groups definitely have a right to their tutoring. I think that's very good. It's just that it felt a little weird calling it tutoring for underrepresented groups, but it's not LGBT people. It was kind of a weird label thing.

While trans* individuals are numerically underrepresented on West University's campus relative to cisgender individuals, the tutoring program was specifically intended for people of color and people from low socioeconomic backgrounds. Both Kristy and Aaron perceived that the university's lack of sensitivity toward intersectionality meant that LGBTQ+ students did not receive necessary educational support. To transform the university from an inequality regime to an equity regime, universities must center LGBTQ+ students' educational success at colleges through institutional support that prioritizes intersectionality.

At Christ College, LGBTQ+ students also recognized the importance of intersectionality. As a gay man, Josh described how intersectionality allows him to ally with women against broader toxic masculinity and patriarchy:

> I really align with the feminist movement. So I feel like that's where I can recognize intersectionality the most. I have a lot of friends who are women, and I just recently have come to this realization that my experience as a gay man is really tied to the experience of especially cis women. We're sort of discriminated by the same force but also oppressing each other simultaneously. . . . Like, the overarching toxic masculinity. I would say that is maybe the root of homophobia, the same force that kind of creates the wage gap or makes women feel unsafe walking home at night. It's the same sort of perpetrators that sort of enact homophobia.

To Josh, toxic masculinity is both the root of homophobia and the force that produces inequality between women and men. At the same time, he recognizes that patriarchy offers gay men privileges that are not available to women. In this system, gay cisgender men are advantaged over women as men, but their queer sexuality disadvantages them relative to those who identify as heterosexual.[20] By aligning himself with the feminist movement, Josh expresses his hope that women and LGBTQ+ folk can fight against the patriarchy that oppresses both of them along lines of gender and sexuality.

Reese, a gay, cisgender Filipino who uses he/him and they/them pronouns, described how intersectionality affects him:

> Communities of color are still trying to open themselves up to queer issues, and queer issues are still very racist and very White centered. But then again, I'm a cisgendered gay man, and so within the LGBTQ com-

> munity, cis men and gay people have the most privileges, and then in communities of color, I am Filipino. So even in Asian circles, . . . that's a weird identity to me, but then in the greater context, . . . we don't experience as much oppression as Black people or Indigenous people, and so I am still privileged in the context of race, but in the context of White supremacy, I'm not. But then, I do contribute to White supremacy because of this . . . colonization mentality and generational traumas [*laughs ironically*]. There's a lot of layers. So, I experience oppressions as a person of color, but I do contribute to the oppression of other people as a cisgender man and as a Filipino. Like, I'm very peripheral in most movements, and I'm still trying to learn how to advocate while being peripheral and while not taking up too much space in that.

Reese observes that many communities of color are homophobic, while many queer communities are racist. This creates a conundrum for him: as a gay man, he understands that he is privileged among the LGBTQ+ community, but his race unsettles that privilege. At the same time, he perceives how the racial structure in the US advantages him relative to Black and Indigenous people, but all racialized minorities are oppressed relative to White supremacy. These many "layers" of privilege and disadvantage make it difficult for Reese to navigate how and when to advocate without "taking up too much space" in the LGBTQ+ community.

For these students at West University and Christ College, achieving LGBTQ+ inclusion and equity also requires recognizing intersectionality and diversity within the LGBTQ+ community. Sometimes this means looking at their own communities critically and observing how certain groups, such as White, gay, cisgender men, remain the most visible at the expense of other groups. Sometimes this means examining one's own social identities relative to others and evaluating how they may be complicit in the oppression of others, even as they themselves are marginalized on other social axes of privilege. Students also observed the need for universities to support disability and mental health in addition to race when it comes to their LGBTQ+ students.

Scholars and LGBTQ+ activists have long noted how LGBTQ+ movements often prioritize gay and lesbian people and cisgender individuals over trans* and nonbinary people.[21] LGBTQ+ people of color and those with other marginalized social identities are often disproportionately affected by discriminatory practices, structural disparities, and violence compared to their White counterparts.[22] In naming these criticisms, scholars and activists are demanding that the LGBTQ+ community work for equity both within and beyond their own communities.

Challenges and Futures

The LGBTQ+ students in my study actively called for change and imagined how diversity, equity, and inclusion might look for their communities in different university contexts. LGBTQ+ students at both Christ College and West University sought to make organizational changes and labored for the LGBTQ+ students who will come after them. They also imagined cultural changes that moved thinking about gender and sexuality beyond binaries, cisnormativity, and heteronormativity. At Christ College, students also spoke of expanding the discourse of reconciliation to encompass LGBTQ+ students, thus expanding how diversity and reconciliation are understood on their campus.

Nonetheless, challenges remain, as students at both West University and Christ College continue to fight for their belonging in places where their exclusion and lack of equity are built into the very structures of their universities. At Christ College, students continue to battle against homophobic and trans*phobic policies and statements. At West University, students continue to call for the expansion of policies that consider different intersectional needs. What is clear, however, is that LGBTQ+ students will persist in imagining diversity, equity, and inclusion for themselves from a power analysis framework. They will continue to do the work of imagining and laboring to make their universities equity regimes.

In addition to calling for organizational changes, LGBTQ+ students observed that true equity and inclusion for their communities would require addressing the places of inequality that exist within the LGBTQ+ community. Students recognized the importance of considering intersectionality, not only for creating an equitable learning environment but also in how different privileges and marginalized social locations shape their interactions with each other. The challenges and futures of diversity on campus are ultimately twofold: inward and outward facing.

7

Asian American Students

At Christ College and West University, Asian Americans tell me about how they imagine diversity in an ideal world. Peter, a biracial Asian American cisgender heterosexual man who attends Christ College, speaks of celebration with a dose of pessimism: "In an ideal world, I think we're able to hold onto our uniqueness, celebrate that while 100 percent respecting that other person's culture as well. I don't think it's realistic, but in an ideal world, we're all different and unique, and we all don't have to compromise to be ourselves and hold onto that."

Across state borders, Aiden and Diana, Asian American students at West University, concur. Aiden, a heterosexual cisgender man, also envisions diversity as a celebratory mindset in which sharing of cultural differences is common:

> We should be not trying to hide the fact that we are all different, right. . . . For example, we know that Caucasian people look differently, maybe talk a little bit differently, have different experiences generally than Asian Americans. And that's okay. We shouldn't hide the fact that different ethnic groups, . . . have different experiences than us. Instead, we should celebrate that fact, and we should have everybody contributing their ideas and experiences. . . . So instead of homogenizing things, we're saying like, "Oh, I don't see color." Like, I don't think that's a good approach to diversity. Instead, we should say, "Hey, I see that you're Caucasian and I'm Asian, and hey, maybe we can talk about the differences in our culture," find some commonalities, like, "Oh, I can show you dumplings, and you can show me hockey or something."

Diana agrees with Aiden and Peter. She speaks about taking pride in where she comes from: "I think in an ideal world, diversity is celebrated. I think that the world shouldn't necessarily be divided, but I think that everybody should be proud of their differences and celebrate them as opposed to just brushing them under the rug for like one American identity, for example. I think it's important for people to be able to take pride in where they're from and how they live." Peter, Aiden, and Diana imagine a form of diversity that allows them to share their cultural differences. Aiden's ideal world eschews color-blindness, while Diana's rejects assimilation into "one American identity." They all stress the importance of retaining their ethnic heritages and the desire to see these differences celebrated, honored, and respected.

In this chapter, we examine the challenges Asian Americans face in achieving diversity, equity, and inclusion for themselves. Their narratives reveal that supposedly neutral university traditions are not neutral. Asian Americans do the difficult work of supporting racial diversity on their campuses even as they try to create communities for themselves through their student organizations. Asian American students also recognize the need to move beyond a Black and White binary understanding of race in discussions of racial diversity on their college campuses. Finally, like the LGBTQ+ students discussed earlier, Asian Americans observe the need to understand diversity and equity within the heterogeneity and various intersections of their own groups.

University Traditions and Programs

Universities often have cultural traditions that are meant to appeal to the student body and bolster a sense of identity and solidarity among current students and alumni of their university. This may be exemplified in sports rivalries. For example, Harvard versus Yale, Stanford versus UC Berkeley, and UCLA versus USC are just some examples of storied rivalries in which university sports are meant to foster a sense of loyalty to one's campus. Yet, university traditions raise the question of whom these university traditions are for. Wesley, a queer biracial Asian American at West University, described this well:

> There are cultural orgs, but, like, those are student groups. It's not institutionalized. The institution only is [for] one type of student. . . . That's one of the problems I was having is, like, all the West University events, the West University programming, it's about equality, not equity. . . . They're creating these neutral programs. . . . They have a bonfire at the begin-

> ning of the year, they have quote unquote "school traditions," and I was, like, . . . Why is that what the school has determined to be relevant and valuable for the entire student body as a whole, right? . . . Why do cultural orgs have to fundraise and scrap, you know, embarrassingly and demeaningly for money? . . . We have to apply for money to have a cultural program, and that's just taken for granted. . . . That's ridiculous, that you have to basically beg the school for money to have something about like a Chinese culture night or whatever. Like, that's not something that West University is willing to have [as a] West University thing to be institutionalized, but we're willing to have West University versus East University.[1]

Wesley's critique of the traditions that West University encourages its students to participate in raises important questions about what West University values and how, if at all, it values diversity. In the examples Wesley raises, none of West University's student traditions appear to center diversity. Events that promote diversity are not institutionalized as part of West University's identity, nor do they receive the same kind of financial support or promotion.

Indeed, student leaders of AAW described the difficulties of raising money for their events. For example, Darren, a heterosexual cisgender man involved in leadership in AAW, noted,

> For AAW's cultural night, we do have to work a little bit harder, because there isn't as much as a unified community. So, for example, for [an Asian ethnic student group], [a public figure] donates. So, it funds a lot of their [cultural] show; whereas we do a lot of funding from our own friends and family and through fundraisers, and we do get some from funding apps, but there's a lot that gets left uncovered. And then, I think for [another Asian ethnic student group]—they have an airline that funds most of their show. Everyone else . . . 'cause they're a lot more unified, so they're able to land one big thing to cover everything, whereas we have to try to put together what we can.

Darren contrasts AAW's resources with those of other Asian student groups on campus. Other Asian student groups also host large cultural events, but he explains that they receive support from outside donors. From his perspective, AAW is not as well funded because of internal divisions among AAW's ethnic group, which he thinks detracts from a unified identity and limits the organization's ability to raise funds. In contrast to Wesley, however, Darren does not question how West University centers some traditions over others or how supposedly neutral university events are better funded even as the university purports to value diversity.

AAW's large cultural night is expensive. Joyce, who planned one of AAW's cultural nights, outlined the responsibility and costs:

> I had to write the script [for the cultural night's play]. I had to find actors. I had to find people for my board. So, there's a lot more responsibility because it was a show that's held in our [university's auditorium], and that's a $30,000 production. So I had to find out how to get all the financial resources and how to make the show's story appealing to an audience and also stay in contact with all the other aspects that are involved, like we do . . . cultural dance, . . . hip hop, . . . [martial arts] to incorporate Asian aspects into the script and the play itself.

A perusal of AAW's efforts in 2023 revealed that the group was trying to raise $45,000 for its cultural night.

As we saw earlier, the DEI office provides avenues of funding for different organizations to host events. Students from other organizations, such as LGBTQ+ organizations, also described applying for and receiving funding from the DEI office.[2] The DEI office plays a key role in providing financial and symbolic resources to student organizations that hold events that promote the office's values of diversity, equity, and inclusion.

Giselle, a recent graduate and a heterosexual cisgender woman, described how AAW received symbolic support from the DEI office: "They supported us in writing a letter just stating [the DEI officer's] support for our cultural night. . . . I don't remember how new this diversity department was, but we reached out to [the DEI officer] because we reached out to . . . different people in the upper levels of—I don't want to say management—in higher ed in our school and that it would be great to have someone support and represent us, and he was one of those people." Wesley, Darren, Joyce, and Giselle suggest that cultural nights hosted by organizations, such as AAW and other racial and ethnic student organizations, are often expensive. Yet their funding is uneven; AAW must often rely on outside donors. Leaders at AAW have also sought and received support from the DEI office. That these cultural nights are promoted through the DEI office rather than championed as core to West University's identity reveals how these cultural nights do not have the same institutional legitimacy as other supposedly "universal" events, such as the bonfire and college football game that Wesley mentions.

At Christ College, students also struggled to raise funds for racial diversity events. Dana, a biracial student in diversity leadership, described working to create a multicultural worship night:

> We needed money because we had used all of our budget, but we just needed a thousand-dollar deposit that may not even be used to rent the gym for a rain plan for a multicultural night of worship. Super easy. The university may not even need to spend it. It's their own money because they are paying for the gym, so we went and proposed [it] in the student senate. This student—White male . . .—had this history of kind of asserting his power visibly on campus. He was a senator, and so we were asking for this money, and . . . he turned our request for money into "Are you using your money well?" Like, "Why is this being promoted? Why do you want to promote multicultural Christianity?" in the senate, so he turned the senate around. It was a really weird experience where we thought we were going to go in, out, get this money super easy. And he just started using narratives to turn people around to make us seem irresponsible, . . . and then we'd also been in senate when the other event group . . . wanted a reindeer for . . . the big Christmas [party] they put on. They got it. It was more expensive.

Racial diversity is something Christ College supposedly values, as witnessed through its rhetoric of racial reconciliation and its hiring of a DEI officer, yet Dana's request for resources was denied while another group was able to acquire funding for a reindeer. To Dana, it was absurd that the reindeer was funded over their event, which promoted Christ College's goal of diversity through a multicultural worship night. Dana went on to reflect on the experience: "For me, that was an instance of the system. . . . I think that memory is more hurtful because it was the diversity statement essentially of what Christ College hopes for, of students being empowered, different students, being denied because one student was able to turn around [the senate]." To her, the incident reflected a lack of commitment to valuing diversity among the student body and the university. For those who opposed the multicultural worship night, they viewed a Christmas party at a Christian college as neutral and innocuous.[3] A multicultural worship night, by contrast, centers racial and ethnic diversity and has the effect of unsettling the White evangelical culture of the campus.[4] White students at evangelical Christian colleges may value racial diversity in name, but when the rubber hits the road, they are less inclined to center race in concrete actions and events on their campuses.[5]

Peter also described the difficulty of obtaining funding after starting a student organization:

> Multiethnic clubs, it is very hard to get funding for our clubs. . . . First of all, if you're a first-year club, you have no budget at all, and you need to go through this long process of getting approved if you wanted to do an event. . . . Even as a second-year club, you only get really small amounts of money. . . . If [diversity's] your slogan, like statement, I feel like they should put even more of an emphasis on supporting multiethnic clubs on campus. Like, if you want to throw a big event, it shouldn't be months and months of planning on how we're going to get the funds. It should be a quick "Let's do this." That way it really should be able to spread awareness and promote, like, people come from these backgrounds, and this is a culture they're connected to.

As Christian colleges, including Christ College, become more racially diverse, students of color may start different student organizations to create spaces for themselves.[6] Peter feels that the funding structure at Christ College deters the success and survival of new student organizations. Yet these student organizations are important for creating a sense of belonging for students of color at historically and predominantly White institutions.[7]

Peter depicted this dynamic well:

> I think speaking from personal experience, there aren't a lot of Asian students on campus. Christ College has a specific White Christian cul-

> ture here, and I say that it's difficult to find a space or a group of people that are, I guess, like interested in sort of learning a bit more about our roots. . . . For me, I had to actually create something for it to happen. So I think that's a challenge that [we] might face, just kind of trying to find our own in this kind of dominant culture on campus, if that makes sense.

Peter focuses on how the lack of Asian Americans and a dominant "White Christian culture" at Christ College propelled him to start his own student organization. He started an organization to create space for Japanese students and interested outsiders to learn more about Japanese culture and history. As the leader of a new club, he encountered barriers to funding and organizational red tape, which he felt was holding back student organizations.

These narratives reveal several important dynamics about diversity. As we have seen, students interpret the presence of student organizations as an index of a diverse student body and a robust campus life. Universities promote student-driven organizations to implement diversity as social difference. This creates possibilities for students to construct their own communities around common social identities and social interests. This suggests that there is space for *all* types of difference: if you cannot find a place that suits you, all you need to do is create your own (provided that you are willing to jump through some bureaucratic hoops). This is what Peter did at Christ College. Students' comments about university culture and traditions, however, reveal how universities do not institutionalize their supposed commitment to diversity by failing to integrate diversity into their university traditions.

These students' observations suggest that university programs and traditions imagine a certain kind of student. At West University, this imagined student is largely denuded of any social characteristics except being enrolled at "West University." Wesley reminds us that this denuded West University student, who is absent of social characteristics, does not exist. Rather, the university imagines this student as embodying the dominant characteristic of being White, where Whiteness is invisible or seen as neutral.[8] At Christ College, students articulated how the university culture was largely "White evangelical" and reflected the White racial and religious demographic of the university. The ideal student does not come in already made. Instead, the university's traditions and culture shape student identity. These university traditions, norms, and culture do not center racial diversity and equity. To transform the university into an equity regime, the university must reevaluate what kind of ideals it wants its students to embody and transform its traditions. The reality, however, is that promoting the value of diversity is sequestered to university DEI offices and, as we will see, to the efforts of student organizations.

Bifurcated Cultural Belonging and Education

Some conservative critics have argued that racial or ethnic student organizations, by their very existence, create divisions by being exclusivist to a racial or ethnic group.[9] These bad-faith arguments, however, do not recognize how racial and ethnic minority students must navigate a *bicultural identity* between the dominant White culture and their own ethnic culture and are always managing the demands and power differentials of both.[10] Even as students made clear that they felt their organizations were for their own ethnic group or for panethnic Asian Americans, which provided them with a sense of community and belonging, students consistently mentioned programming directed at outsiders to their group.

As a second-generation Asian American, Orlando comments on the importance of AAW to him:

> As Asian Americans, we are kind of stuck in the middle between an American culture and our heritage culture. So I feel like what AAW did for me is that I realized that there's a difference in culture between not just White Americans but also like Asians from Asia. . . . I've always been in California my whole life. Growing up, I thought I was [ethnicity]. . . . I'm not from [country], . . . but I realized that's just one thing, but when I met people here who are actually from Asia, I realize there's a big difference between us as well. So I feel like the club gives space for people who are stuck in the middle. Like, Asian Americans are kind of stuck between two cultures. It gives us a place where we can relate.

Orlando describes the "in between" feeling that second-generation Asian Americans feel about being Asian while also being American.

AAW and other racial or ethnic student organizations provide spaces where bicultural students can meet others and develop a sense of belonging, but these same racial or ethnic student organizations may also struggle because of the competing demands of members' bicultural social locations.[11]

Bicultural students and organizations navigate the mainstream and dominant culture and that of their ethnic culture.[12] Neither culture, however, is static; both interact with different structures of power. In higher education, Whiteness remains prevalent and is interwoven into the university's structure even as racial diversity increases.[13] One way bicultural students navigate this challenge of Whiteness on their campus is to craft their student organizations as places of *education*. This educational focus allows them to simultaneously learn about their own ethnic history and provide educational opportunities for people who are not Asian American or part of their ethnic group. In this way, racial and ethnic student organization activities incorporate aspects of the diversity rationale by aiming to educate others, even as they seek to educate and create community for themselves. This means they navigate creating community for themselves while also maintaining an openness to the dominant group and other groups. It is important to note that AAW students and the Asian American groups at Christ College did not primarily see their groups as political groups, even if their activities occasionally touched on politics.[14] This was to the chagrin of several students I interviewed. Instead, Asian American students primarily saw their campus organizations as social, cultural, and educational, skirting the line between creating community for people who identified with their group and educating outsiders (and their own) about history and culture.

Ellis, an Asian American cisgender woman involved with AAW, described how AAW's dual identity works as both pan-Asian and ethnically oriented:

> We're more pan-Asian than we are [ethnic identity] per se. But it's like we definitely do a lot of things to push the [ethnic identity] awareness. For example, . . . our cultural night is always about some sort of [AAW's ethnic] identity. . . . We have a lot of cultural events that are exclusively about [AAW's ethnic] culture as well, so instead of other pan-Asian cultures.

> I think in terms of pan-Asian involvement, it's just basically that we tell members that you don't have to be [our ethnic identity] to join this. . . . You don't have to be [ethnic identity] to learn about [our ethnic] culture, you know.

Henry, a heterosexual cisgender man who is not of the ethnic identity that AAW identifies, agreed with Ellis's assessment of AAW's openness: "I feel like their [AAW's] whole goal is to mainly spread the culture and traditions of [ethnic group], and it's not limited to just [their ethnic group], because they want to kind of like show their history, explain their history, to more than just [their ethnic group]—to everybody, you know? That's why they welcome everyone—doesn't matter where you're from. They just want to get their word out." Alice described the educational aspect of AAW's various events and how they move between different audiences:

> I think part of the assumption with AAW is that we're assuming very heavily the American part of [ethnic identity]. So for example, we have a general meeting on Wednesday, and . . . they're like teaching based. I remember one we did was about . . . traditional medicine. We taught people what these herbs are. These are what they're supposed to do. Like, we made some of it to try—like, a tiny little cup. . . . I think we very much just want to teach people about culture, 'cause I think we understand that there are a lot of things that we don't even know about [ethnic] culture.

Alice uses the example of traditional medicine to describe an area that Asian Americans may not have a lot of knowledge about. While she talks about wanting to teach "people about culture," it is also clear that the "people" she is talking about is the "we" of the Asian Americans in AAW, who are "very heavily the American" part of their ethnicity. Like Orlando, she recognizes that the group is geared to the American part of being Asian American—a reference to those who are second generation or born in the states. Alice and Orlando both want to know more about their cultural heritage.

When we moved to discussing AAW's cultural night, Alice noted being careful about the use of language to be inclusive of outsiders: "In [our cultural night], very often we use [ethnicity's language] phrases and, like, that to a certain degree, like, using ["little sister" in ethnicity's language], for example, that's a very common phrase. I think we'll do that, but we try not to go to anything higher than that. 'Cause I feel . . . culture nights are supposed to be this universal experience. If you say lines that people don't understand, then it's like you're missing out on some of that tone." Alice's comments reveal how AAW tries to educate its own members while simultaneously reaching out to those who do not belong to their ethnic or racial group. AAW's cultural night, which delves into a piece of their history or some social issue, is designed to be inclusive by using common language terms without making it appear too particular and thus losing what Alice calls a "universal" appeal. This "universal" appeal is not universal but, rather, strategic. The goal is to incorporate Asian Americans who do not speak the language, those who do, those who belong in the ethnic group, and those who do not.

Ellis, Henry, and Alice all describe how AAW works to include multiple different groups. They do this by stressing the importance of appreciation and education. Appreciating and learning about history and culture are something that *all* groups—both those who identify with AAW's ethnic group and those who do not—can do. This centers the diversity rationale as the point of entry for both outsiders and insiders. This is quite different from the university traditions described earlier and the social and cultural nature of AAW. Events like West University versus East University or an annual bonfire are *not* educational. They are designed to be social and to foster community and a sense of identity. Large cultural events put on by student organizations, like AAW's cultural night, are designed to be *educational* and *celebratory*. Racial and ethnic student organizations do the heavy lifting of creating community for themselves while also educating others, thereby fulfilling the diversity rationale and upholding the university's orientation toward diversity as difference through their existence and events.

Students at Christ College also described the importance of racial and ethnic groups as being social, cultural, and open to everyone. As at West University, students at Christ College described the difficulty of managing these different desires. John, a biracial Asian American, described the need for student organizations to be open to others even as they offer a place of commonality for some students:

> I know personally a lot of people from Hawaii get homesick, and being with other people from the same place [in the Hawaii Club] really helps them feel at home. As long as they're open to the public or as long as they're open to other people, I think it's perfectly fine. . . . As long as it's not that you have to be born in Hawaii to come here, 'cause I've been to the Black Student Union a few times, and there are a lot of non-Black people there. And like, that's great. The people who are Black, who want that Black Student Union, they love it, and it's a good time for them to feel, I guess, at home with people they share a lot in common with. I feel like as long as it's open to people of other backgrounds, then I think it's a really good thing.

For John, student groups provide a place for students to experience belonging around a certain identity; however, he does not think these groups should be exclusionary to their own group. He points to the Hawaii Club and the Black Student Union at Christ College as student groups that provide community while also being open to outsiders.

In contrast to John, Jason ruminated on the differential experiences of ethnic and racial minorities and the dominant (White) group at Christ College:

> I think it [ethnic student organization] is needed. Just speaking from my own perspective, it's that you lose a sense of yourself a lot of time when you're in a community that doesn't affirm your roots or, you know, things that are part of your culture. So I think that it is needed, but at the same time, when someone who's not of that racial group or ethnic group comes into that group, I can see that being sort of—might feel bad, I guess. I guess, if we make everything in perspective, that's sort of how a lot of immigrants feel; that's how a lot of minorities feel in their everyday lives.

Like Orlando and Alice at West University, both of whom recognize the importance of AAW as a bicultural organization, Jason recognizes how racial and ethnic minorities need racial or ethnic student organizations because the university in its practices and culture does not affirm their culture or roots. At the same time, he describes how outsiders who join their groups may be forced to put themselves in their shoes and experience what it feels like to be a minority or an immigrant traversing a space that is not theirs. This experience, however, is voluntary. Students who are not Asian American are not obligated to participate in AAW or any of the Asian American groups at Christ College. This contrasts with Jason's sense that his daily life at Christ College is accompanied by a lack of affirmation for his roots and culture.

Ian, a heterosexual cisgender man, characterizes student organizations as important educational spaces that can dispel racial stereotypes:

> I know plenty of Asians, including myself, who aren't straight-A students and such, so I feel like just these stereotypes make it more difficult to relate to other people because then they're like, "How come you're not this? You're not who I expect you to be?" Whereas on our side, I feel like most of us [Asian Americans] have a more open mindset towards other people. Like, in [our organization], we're always very open to people of other ethnicities to come and join even if they're not Korean or not Chinese or Asian. We always welcome their point of view and try to teach them more about our culture, which I think is really important, because it kind of helps to erase those types of stereotypes.

For Ian, Asian American student organizations play an important role in "teaching" outsiders about Asian culture. Like Jason, Ian recognizes the cultural and power imbalance in running a bicultural organization. To him, Asian Americans (and perhaps other racial or ethnic minorities) are more open to the dominant group—White people—than White people are open to them. The dominant group may stereotype, misunderstand them, and be unwilling to step out of their comfort zone to learn about them. In this way, White people can live in ignorance of others; when they do enter diverse spaces, they may do so without engaging in the messy reality of inequality.[15] Despite this imbalance, Ian's student organization welcomes others.

While Ian and Jason concurred that there was a power imbalance to their student organizations as bicultural organizations, Jason also focused on how an open attendance could detract from building a core community of Asian Americans:

> A lot of what we've been doing is trying to have events that are attractive for people to come to, and so a lot of that would be food events. You

know, we'd try to have events where people can come and make food or come and maybe we'd go out to eat. . . . We'd be able to just experience what [ethnic] food is like, and in hindsight, for us as leadership, I think that was a mistake on our part. . . . I think we were focusing too much on trying to get people to come versus creating an actual community.

David felt similarly to Jason, describing his hope for the student organization: "We pretty much wanted a core group. A space where [ethnic group] and, I guess, anyone who's related to the [ethnic] nationality, I guess, comes in and has a place to express themselves and find common ground with people. And yeah, that was kind of our vision. We just wanted to have a good group that would have lasting relationships." Ian's, Jason's, and David's comments reveal some of the conflicts their group experienced. They all belonged to the same Asian American group at Christ College, one oriented toward an East Asian ethnic identity. Their different narratives reveal their conflicting desires in wanting people of all backgrounds to attend their events while also desiring to have a core group for "community" and "lasting relationships." When student groups position themselves as "educational" to outsiders, this may hinder their ability to focus inwardly on building community.[16] Students at Christ College and West University wanted to do both, but at Christ College, their small numbers and the power imbalance that bicultural organizations must navigate made this difficult to attain.

Students navigate multiple audiences and competing goals and hopes for their racial or ethnic student organizations. They aim to provide a sense of identity and community for their own *and* to provide an education to outsiders. The Asian Americans I spoke with at West University and Christ College were therefore proponents of the diversity rationale, but this came at the cost of core community—as in the case of Christ College's student groups. It sometimes also came at the cost of rejecting a more explicitly political focus. For example, Daniel described his ambivalence toward the Korean ethnic student organization he was part of at Christ College: "If anything, it made me realize that they weren't as concerned with certain social-political things that I was concerned about. I felt like a lot of the Koreans who were running the club were more interested in getting Korean BBQ and stuff like that than talking about the North Korean–South Korean conflict or ways that we can be involved with the community. It was very social."

At West University, Madelyn, a heterosexual cisgender woman, theorized as to why AAW is not more political: "Well, the political—it's kind of more difficult for us to—because AAW doesn't have a political stance. We're politically neutral. So there's not much that we've been sharing or doing with the members, since we are mostly a social-cultural organization. But we were hoping to spark political conversations and discussions about Asian American activism and also how the cultural night this year is tied to the era of Vincent Chin, stuff like that—just to get our members thinking about our ancestors' past and just all the history that's made us who we are today." Although AAW includes "politics" as one of its four core areas, with the other areas emphasizing its social, cultural, and community-oriented goals, AAW's position is to be politically neutral. It tries to promote political conversations and activism through education about members' ethnic and racial history. For example, in AAW's annual cultural night, members told the story of Asian American responses to Vincent Chin's murder. A Chinese American man, Vincent Chin was brutally murdered in 1982 by two disgruntled White automobile workers who blamed Japanese automobile imports for layoffs in the automobile industry. The two men received a sentence of three years probation and a $3,000 fine for murdering Chin. Asian Americans across the United States protested the injustice.[17]

Later on in the interview, Madelyn told me that she feels one of the biggest challenges Asian Americans face is being more politically aware: "I think what a lot of Asian Americans on this campus, challenges they face, probably just activism, . . . just getting more Asian Americans . . . to be politically aware of what's going on around us. Like, there's that stereotype where Asians are reserved, submissive and stuff. Like, just trying to get everyone out of their bubble and to actively participate. That's also a challenge because that's sometimes—it's not their priority. But I really think that a lot of people should be aware of what's going on because it does affect them."

None of the students affiliated with either AAW or the Asian American student organizations I interviewed at Christ College were primarily oriented toward politics. AAW tries to include politics through education—that is, by teaching about Asian American history and issues. Similarly, one of Christ College's Asian American groups hosted a film on North Korea to educate students about the North Korea and South Korea conflict. Leon, an Asian American, gay, cisgender man, explained, "We tried to collaborate with LNK—Liberty [in] North Korea—so we tried to host a trailer film night. . . . It was the actual complete film. Specifically for colleges, they were only showing it for college at the time, so we hosted one of those." These student organizations often promote political discussions through educational events, such as through a cultural night or watching a film together. They are not primarily activist groups, which was sometimes disappointing to people, such as Daniel, who wanted more political engagement.

Ethnic student organizations are important for inclusion, developing leadership skills, and navigating and developing a sense of identity.[18] Research has also shown that involvement in ethnic student organizations promotes greater commitment to the interests of one's ethnic group.[19] At the same time, some conservatives criticize racial or ethnic student organizations for promoting balkanization and self-segregation.[20] Their arguments, however, fail to recognize how ethnic student organizations navigate dominant Whiteness in the university culture and structure. Student narratives and experiences reveal the complex ways in which these organizations promote and navigate the competing goals of their organizations as bicultural organizations. These goals include creating space for themselves, but they are also not exclusionary. They position themselves to outsiders through education and appreciation, thereby fulfilling the diversity rationale. But this ultimately comes at the cost of community and political action.

Beyond the Black and White Racial Binary

As we saw in chapter 5, Asian Americans often struggled to make sense of their inclusion in university diversity programming due to narratives about their numerical representation. They sometimes saw themselves through the model minority myth or observed how others perceived them through the model minority myth. As I spoke with Asian American students about their hopes and concerns, some students described feeling estranged from dialogues of racial diversity on their campuses because they primarily focused on Black and White understandings of race.

At Christ College, David described how Asian Americans were absent from discussions of diversity on the campus several years ago:

> Two years ago, I think we had this whole debacle of faculty members not being diverse enough or something. And so, all this stuff—talk—went through two years ago, but it was mostly on African American versus White. So I kind of feel like in terms of Asian ethnicity, it's not as represented or not as pressing as maybe like African American versus White. . . . I think that Asians have been historically or at least in my experience have been put on the back side of the racial talks or just cultural talks in general. . . . The whole if I were to go back to the [history of] Japanese internment camps, it is something we talk about in high school now, but . . . some people don't even know about it or other Asian things or Asian history. . . . I think the focus on this university right now is more of the popular subjects, like African American versus White. But I don't necessarily see a lot of other cultures being incorporated into it. So maybe seeing something like that would be nice.

David describes the push for diversity at Christ College that led to the creation of the DEI officer position. David notes how the discussions for diversity felt very Black and White to him; other students of color were not incorporated into the conversations about diversity on campus. Although he acknowledges that Asian Americans have a history of oppression as well, he feels that this was invisible in university discussions.

Daniel, for his part, critiqued approaches to racial reconciliation at Christ College:

> Racial reconciliation for me as an Asian American is understanding my place and where I stand in the dynamics of racial America, because it is racialized and race does play a factor. Asians are very, as a whole, muted, ignored, left out of the conversation, but even that's a position that's in place. I think our place has been a harder place to find simply because it has been muted and it is shut out. Our experiences are lessened than [compared to] others, so racial reconciliation is merely acknowledging that they exist, for me, and finding others who will acknowledge them, though I haven't yet.

Even though Daniel told me that he learned about the model minority myth from one of the leaders of the Center for Racial Reconciliation at Christ College, he observed that Asian Americans remained largely missing from narratives of racial reconciliation. He wanted to see Asian Americans further highlighted and recognized in racial reconciliation efforts.

Racial reconciliation among evangelical Christians started as a way to understand race in response to the civil rights movement, in which Christians primarily focused on Black and White racial concerns.[21] White evangelicals eventually used racial reconciliation to promote color-blindness by emphasizing religious identity over racial identity.[22] Although Asian American Christians may sometimes find racial reconciliation appealing because of its emphasis on religious identity over racial identity, it is also clear that some Asian Americans reject the view that racial identity and experiences of racial inequality should be subsumed under religious identity.[23] Like the LGBTQ+ students discussed in chapter 6, who longed to see LGBTQ+ students incorporated into a type of reconciliation (which included structural changes), these students wanted to see Asian Americans incorporated into racial reconciliation as well.

At West University, Asian American students also questioned Asian Americans' inclusion into diversity efforts when they considered other racial groups. Alice explained,

> I feel like out of the other ethnicities and cultures, like Asian Americans, our communities are pretty—I wouldn't say well understood—but like, well recognized. . . . And I think West University, probably because we have such a high Asian concentration, but it's like we have good recognition of Asian American diversity. I think it definitely stresses more on Chinese, 'cause a lot of people don't really understand the differences between, like, not even just Japanese, Korean, and Chinese but also, like, Malaysians, Singapore. Those are very, very underrepresented. People don't know as much about them. . . . I know there are like Black Lives Matter groups on campus and stuff. And I remember seeing a girl with a shirt with "Black Transfer Pride"—like Black student transfers, which I felt was a very specific group that I never thought [of]. I feel like Asian Americans—we could get better representation, but it's like I don't know

> if we really care. I feel like we don't feel as disenfranchised as some other groups, and so, because of that, we don't push, and we don't really feel like we need those kind of groups.

Alice feels that Asian Americans are well recognized on West University's campus due to the size of their population. This reflects an understanding of diversity as numerical representation. As her comments continue, Alice contrasts Asian Americans' lack of engagement with Black student affinity groups. In her view, Asian Americans do not seek more interventions because they do not feel as disenfranchised. When I asked Alice why she thinks Asian Americans do not feel disenfranchised, she told me what she learned in an Asian American history class:

> When I was thinking about my story, I talked to a TA . . . for an Asian Am[erican history] class, and it was very interesting. She told me about how the Vincent Chin protests ultimately kind of failed because you have an Asian American community or a Chinese American community that's split into people who are, like, they're more or less assimilated. They feel like they can speak out against the American government and society. And then you have the more recent immigrants who came here with the intention to be successful under the American system. And I think that still remains, even though that was like [a] 1980s concept. . . . We know that our parents came here because America is America. It's not like we came here not out of our own choice, so I think that's why we're very reluctant to, like, say and speak out against certain things.

Alice learned how the responses to Vincent Chin's murder reflected a fragmented Chinese American community: one that was split between those who felt they could oppose American society through protesting and recent immigrants who "came here with the intention to be successful under the American system." She feels that this divide remains and is why Asian Americans may not be involved in discussions of racial diversity on West University or seek racial changes on campus.

Diana, an Asian American, heterosexual, cisgender woman at West University, pointed to the model minority myth and Asian Americans' attempts to obtain White privileges to explain Asian American students' reluctance to get involved with racial discussions on campus:

> Back in the civil rights movement and stuff, Asian Americans I felt were a lot more active in politics and such than we are now. . . . By raising one minority above the other, Asian Americans have been allowed to feel comfortable about their place in society by, I guess, attempting to reach the same privilege as White Americans. . . . Or they feel that because they have made it, they do not need to support other minority groups and, I guess, strive for better in our community. . . . I feel like there's a lot of complacency. So the [model] minority myth just kind of adds on to that, in the sense that we are Asian American, so we will succeed because we are Asian American, not necessarily because of our own ability, . . . when it negatively affects other Asian American groups, like Southeast Asians or just small Asian groups, that are brushed under the rug because according to the model minority, they are meant to succeed in society. I think that's very unfair.

These students recognize that Asian Americans are largely missing in discussions of racial diversity on their campuses. Daniel suggests that "Asians are very, as a whole, muted, ignored, left out of the conversation, but even that's a position that's in place." Diana describes how "raising one minority above the other" has made Asian Americans complacent as they attempt to "reach the same privilege as White Americans." Alice discusses different immigration waves and issues of assimilation that shape political engagement. Their comments reflect how processes of racialization and racial triangulation have shaped Asian American engagement, visibility, and invisibility in racial discussions.

The political scientist Claire J. Kim argues that Asian Americans are pulled toward the privileges of being White and away from Blackness because US institutions and structures are built on anti-Blackness. This pulling and pushing ultimately positions Asian Americans between these racial groups such that White supremacist and anti-Black structures are maintained.[24] For Asian Americans, a power analysis frame of diversity means recognizing the White supremacy and anti-Blackness of the racial structure in which Asian Americans are positioned. This position in the US's racial structure is both stable and shifting within different institutions and political contexts, often serving different racial ends.

In higher education, Asian Americans move between invisibility and visibility. When White conservatives promoted Asian American achievement as a reason to end race-conscious affirmative action in higher education and when Asian Americans themselves supported such a campaign, they participated in maintaining the racist racial hierarchy in which they are positioned.[25] This racial hierarchy upholds White privilege and structural anti-Blackness by extending limited White privilege to Asian Americans. At other times, Asian Americans' relationship to the racial structure is more precarious, as when they are portrayed as being too populous in educational settings, carriers of disease during the COVID-19 pandemic, or foreign spies in STEM fields.[26] At the same time, Asian Americans can and have asserted themselves in these conversations, sometimes pushing back against racist narratives about themselves and at other times wielding the model minority myth to different racial ends.[27]

The students I interviewed recognized that they were missing from discussions of race on campus or that Asian Americans themselves did not engage in conversations about diversity because of the model minority myth or the lures of proximity to Whiteness. They understood why they were missing and wanted to see themselves included.

Diversity and Division Among Asian Americans

Asian Americans were also vocal about issues of diversity and inequality within the "Asian American" category.

Randy, a gay Asian American student at West University, enumerated multiple stratifying lines to illustrate the diversity within the "Asian American" category:

> [Asian Americans are] 10 percent of America or less, . . . and within that, you have, like, a kajillion different ethnicities. . . . Even though I may belong to the majority, which is Chinese, . . . within that Chinese category, there is even ethnic discrepancies. . . . So you have the generation that came during the gold-mining period, and they have a legacy here now, and they are more assimilated into America—or should be. . . . With regards to people like me who have had parents come from Vietnam, technically, even though we're technically Chinese, we still had to kind of come from the ground up. . . . And then you have people coming from the communist revolution who may be businessmen and already had a sense

> of education. . . . And even to speak more specifically amongst the Southeast Asian community, it's like you have all these countries—all these immigrants coming from war-torn countries coming into America, coming into another country that depends on capital.

According to the 2020 US Census, Asian Americans make up around 6 to 7 percent of the US population.[28] This small percentage includes roughly twenty-two million people from over twenty countries, with various religious traditions and languages.[29] Sixty percent of this population are immigrants.[30] Given this diversity in national origins, immigration patterns, and more, Randy asserts that it is difficult to talk about Asian Americans as a whole.

Jason, at Christ College, pointed to racial divisions due to historical conflicts and the need for healing between ethnic groups. He described this in the context of racial reconciliation:

> Well, reconciliation meaning there's been a historical conflict, and so, I guess that would mean that historically, two ethnic groups have had some ugly history. Racial reconciliation would be acts that would be in an attempt to change [the] perspective [of a] group to acknowledge that, keeping our minds on the fact that that happened and moving towards an action that sort of improves tolerance between one group. Actually, when I think about this, I think a lot about how my parents [are]. . . . They don't think well of Japanese just because of how Japan colonized Korea. . . . There's still a lot of rooted resentment just in culture. Anything native Japan, you don't want to buy that. Like, just those small things. So in that sense, racial reconciliation would look like things that acknowledge that that happened and that would, as we look at that in the past, we try to do things not like that. I actually think a big part of why that conflict still arises is because of the fact that Japan as a government has not acknowledged a lot of its war crimes, and so I guess racial reconciliation would start with that.

Jason draws on generational trauma to explain why reconciliation is needed among different Asian ethnic groups. Jason, in other words, recognizes how these groups have their own histories of conflict before coming to the US. These conflicts and traumas do not necessarily go away when one comes to the US. For Jason, achieving reconciliation among different Asian groups would require addressing these past wrongs.

Inclusion and diversity among Asian Americans also meant recognizing mixed racial and ethnic heritage within the Asian American population. Jacqueline, a biracial student who is both White and AAW's ethnic identity, told me about a time a student questioned her involvement with AAW:

> It was actually at an AAW meeting last year at the beginning of the year, and I was talking to some freshmen, because I was a second year and I had like gone through AAW . . . so I could answer some of their questions when there wasn't [leadership] around. And then there's this first year who asked me, "Oh, like, why are you here though?" 'cause I guess he assumed that I wasn't [AAW's ethnic group] at all and, like, there was no reason for me to be here if I wasn't. . . . And I was like, "Okay, first of all, I am [of that ethnic group]; two, you can be here if you're not, . . . and there are a lot of people here who aren't and it's fine." That hit me kind of negatively even though it wasn't [an] intentionally harmful question.

Jacqueline was questioned for her involvement with AAW because she appears racially ambiguous. She pushed back by reminding the student that AAW includes people of various races and ethnicities, but the assumption that she should not be there because she did not look stereotypically Asian was an unwanted experience.

When students spoke of Asian American inclusion in chapter 5, they sometimes did so in ways that were uncritical of the differences and inequalities among Asian Americans. For them, simple numerical representation was sometimes an indicator of their being part of a diverse campus. Here, students complicated this view by considering the diversity and inequality among Asian Americans as a group. They pointed to differences in ethnicities and national origin, immigration patterns, class inequalities, interracial identities, and intersectional factors that need to be addressed for equity and inclusion to be obtainable.

Challenges and Futures

In this chapter, we have examined some of the challenges Asian Americans face in building community for themselves on their campuses. Students shared their thoughts on tackling larger issues, such as where they fit in the US racial structure, diversity among the "Asian American" category, and how to balance competing needs for community, cultural appreciation, and education. These challenges reveal organizational and cultural elements of diversity on their campuses that need to be addressed for Asian American diversity, equity, and inclusion.

First, Asian American organizations and other ethnic organizations are important for building community for Asian Americans. This is not surprising since other scholars have long shown the importance of ethnic organizations on college campuses for inclusion, but Asian Americans' understandings of the purpose of their organizations reveal competing concerns that have implications for the possibility of equity regimes on their college campuses.[31] Their organizations allowed them to understand their bicultural identities as people who were Asian and American.[32] Yet, they often took an educational stance when it came to outsiders, thereby supporting the diversity rationale. Their organizations played dual roles in being both inward and outward facing.

The need to play dual roles is the result of the racial power imbalances embedded in universities as inequality regimes and fostered in the university's myopic approach to diversity that uplifts the diversity rationale. I am not denying that there are true benefits in interracial relationships that racial and ethnic student organizations may help facilitate in maintaining openness to people of other racial or ethnic groups.[33] Instead, I am pointing out how the racial power inequalities in universities create a context that Asian Americans cannot opt out of in the same way White students can opt into "experiences of racial diversity." Asian Americans and other racial or ethnic minorities must navigate the dominant structures of Whiteness, while White students do not need to navigate realities of systemic racial oppression. As we have seen here, even in creating a community for themselves, they must still consider the feelings and epistemic experiences of White students. White students, however, can choose to celebrate racial diversity without working toward making a more racially equitable and inclusive campus.[34] Again, this is reflected in how universities prioritize traditions that do not center diversity, while student organizations encourage the diversity rationale with little funding.

Asian American students were aware of this inequitable dynamic in their organizations and at their universities. The multiple hats that these Asian American student organizations must wear in responding to their own needs without excluding people outside their racial or ethnic group might also contribute to why student leaders did not make their organizations more overtly political. Instead, engagement in politics was promoted through education. Some students were dissatisfied with their group's level of or approach to political engagement. The lack of political engagement meant that these groups were potentially missing the opportunity to be stronger advocates for institutional changes that could bring greater equity to Asian Americans and other racialized minority groups.

Notably, Asian American students also recognized that there were ways they did not fit into campus conversations about racial diversity because of a Black and White binary understanding of race. This dynamic existed at both campuses, despite the numerical difference in their Asian American populations and the different religious and secular orientations of their universities. The future of racial diversity and equity depends on recognizing the complex ways that the US racial social structure operates to create inequality and sustain White dominance and anti-Blackness. Processes of racial triangulation that place Asian Americans as a monolith between White and Black must be challenged while also recognizing the intersectional inequalities among Asian Americans.

Conclusion

In this book, I have argued that universities' approaches to diversity act as inequality regimes on campus. Students' experiences of diversity policies and the tensions West University and Christ College face around different types of social difference illustrate the limits of diversity statements and programming in bringing about equity.

We saw that students defined three different types of diversity frameworks: *diversity as difference*, *diversity as numerical representation*, and *diversity as power and equity*. When universities adopt either of the first two approaches, they are likely to implement diversity in ways that perpetuate inequality on campus. Inequality is perpetuated along *multiple lines of social difference* through the language and practices of diversity as difference and diversity as something that can be numerically quantified. When students and the university describe diversity as difference, they understand diversity as the inclusion of multiple forms of social differences, such as social identities, worldviews, and more. They frequently justify diversity as an educational benefit for students.

The diversity as difference framework reproduces inequality because it operates from an assumption of abstract equality among all types of difference. This framework is present in both secular and religious contexts, and it undergirds West University's and Christ College's approaches to diversity. Practices such as publishing diversity statements and authorizing identity-based student organizations indicate that a university values diversity as difference, but these practices, in and of themselves, do not address the realities of social inequality or how exclusion can still exist on the college campus. These realities are exemplified in issues of speech on West University and LGBTQ+ inclusion at Christ College.

Diversity primarily understood through a framework of *numerical representation* also reproduces inequality. Numbers do not exist in a vacuum. Cultural interpretations of numerical representation can lead to inequitable understandings of diversity and exclusion. This is exemplified in how Asian American students interpreted their levels of campus inclusion and whether diversity programming is intended for them, with students expressing ambivalence based on their share of the campus population and educational outcomes. The diversity as numerical representation framework is especially prone to perpetuating racial inequality and racial hierarchies when interpreted through cultural essentialist narratives, such as the model minority myth.

Students often critiqued these limited diversity frameworks through what the sociologist Natasha Warikoo calls a power analysis frame of diversity.[1] Diversity understood as *power and equity* is the most promising approach to diversity, because it highlights the need for organizational and cultural changes. This framework centers equity over abstract equality and inclusion over tokenism. However, we also saw that even diversity practices based on a power analysis frame often fall short of institutional change because of uneven implementation and cultural inertia. Students, faculty, and staff must be vigilant in transforming universities into equitable and inclusive environments. Thinking of diversity as power and equity challenges us to continually think about whom and what colleges are for.

Diversity in a Post–Affirmative Action, DEI-Ending, Anti-CRT World

To be critical of how universities have approached diversity at a time when race-conscious affirmative action in college admissions has ended and legislators and politicians across the United States are attacking DEI (diversity, equity, and inclusion) programs in higher education may seem dangerous to those of us who firmly believe in the need for DEI, even as we understand its flaws and limits. Florida and Texas have passed bans on DEI policies in public higher education.[2] In my own state of Wisconsin, Republican lawmakers have successfully forced the University of Wisconsin's hand to phase DEI positions into other roles.[3] Opponents of DEI programs cast them as inherently unfair and unnecessary in a world of equality. Harking on DEI's acronym, Governor Ron DeSantis of Florida has called DEI programs discriminatory, exclusionary, and indoctrination.[4] If equality existed in our social structures, then DEI programs would certainly need not exist, but we do not live in a structurally fair world. To pretend we do is not only factually inaccurate but unjust and inhumane. DEI programs exist because the world we live in is deeply discriminatory, exclusionary, and indoctrinated such that we do not see the realities of historical and systemic injustice that prevent *all* people from truly living and thriving.

Across the country, evangelical Christian colleges are also facing opposition to DEI-like education and policies. Faculty who teach on race, gender, and sexuality at Christian colleges are being removed.[5] Boards of trustees and denominations are tightening their grip on Christian colleges, fearing that exposing students to critical discussions on social inequality and identities, or changing their policies on gender and sexuality, would deteriorate their colleges' commitment to supposedly Christian values.[6] To them, teaching critical race theory (CRT), gender and sexuality theories, and more goes against Christianity.[7] These powerful and influential figures in evangelical Christian circles and higher education do not see how more inclusive and equitable policies would instead fulfill their mission to live out unconditional love and justice.

These opponents of DEI policies at public universities and their corollaries at Christian colleges reject a power analysis understanding of diversity. Instead, when not pontificating outright discriminatory and dehumanizing views, they more closely cleave to an understanding of diversity as difference, in which abstract equality guides their thinking and seeing. Yet diversity understood through a power analysis frame helps us see the flaws and real tensions of this thin diversity framework.

I do not want this book to be read as another academic exposé of the problems with current understandings of diversity. Instead, my hope is to demonstrate that an expansive power analysis understanding of diversity can lead to community and coalition building. Indeed, amid backlash against DEI, the end of race-conscious affirmative action, and anti-CRT movements, coalitions and community are needed more than ever. Students of color and LGBTQ+ students will continue to fight for their places, but they need allies. Students, faculty, and staff who sit at the most privileged intersections need to speak up about the importance of these programs, not only because diversity provides educational benefits but also because DEI programs are about making the social world more just and equal. Students, faculty, staff, and university community members should contact their legislators and demand they maintain and fund DEI programs at public universities. It is important to let state legislators know that these offices and programs are valued and are consequential to student success on college campuses. At Christian colleges, students and faculty should continue to protest and call for their colleges, boards, and affiliated denominations to do better. Indeed, students at Christ College are doing just that.

I wish to close this book by addressing broad areas of change needed at secular and evangelical colleges if they are intent on bringing about real diversity, equity, and inclusion and transforming from inequality regimes to equity regimes. These recommendations are not exhaustive. Many of these ideas are admittedly tentative and may even be dissatisfying to some readers. To others, some recommendations may even seem foolish, but imagining a better world is the first step to bringing it into being.[8]

Creating Equitable Participation in Speech

There is no easy remedy for issues of speech on campus, especially at public universities. Before discussing strategies for equity and inclusion, it is helpful to step back to remind readers that the idea of "free speech" embodies political struggles and what counts as "free speech" is a social construction, a changing ideal rather than an immutable principle.[9] A cursory review of the contradictory rulings in the many cases regarding speech argued before US courts makes this clear.[10] Only in recent years have we seen a steady move toward absolutist approaches to speech. Because speech occurs in multiple areas and levels of the university, I have outlined different areas on campus where issues of speech can be addressed in this section.

In classroom environments, where discussion is central to learning, participants can agree on ground rules that make the conditions for speech more equitable. Notice that this is not about making dialogue spaces "safe." Indeed, scholars have pointed out that making dialogue spaces "safe" does not protect groups who sit at intersectional margins; instead, it favors the emotional states of privileged groups. Discomfort is a necessary part of growing and learning, and emotional engagement is an important part of intellectual growth, especially when it comes to learning about uncomfortable truths about our social world.[11] Importantly, this emotional discomfort is different from what one experiences at the receiving end of targeting speech. Targeting speech, such as racist comments, creates barriers to learning and brings into question the full humanity and participation of a student.[12] Such speech should not be tolerated to ensure the equal participation of all students. The kind of discomfort that occurs as the result of learning, or the rupturing of taken-for-granted beliefs, however, should not be avoided. Faculty and instructors should encourage students to seek to learn through these embodied emotions because learning is not just a mental process. It is also an embodied one.[13]

Establishing an equitable space in the classroom may also mean introducing practices that allow students to participate in various forms, including those that do not center the act of speaking. Students can be encouraged to demonstrate their knowledge and growth through various modalities. As a student, I always found it difficult to speak in class. I found it difficult to gather my thoughts coherently, worried whether I understood the material correctly, that I might simply be wrong, be misunderstood, or fail to deliver my ideas in an articulate manner. This was true even during graduate school, where courses centered on dialoguing over complex readings. Giving students structured space to write their thoughts or illustrate their knowledge outside of verbal speech acts may allow students to engage on a deeper level. Difficult readings can be accompanied by guiding questions that help students reflect intellectually and emotionally on what they are learning and feeling.

These interactional methods may work toward equity in classroom and discussion-based environments, but what about the times when campus organizations, or the campus administration itself, invite speakers with whom some students disagree? Classroom environments are different from the university quad and student organizational spaces. In the case of contentious politics, right-wing speakers and organizations sometimes depend on the publicity generated by students on liberal campuses protesting, shouting down, and creating a ruckus in response to speakers presenting views they find abhorrent.[14] One option for students who disagree with these speakers is simply not to show up, because showing up plays into the conservative handbook for legitimizing their views and promoting distrust in higher education. It may be difficult for students to ignore these speakers, but it is also a good reminder that students are not obligated to attend. Indeed, students ignore many events on college campuses every day simply because they are not interested in attending them. Treat these speaker events in the same way.

Republican student organizations often receive financial support from wealthy external supporters in ways that liberal student groups do not. Some of these wealthy external organizations actively encourage and financially support Republican student organizations to host provocative events on college campuses as part of a broader strategy to delegitimize educational institutions. Republican students do not always agree with their funders' suggestions and sometimes reject the strategy, but these external, right-wing organizations nonetheless play a powerful role in shaping university politics and conservativism on college campuses.[15] For conservative students on college campuses who find the methods or views of these organizations abhorrent, I encourage continual resistance and working to create events that model the kind of generous and thoughtful politics they wish to see.

Events that are intended to provoke a media-friendly form of outrage are different from good-faith discussions that students may desire to have across the political spectrum. Some of these good-faith discussions are sponsored by student groups that resist being pigeonholed into one political party or the other.[16] Every day, people choose whom to speak with and how to engage with their interlocutors. Choosing to dialogue across difference in smaller groups that are not oriented around a specific political identity is different from attending events focused around incendiary speakers. Knowing how to dialogue across differences is an important civic skill, and I encourage students to do so in the classroom (whether online or in person) and in other dialogue spaces designed to facilitate these discussions. Despite the concerns that student facilitators raised about intergroup dialogue in my study, studies show that intergroup dialogue has a positive effect on students' attitudes, critical consciousness, and identity.[17]

I understand that the recommendation that students be thoughtful about when they choose to engage in debate may be unsatisfactory to some readers. After all, emphasizing choices is an individualistic strategy. What, then, about broader structural and cultural changes to facilitate generative and equitable approaches to speech on college campuses?

The sociologists Wendy Leo Moore and Joyce Bell suggest that universities ought to center the Equal Protection Clause in issues of speech.[18]

In doing so, universities would emphasize equal educational access for their student body. Moore and Bell provide an example of how a university might orient its community values through three points. Their points focus specifically on issues of racism, but it is not difficult to substitute this with other forms of exclusion, such as sexism, homophobia, and trans*phobia. Specifically, they recommend that universities adopt the following stance regarding free speech:

- At a public university, all students, regardless of race, must have substantively equal access to the institution.
- Racist speech and expression is considered by this university to be fundamentally exclusionary and potentially threatening in that it affects the ability of students of color (as well as faculty and staff of color) to meaningfully engage in the institutional community and to benefit from the resources of the institution to the same extent as white students.
- Whether or not First Amendment law permits the university to take punitive action against those who engage in racist speech and expression in our university community, we will take all legally permissible action and utilize our own institutional power of speech to sanction and criticize these forms of expression in order to protect the rights of students of color to attain their education free from the threat of dehumanizing or violent expressions.[19]

Moore and Bell focus on ensuring access to education for racialized minorities. Although they recognize there are limits to the actions universities can take under existing norms, they also suggest that universities should take legal action when possible when speech is threatening or violent.[20] Other scholars argue similarly, suggesting that universities can and should limit speech because the institutional purpose of higher education is *education* and everyone should have *access* to education without being dehumanized, harassed, or incited against.[21]

What these scholars have in common is the recognition that public universities are *universities first*. Therefore, everyone should have access to their education without the hindrances and consequences of dehumanization and violence. Some readers may object to this approach, arguing that it makes speech secondary to education, but this critique fails to recognize that free speech is only possible when all peoples are truly equal—that is, equally able to participate.[22] The current legal constraints at public universities favor absolutist perspectives of speech. This limits a public university's ability to create inclusive and equitable environments.[23] While absolutism is the current prevailing norm on public universities, this does not mean that it will always be so.

Advocating for LGBTQ+ Students at Christian Colleges

For those who work in Christian higher education, what might it look like to build a more equitable and inclusive campus for LGBTQ+ students? I acknowledge that my experience in Christian higher education is limited. I have never attended a Christian educational institution, but I am the child of an Asian American evangelical Christian minister. I grew up hearing theological beliefs about gender complementarianism and heteronormative sexuality, and I called many of these theological beliefs my own throughout my youth and early adulthood.[24] I participated in condemning gender presentations and expressions of sexuality that did not fit what I had then believed to be holy. But in the same way that I changed my views from my conservative evangelical upbringing, I believe that organizations and the people inhabiting churches and Christian higher education can also change.

Oneya Okuwobi, a wise sociologist, Christian, minister, and friend of mine, once said, "Theology tells us how to live. Sociology tells us how we are doing with that." Sociology can also tell us how theology operates, pointing to failures in theology. In a study of LGBTQ+ student groups and nondiscrimination policies at Christian colleges, the sociologist Jonathan Coley found that Christian colleges that were more communal in their theology were more inclusive with regard to having LGBTQ+ student groups and nondiscrimination policies.[25] In other words, universities that were less oriented around individualism and individual piety were more likely to have officially recognized LGBTQ+ student groups and nondiscrimination policies to protect LGBTQ+ students.

Much scholarly ink has been spilled in demonstrating how individualistic tendencies in evangelical Christianity have also hurt people of color. White evangelicals look at racial inequality and deem it the result of individual actions; accordingly, they advocate for a process of racial reconciliation that focuses on interracial relationships.[26] This shifts engagement from changing policy and structures to individual relationships. If theologies of individualism are ultimately breaking communities, excluding LGBTQ+ folks, people of color, and other marginalized groups, then there may be something fundamentally wrong with the way individualism has shaped theology and engagement. Individualistic orientations center people at the privileged intersections at the cost of building greater inclusion and equity for LGBTQ+ folk and people of color.[27] What might a more community-based orientation toward building inclusive Christian college campuses for LGBTQ+ students look like?

Students voiced several ways Christian colleges can move toward inclusion. Some of these are basic strategies that rely on the diversity as difference framework, such as allowing LGBTQ+ students to meet on campus and create an officially recognized student group. Students told me repeatedly how the existence of Harbor helped mitigate some of their fears about attending Christ College.[28] Although these students still faced challenges on campus, they were able to find community with other LGBTQ+ students and benefit from their advice on how to navigate the university. Still, Christ College's official recognition of Harbor remains somewhat of an exception among evangelical Christian colleges.[29] The simple act of recognizing student groups is one step many Christian colleges can take but must not be the only action taken.

It should also not be the responsibility of LGBTQ+ student groups to envision or enforce changes to university policy. For example, Harbor provides information on how Christ College's counseling services are affirming of queer and trans* identities. Harbor members argued that this information should be readily available on the mental health services website, rather than something that is only known and passed among Harbor members. This simple shift removes the onus from Harbor to provide this knowledge to its network by making it readily available to all. Indeed, not every LGBTQ+ student will end up at Harbor, yet every LGBTQ+ student who looks up Christ College's counseling services online should know that they can receive counseling services that will not denigrate them or put them through conversion therapy.[30] Resources for LGBTQ+ students should be institutionalized and publicized.

Many Christian colleges also maintain exclusionary policy statements regarding gender identity and sexuality. At Christ College, Harbor exists alongside policy statements that suggest that its members' sexuality or gender identities are in conflict with the university and broader Christian belief. LGBTQ+ students often felt that Christ College's conflicting stances toward their presence on campus reflected a need to please conservative alumni and donors and their university's affiliated denomination. This situation is not unusual, as Christian colleges must grapple with the different and often competing demands and visions of their donors, denominations, and students.[31] To put it simply, Christian colleges should remove these cisgender and heteronormative statements regarding sexuality and gender identity. This is, of course, easier said than done, as evidenced by the ongoing opposition from the Board of Trustees to removing Christ College's statement on gender and sexuality.

Opponents of developing a more inclusive campus environment at Christian colleges often depict the discussion in terms of a "culture war" or an attack on unalterable theological beliefs.[32] I urge trustee members, denominational stakeholders, and other stakeholders who oppose LGBTQ+-inclusive policies to consider whether a "culture war" is really the right way of framing these conflicts.[33] What new possibilities for healing and reconciliation emerge if we stop fighting "wars" and instead sow seeds of life? I encourage those who feel that changing their views on gender and sexuality requires changing their theology to critically evaluate their theology. Faith is not living unless it has room to breathe and change. Even if stakeholders' personal positions do not change, I urge them to imagine these exclusionary policies not from distant positions of power but from the way living and breathing students experience these policies.

Some skeptics ask why LGBTQ+ students would want to attend Christian colleges that are either demonstratively or stereotypically known for discriminating against them. Asking this question preempts any possible change and assumes that LGBTQ+ students do not belong at Christian colleges (and sometimes in Christian communities more broadly). This question also centers individual choice and assumes that LGBTQ+ students have a range of collegiate choices. In my interviews, LGBTQ+ students attended Christ College because the Christian family members who were helping them finance college would only do so at a Christian college, because Christ College was the most financially viable with regard to scholarships, because other family members had attended the college, or simply because Christ College was the only college that admitted them. Other research on this question shows that LGBTQ+ students may attend Christian colleges to build their faith. Some may not have yet realized that they are on the queer or trans* spectrum.[34] Instead of asking why LGBTQ+ students would attend a Christian college, the question should be turned inward. If the default is to be exclusionary and ask, "Why would you come here?" then perhaps there is fundamentally something wrong with the way belonging is being conceptualized.

Christian colleges, like public and secular universities, need to provide gender-inclusive housing options. These housing options should not cost students more than gendered housing options. Universities can design more inclusive roommate matching surveys to allow LGBTQ+ students to match with other LGBTQ+ students or allies.[35] Many of the recommendations I have made on speech apply to LGBTQ+ inclusivity in the classroom. Other recommendations include normalizing the sharing of pronouns and expanding the curriculum to include LGBTQ+ authors. Moreover, Christ College and other Christian universities should actively hire LGBTQ+ faculty without tokenizing them.

In this book, we have seen that LGBTQ+ students at Christ College and West University labored to bring changes to their campus. While the preceding discussion focuses on Christian colleges, both religious and secular universities need to continue to assess their policies and how they might affect LGBTQ+ students. We saw that LGBTQ+ students on *both* college campuses were concerned about housing, treatment in the classroom, and the heteronormativity and cisnormativity they faced. These are areas that students, faculty, and staff can continue working on while centering the lived experiences of LGBTQ+ students.

Racial Equitable Futures

Part of what motivated this book was the desire to understand how "diversity," as a term, encompasses differences beyond racial diversity and the consequences of diversity's capaciousness for social inequality. Nonetheless, in my research, I found that the majority of students defined diversity in relation to race. This book has focused on Asian Americans as a racial group to examine issues of diversity. It has specifically highlighted them in relationship to issues of numerical representation, but these students' experiences also help us understand how the need to bring about racial equity requires tackling the racial structure writ large. In other words, racial equity can only be possible when we understand and dismantle the US's racist racial structure.

This is a tall order. In the US, racial groups are stratified in complex ways that pit different racialized minority groups against one another to maintain systemic White supremacy. Ultimately, these intersectional processes combine to maintain the structural, material, and cultural dominance of people racialized as White and keep people racialized as Black at the bottom.[36] The key to establishing racial equity is dismantling the White racial supremacy and anti-Blackness embedded in our structures.[37] Color-blind perspectives on race are unable to tackle these systems and only serve to perpetuate laws, policies, organizational configurations, processes, and practices that maintain the privileges and power of White people.[38] This is because *not* recognizing the significance of race to these processes and structures allows their racialized nature to persist. Many of these interlocking systems that maintain racial injustice are beyond the university and intersect with other forms of injustice and oppression, but there are some things universities can do to push against systems of White supremacy and anti-Blackness on their campuses.

Secular and religious colleges must recognize and change organizational practices, policies, and cultural norms that center White students. Many of these colleges were built on what Chris Corces-Zimmerman and colleagues call the "historic scaffolds of whiteness."[39] These scaffolds include policies that maintained campuses as racially White and institutionalized practices and culture that centered White knowledge and feelings.[40] For universities to become racial equity regimes, they will need to actively dismantle the scaffolds of Whiteness. This will not be easy for institutions that have been White from their inception and that were intended for White people. Even universities that were not White at their inception, such as historically Black colleges and universities (HBCUs), may draw on the racial language of predominantly White institutions.[41] Universities, therefore, must be vigilant about how their organizational practices, policies, and cultural norms may be maintaining racial and other forms of social inequality.

First, universities must become aware of how their language of racial diversity obscures racial inequality and actively work against such obfuscation. Scholarship—this book included—has demonstrated this problem of racial diversity discourse in higher education and other organizational spaces.[42] Challenging White approaches to diversity means changing the language around racial diversity such that it centers equity rather than just diversity as difference. In a post–affirmative action world, in which political systems have found diversity wanting, there is space to imagine new avenues for racial equity. Not long ago, the language of diversity replaced multiculturalism in the United States.[43] I urge readers to consider what new words and concepts can capture our ideal for racial equity and inclusion without falling into the same problems as "diversity."

Numerous universities require general education courses on diversity. Studies show that diversity courses positively shape students' behaviors, develop critical thinking, and reduce bias, even if the effects are moderate.[44] But these policies are easily challenged, as we have seen in the rollback of DEI educational policies in several states. While universities should continue to promote and protect these educational requirements, a broader understanding of equity in education requires integrating teaching about social inequality and equity in *all* courses. This includes classes in which social issues might, at first glance, appear to be outside the purview of the class. Even having just one lecture on social consequences, such as "science outside the lab," can help advance students' knowledge and expand their critical thinking skills.[45] More importantly, including how course material relates to racial inequality and other forms of social inequality across the curriculum centers social equity as a key part of the university's values—not just something sequestered to a "diversity requirement" in general education.

Universities also ought to evaluate their traditions for inclusivity, asking whether these traditions truly promote their community values. As we have seen, Asian Americans were aware of how their university's promoted traditions were not race neutral. Indeed, these "race neutral" events, often promoted to build identification with a university, did not actively embody the university's purported value of diversity. Universities should carefully consider how their treasured traditions embody their values. Both Christian and secular universities need to ask this question. Students of color want to see their cultural heritages celebrated and honored. Universities should support these functions as core to the university identity by providing funding for cultural events, actively promoting them, and even integrating them into university traditions. Celebration, however, should not replace the difficult work of building racial and intersectional justice.

In a post–affirmative action world, universities are rethinking how to increase the numerical racial diversity of their college campuses. At stake is the educational access of racialized minorities who continue to be barred from higher education. In the state of California, where affirmative action was banned in 1996, advocates have utilized various strategies and policies to increase the number of underrepresented racial and ethnic minorities on their campuses.[46] Without race-conscious affirmative action, the number of Black and Hispanic students dropped across the public university system, with the most precipitous declines at the most selective campuses of the University of California (UC).[47] The UC system implemented the Eligibility in Context Program (ELC) to admit top-performing students across state high schools and also incorporated holistic admissions practices.[48] Administrators and staff also worked tirelessly to increase the racial diversity in the pool of applicants through different outreach programs. A mix of these policies and outreach programs has helped increase the presence of Black and Hispanic students on UC campuses, but their numbers are still disproportionately low.[49] Decades out, scholars have shown that the ban on affirmative action in California affected more than enrollment: it affected the earning power of Black and Hispanic adults, the experience of student organizations, and the campus climate.[50]

Scholars, administrators, and advocates are researching and considering various possibilities to increase racial diversity on campus. As in California, some of these measures include holistic admissions that consider contextual factors, such as high school and neighborhood socioeconomic status.[51] Some have argued for a lottery system at selective colleges; however, simulations suggest that a lottery system would not achieve a diverse student population.[52] Some universities have adopted test-optional policies for the SAT and ACT, with research showing mixed results in increasing racial diversity and creating equity.[53] Whatever the future for college admissions, it is clear that increasing access to education for racialized minorities will remain a work in progress.[54] There is no magic bullet—including affirmative action policies—but we cannot give up on advocating for equitable access to college.

What about Asian Americans? At West University, Asian Americans are the largest group within a plurality. It is helpful to remember that Asian Americans' enrollment on college campuses tends to be at nonselective universities and is concentrated in around ten states. Across the country as a whole, Asian Americans make up around 6 percent of all enrolled college students.[55] Yet, at selective campuses and in states where Asian Americans are more populous, their enrollment numbers are often used to discredit systemic racism. Opponents of affirmative action have drawn on cultural arguments like the model minority myth to raise up the academic performance of Asian Americans and to argue against inclusive and equitable college policies.[56] Policy makers, university administrators, and Asian Americans themselves must fight against these false narratives that fail to recognize how Asian Americans are racialized in ways that maintain a racist hierarchy and ignore intra-Asian inequality.

Asian American students' experiences of their universities vary significantly. Studies have found that they experience chilly campus climates, but this varies by ethnic group.[57] Even on campuses like West University, where Asian Americans' numerical representation is substantial, Asian Americans experience marginalization through microaggressions, the lack of representation in leadership, and the undercurrent of White cultural dominance on campus.[58] Asian Americans' experiences should not be ignored or made invisible because of stereotypes about their success. Researchers should consider the experiences of Asian American students at different types of universities, including nonelite universities and religious institutions, to develop inclusive recommendations for improving equity and belonging.

Policy makers and university communities should also be attentive to differences among Asian Americans. Asian Americans are a diverse group with wide-ranging socioeconomic statuses, educational attainment, and more.[59] Some ethnic groups within the broader category have low college enrollment and high poverty rates.[60] Treating Asian Americans as monolithically successful overlooks the experiences of some Asian American groups in higher education and in scholarship opportunities. For example, the National Science Foundation (NSF) does not consider Asian Americans an underrepresented minority in STEM, even as Hmong students, for example, are rarely found in collegiate and workplace labs.[61] Focusing on the numerical representation of Asian Americans as a homogeneous group fails to recognize how access to and the ability to enroll in college are shaped by broader structural and intersectional factors. Researchers should continue to examine intra-Asian outcomes, and policy makers and administrators should not treat Asian Americans as a monolith when considering opportunities and disadvantages.

In a recent survey, the majority of Asian Americans reported not knowing much about Asian American history. They turn to the internet and media to learn about Asian American history, though a substantial minority also learned about Asian American history in college.[62] On the one hand, Asian American history should be taught at all stages of education and be recognized as part of the US's history. On the other hand, it is also important that Asian American history be taught alongside other racial histories and be connected to US structures and institutions.[63] In Florida, Governor Ron DeSantis mandated that schools teach Asian American history, but the signed law coincided with a rejection of DEI programs, the curbing of African American and Black history, and the censoring of gender and sexuality education.[64] Asian American history should not be taught to the exclusion of other racial histories. Rather, it should be taught in a way that helps people of all racial groups build mutual understanding about the US's unjust racial system and how coalitions and communities can dismantle intersecting systems of White supremacy and anti-Blackness.

It is also clear from this study that racial and ethnic organizations, like the Asian American ones at West University and Christ College, are important to developing a sense of community and belonging. Students of color and these organizations must be supported while recognizing the unique challenges they experience within the unequal racial dynamics of their universities. Whether students envision their organizations as havens away from home, educational spaces to learn about themselves, or a social club, Asian American students can also strive to develop a sense of linked fate with other racial and ethnic minorities on their campuses to challenge their universities' inequality regimes. Linked fate, the sense that one's own group's thriving is linked to those of another, can help develop racial coalitions and communities that honor the uniqueness of each group while working together to bring racial equity and inclusion.[65]

Beyond Numbers

Finally, it is necessary for us to change how we think about numeric representation. Numeric representation and quantitative measures of outcomes are important and powerful. They can be marshaled in support of building equity regimes, but they do not tell the whole story regarding equity and inclusion. As we have seen, focusing on numeric representation can lead to tokenizing, overshadowing the structures that shape numeric representation and perpetuating myths like the model minority. When groups are represented quantitatively, we need to ask how they are being talked about. Is this narrative leading to greater inclusion and equity, or is it perpetuating stereotypes and upholding structures of inequality?

We also need to ask what our end goal is in discussions of numeric representation. For example, do we want racial representation on colleges and other sectors to match US Census statistics of race in the United States? What does this mean for groups, like the LGBTQ+ students in my study, who did not primarily think of their inclusion through numbers?[66] More importantly, how do we understand representation beyond a single axis that captures the intersectional complexity of the world we live in? Numeric representation focuses too narrowly on individuals with different characteristics rather than turning our attention to structures of inequality that privilege and dispossess people on the basis of those characteristics. If we want inclusion and equity that reflects our multifaceted world and the people who live in it, then discussions of under- and overrepresentation are not enough. They offer a starting diagnostic to look at our structures of inequality, but we must also attend to people's lived experiences and the social systems that shape experiences and representation.

Closing Thoughts

I walked away from my interviews at West University and Christ College feeling the mixture of hope and pessimism inflected in my students' voices. They recognized the power of a term like "diversity" but also how vacuous it became once divorced from broader organizational and cultural changes. They wanted to see their universities do better and do more. But they also recognized that their universities were not just for them. Any improvements to their university's approach to equity and inclusion would benefit the many students who would come after them.

That is the odd thing about universities. Traditionally enrolled students may only be there for around four to five years, yet within those years, they are expected to experience intellectual, emotional, and social growth. They are expected to emerge as responsible, civically engaged, and thoughtful adults who will shoulder and inhabit the institutions that make up society. As a young person, I liked to think of college spaces as a social experiment of what community could be like. Living in community is challenging, and building a community necessarily raises the question of what we value, how we build our institutions, and how we treat one another. The students in my study were thinking about these things: What do we value? What do we want our institutions to look like? How do we want to treat one another? That they were critically evaluating these things on their college campuses means that they took seriously the vision of a diverse community and the struggles of living together in an inequitable world. In the limited time and space of college, they fought to make their values known, to change the university to be more just and inclusive, and to treat one another with empathy.

Yet the reality is that the questions of what we value, how we build our institutions, and how we treat one another are not, and cannot be, limited to the college experience. They are more broadly about us as social beings and the socially unequal and unjust world we live in. We live in an increasingly diverse world, and we are left with the same questions. I hope the student narratives presented here challenge us to think about what a diverse, equitable, and inclusive world can look like, not only on college campuses but also outside them.

ACKNOWLEDGMENTS

Someone once told me that it would take a decade from the day I started conceptualizing this project to seeing it published as a book. And they were right. So much has happened in the decade from when I started my field research in 2017 to the publication of this book. We have lived through a pandemic and will live through its aftershocks for decades to come. Wars have erupted across the globe. Higher education is pressed from inside and outside. With all this change and uncertainty, it is difficult to find constancy. I am grateful to all the wonderful people in my life who have provided different anchoring points during different phases of this project and my life.

I started this project as part of my PhD at Yale University. During my six years at Yale, multiple people taught me, encouraged me, and breathed life into my various projects, including this one. Phil Gorski: I once joked that you were my "academic dad," to which I recall your quizzical smile. I am grateful for your support of my various projects over the years: science and religion; religion and education; and the many other things I did! Like a good parent, you gave me the freedom and independence to pursue my interests, while asking insightful questions to help me grow as a scholar. Grace Kao: You joined Yale and immediately stepped onto my committee. Thank you for hitting the ground running with me. Though our time was short, I learned a lot from you about teaching, race, and education. Though I was not a K-pop fan then, I am one now! Rene Almeling: Many years ago, we talked on the phone about Yale while I was still at Rice nervously trying to figure out where to go for graduate school. I am grateful to have known you all my years at Yale and for your incisive mentorship. You always eagerly connected me to others, helped me think through my qualitative methods, and supported my various projects.

While at Yale, I also had the great privilege to learn from various scholars. Jonathan Wyrtzen's Postcolonial Theory class was one of the best at Yale. Vida Maralani taught me statistics and mentored my statistics projects. Lloyd Grieger, Philip Smith, and Rourke O'Brien provided me with examples of generous and fun teaching. I am not sorry for laughing too much in Philip Smith's class. Ron Eyerman provided a steady and kind presence. Emma Zang and Rourke O'Brien provided me with guidance during my last year at Yale. Ron Kwon graciously walked with me through my last years at Yale and has not ceased checking in on me. Outside of the sociology department, I am grateful to Joanna Radin and Henry Cowles, whose courses on the history of science shaped my thinking in indelible ways.

Six years also means the delight of creating community and lifelong friendship. Ruthie: My soul friend. You inspire me with your kindness, thoughtfulness, wisdom, and grace. A friend I can go into the depths of the soul with, whom I can always find a good book recommendation from. Ayo: With laughter and depth, you stand on top of mountains and in deep valleys with me. Your courage, steadfastness, and joy enliven me. I would not be who I am today without you. Grace: It was an odd twist of fate that we would be connected through Paul and meet my first year at Yale. You encourage me and ask difficult questions of yourself and of me. I am grateful for how you anchored me in those early years. Denise: You have seen me through my doubts through multiple projects. You encourage me and help me think clearer and better. With fashion and depth, you have changed me for the better. Huseyin: Your stories never cease to make me laugh, from your cultic birth to your near-death scare at an *onsen* in Japan. The places you go and the person you are! I will look forward to seeing you, Ezgi, and Ekin soon! Bill, Patrick, and Josh: A warm thanks for being spiritual guides and mentors to me. At different points of my time at Yale, you spoke words of truth into my life. I hold them close to my heart. I am also grateful to the many others I met at Yale: Amanda, Jin, Nia, Erinma, Jon, Shirley and Lionel, Flo and Daniel, Hannah, Meera, Sarah, Sanjayan, and many others not named here.

Before beginning my journey at Yale, I had the opportunity to work at the Religion and Public Life Program at Rice University. Elaine: A few sentences cannot do justice for all the significant ways you have shaped my life. I would not be the scholar and person I am today without you. You remain to me a standard of excellence that I can only aspire to. I met many wonderful people at Rice University. I am grateful for David Johnson, Jared Peifer, and Brandon Vaidyanathan, who provided encouragement and moments of mentorship during my time at Rice, Yale, and beyond. I am also grateful for all my lasting friendships started at Rice University. Di Di: You are the absolute best. I look forward to growing old with you in academia or retiring early with you to start a restaurant! Our jokes, commiseration, and projects keep me going—we are always adding oil. Adri: You inspire me with your love and care for all the people around you. Your passion is tireless. Elizabeth: My academic older sister, the one before me and always willing to provide me with advice. Thank you for reading my proposal and commenting on various chapters of this book, for sharpening my writing, and for uplifting me. Paul, Catherine, and Kristian: From our car conversations to our present diverging paths, I always enjoy your email updates and food photos. Lilly: You are sharp, witty, and hilarious. Miss you lots and hope we will cross paths more in the future. Dan: I will always tell people I got you the post-bac at Rice, but really, it was you. Grateful we got to know each other through Kelley, collaborate, and have real talk. To all the students who worked with me during my time at the RPLP: You were all such a joy to work with! I hold onto our Friday bagels, our breakfast burrito seminars, and our summer lunch outings. Laura and Hayley, my old guard of RPLP, I appreciate you two so much. I also met many other wonderful people in Houston. To Kelley: I hope you are always enjoying good food and travels! Your advocacy for Asian Americans and justice will always inspire me.

Even after leaving Rice University, the RPLP continues to be an influential part of my life. I thank the participants of the RPLP for reading earlier drafts of chapters from this book and offering feedback. I am also grateful that the RPLP allowed me to meet wonderful scholars like Oneya Okuwobi, Rachel Schneider, and many others. I am also grateful that I was able to collaborate with Sharan Kaur Mehta and Esmeralda Sánchez Salazar on several different projects. You two are so thoughtful and smart and are doing extremely important work.

I now have the privilege of being part of the Sociology Department at the University of Wisconsin–Milwaukee (UWM). Jennifer Jordan: Thank you for helping me onboard to the department during the pandemic and through my back-to-back family emergencies. You were a pillar during those times. As I worked through my book, you patiently answered my anxious questions and provided me with advice. I am also grateful to Aki and John Roberts. Aki: Although we are both homebodies, I am hugely grateful for all the wonderful people you have introduced me to. My friendships at UWM are because of you. John: You always make me laugh while keeping things grounded. Tim O'Brien provides me with an example of sharp scholarship and generous mentoring. When we first met at a conference many years ago, I did not imagine that one day we would be colleagues, and I am forever happy we are! I am also grateful to Noelle Chesley for keeping me on track with the university. Cary Costello, Marcus Britton, and Kent Redding's professional insights have also helped me think more sharply and clearly. Cary Costello's empathetic approach to life is a standard I can only aspire to. Gordon Gauchat's *Lord of the Rings* lore kept things light. Although we did not overlap long, A. Aneesh and Celeste Campos-Castillo were kind and generous to me. I have also had the wonderful privilege of working with excellent students at UWM. A special shout-out to Victoria! It has been a joy working with you and seeing you grow as a scholar. Thank you for reminding me that changing the world does not need to be grandiose.

Other scholars have inspired and encouraged me throughout this journey. At UCSD, John Evans, Amy Binder, Mary Blair-Loy, Jeffrey Haydu, Isaac Martin, and Edmond Chang were all influential in my journey. A warm thanks to Amy Binder for reading a chapter from this book and providing me with feedback both now and when I was a graduate student. I am also indebted to John Evans for introducing me to Elaine and the job at RPLP many years ago. Michael Emerson, Gerardo Martí, Joshua Tom, Jerry Park, Jennifer McKinney, and many others have all inspired and encouraged me in different ways. I will also always recall a lunch with Ruha Benjamin at Yale. Ruha looked at us wide-eyed graduate students and reminded us that academia is a greedy institution, one that a person could never please. As a result, it is important to find the things that ground you outside of academia. I pass this great insight on to my graduate students.

My brothers, Isaiah and Elijah. Though we have met only briefly, it is as if we have always known each other. You two make me laugh, ground me, and encourage me. To be able to collaborate with you both in scholarly research and be the siblings that we are warms my soul. I am looking forward to growing old with you both and seeing the wonderful things you two will accomplish.

Jessica, from our dormitories at UCSD to now, I am grateful for your friendship. I hope we will have a reunion soon.

Thank you to Jennifer Hammer at New York University Press and the anonymous reviewers who helped me improve this book with your comments and recommendations. A warm thank you to Audra Wolfe, whose editorial insights sharpened my writing and thinking. Thank you to Sarah Weidner, who is always on top of things and helped me wade through the process of university reimbursements. I am also grateful for funding from the Society for the Scientific Study of Religion's Graduate Student Grant for providing me with funds to have interviews transcribed professionally. UWM's Advancing Research and Creativity Grant also provided funding for editorial support and a course release to focus on writing this book.

Portions of chapter 5 were also previously published in *Ethnic and Racial Studies* ("Does Diversity Include Me? Colorblindness and Racial Triangulation among Asian Americans on Two College Campuses," 43, no. 12 [2020]: 2217–35).

This book would not be possible without everyone who participated in my study. Thank you for giving me your time and for sharing with me your frustrations, hopes, and apathies. I can only hope that I have done justice to your voices and that your words speak louder than any of my own deficiencies.

Finally, for my family, Happy, and Haneul. In the span of a decade, so much can happen: joys and sorrows, endurance and transitions, scars and new life. What I have learned is how precious time with you all is. How does one distill over three decades of love in a single sentence? I suppose they don't. Thank you for your unconditional love, patience, and laughs, and when I need the occasional scolding, for being a fool with zeroes and not o's. You have seen me through the ups and downs of graduate school, research, and working as a faculty member. Happy and Hani-bear kept us sane and joyful. Thank you for seeing me at my best and at my worst and being with me through all of it.

Momo, you will always be an example of unconditional love to me. Dodo, you always encourage us to be intellectually curious. Joy, your care and self-sacrifice for all the people in your life sometimes drives me crazy, but you are also a reminder of what it means to live a loving life of service. Sharon, thank you for reading drafts of this book from its original to its current form, and sorry for putting you through all the writing torture! You are a writer in your own right: Your writing transcends worlds and recalls that in the end we are all human, who want nothing more than to be loved and to love, to be known and to know, to be seen and to see. To you all, I will always be your annoying one, lovingly and not so lovingly. Love you.

APPENDIX

Semi-Structured Interview Guide

Opening Questions for Students in Diversity Leadership

1. How did you become interested in issues of diversity?
2. How did you come to be [student leader position]?
3. Can you walk me through some of your responsibilities as [student leader position]?
4. How do you think being involved in [leadership position] has changed the way you think about diversity, if at all?
5. How do you think being [leadership position] has changed the way you interact with people different from you, if at all?
6. Are there things you think [position] could do differently?
7. Overall, how has your involvement in [diversity leadership position] shaped your college experience?

Opening Questions for Asian American Students

1. How did you come to be involved with [Asian American group]? Why did you decide to join [Asian American group]?
2. [if leader] What were some of your responsibilities in [Asian American group]?
3. Were you involved with Asian American clubs in high school?
4. How has your involvement in [Asian American group] shaped your college experience?
5. If [Asian American group] and other groups like it did not exist on campus, how do you think your experience would be different? How would you feel?
6. [Asian American group] is openly [ethnic identity] but they are also pan-Asian. Can you tell me a bit about how you think [Asian American group] manages catering to [ethnic group] and other Asian identities?

7. Thinking about Asian American students, what do you think are the biggest challenges Asian American students face on campus?
8. When you hear the word "diversity" at [university], to what extent do you think Asian American students are included in this?
9. Are you familiar with the [DEI office]? Do you think they effectively engage the concerns of Asian American students?
10. Have you heard of the model minority? What does that mean to you? How do you personally feel about the model minority or these stereotypes?
11. Are there ways you see the model minority or stereotypes about Asian Americans operating on this campus? (How do you feel when you see this?)

Opening Questions for LGBTQ+ Students

1. How did you come to be involved with [LGBTQ+ group]? Why did you decide to join [LGBTQ+ group]?
2. [if leader] What were some of your responsibilities in [LGBTQ+ group]?
3. Before coming to [university], were you involved in similar groups or clubs during high school?
4. How has your involvement in [LGBTQ+ group] shaped your college experience?
5. If [LGBTQ+ group] and groups like it did not exist on campus, how do you think your experience would be different? How would you feel?
6. When you hear the word "diversity" at [university], to what extent do you think LGBTQ+ students are included in this?
7. Are you familiar with the [DEI office]? Do you think they effectively engage the concerns of LGBTQ+ students?
8. What do you think are the biggest challenges LGBTQ+ students face on campus?
9. What do you think an LGBTQ+-inclusive campus looks like?

Defining Diversity

1. How do you define diversity? Inclusion? Equity?
2. What is good (or important) about diversity?
3. What is not so good (or even harmful) about diversity?

4. In an ideal world, how do you think diversity works?
5. How do you define discrimination?
6. So now I am going to show you two different diversity-related statements. Take some time to read through them and then walk me through your thoughts on both.
   a. We believe that diversity is critical to the pluralistic university and can broaden and deepen the educational experience and the scholarly environment. We seek to foster open-mindedness, understanding, compassion, and inclusiveness among individuals and groups. We are committed to ensuring freedom of expression and dialogue, in a respectful and civil manner, on the spectrum of views held by our varied and diverse campus communities. We acknowledge society carries historical and divisive biases based on race, ethnicity, sex, gender identity, age, disability, sexual orientation, religion, and political beliefs. Therefore, we seek to foster understanding and tolerance among individuals and groups, and we promote awareness through education and constructive strategies for resolving conflict.
   b. We seek to embody Christ's teachings of love and inclusivity across boundaries of racial, ethnic, gender, socioeconomic, class, age, ability, religious, and other expressions of human difference. Living out the calling and mission of Christ means living within diversity and practicing inclusion on our campus. We believe that all people, without exception, bear the image of God. Because sin has marred each individual, Christ, in His great love, chose to die on the cross for the sake of every person so that all may receive forgiveness for sin and be reconciled to God. Our pursuit of diversity involves fulfilling Christ's command to love our neighbors as ourselves. In submitting to the Lordship of Christ, we seek to eliminate attitudes of superiority.

Campus Practices

7. Are there ways you think the university can change in its approach to diversity?
8. What do you think are the largest obstacles to fostering diversity on campus?

9. Can you walk me through your best experience of diversity on campus? Your worst?
10. Have you ever witnessed or experienced discrimination on your campus?

    (If student can recall a time) How did you respond? How do you think an event like this could be prevented?
11. Have you heard of the (diversity initiative) at (university)? Have you attended any of their programs?

    (If yes) How was your experience? Has it changed the way you think about diversity?

    (If no) Do you plan to? Why or why not?

[For Christ College]

12. Have you heard of the term "racial reconciliation"? If so, can you tell me what that means to you? Are there things you like or dislike about the term?
13. What role do you think (religious) faith plays in racial reconciliation?

Personal Experiences

14. Have you heard of the term "intersectionality"?
    a. (If so) How do you personally identify in terms of your understanding of your intersectional identities?
    b. (If not) How do you identify racially or ethnically? Gender? Sexual orientation? Do you identify with a certain religion?
15. I am now going to ask you some questions related to the identities you mentioned earlier. Feel free to answer these questions discussing your identities together or separately or whatever is most comfortable for you. Can you tell me about a time when you felt your identity/identities were affirmed?
16. Can you tell me about a time when you felt your identity/identities were not taken seriously?

[For religious students]

17. How do you think your faith relates to your identities?
18. How do you think your faith shapes or influences the way you think about issues of diversity?

[For LGBTQ+ students]

19. If you are comfortable, can you tell me a bit about your coming-out process? Have you come out to your family? What about at [university] outside the queer community?
20. [If religious] Can you tell me a bit about how you think your faith relates to your gender identity or sexual orientation?

Responses to Public Perceptions

21. I am now going to ask you to respond to some statements and tell me your opinion. Some people see ethnic and racial organizations on college campuses as leading to separatism. Others see them as providing important support networks and cultural legitimacy to minorities. What do you think?
22. Some argue that affirmative action is about providing opportunities to historically disadvantaged groups and creating a diverse environment where people can learn from each other. Others see affirmative action as admitting students who are ill-equipped to compete in the academic environment. What do you think of these arguments?

    How would you respond to current arguments that White people are discriminated against?

    How about arguments that Asian Americans are discriminated against?
23. At some universities, there have been protests against right-wing speakers. Some people see student protests against right-wing speakers as denying free speech. Others see these as protests against hate speech, sexism, and racism, among others. What do you think?

    How do you think the university should respond to these sorts of invitations?

    How do you think the university should respond to student protests?
24. At some universities, there are memorials or buildings that bear the image or names of individuals some deem offensive. Some people see retaining these memorials and building names as preserving history. Others see them as oppressive and think they ought to be removed. What do you think? How do you think the university should respond?

25. At some religious universities, there have been some controversies over the accommodation of lesbian, gay, bisexual, queer, and transgender students. For some, the objection to these accommodations is a matter of freedom of religion. For others, accommodation is a matter of civil rights. What do you think? How do you think freedom of religion and civil rights issues should be approached on campuses?
26. As you may know, DACA (Deferred Action for Childhood Arrivals) was recently rescinded. How do you think the university should respond? What do you think are some ways for the university to engage undocumented students during this time?
27. Some argue that college students today are coddled—that they are protected from ideas and concepts that they may find offensive through trigger warnings and safe spaces. What do you think?

Closing Demographic Questions

28. How old are you?
29. What are your gender pronouns?
30. What do your parents or guardians do for a living?
31. Are you a first-generation college student? (The first in your family to go to college?)
32. What year of college are you in?
33. What is your major?
34. Is there anything you want to add or any other thoughts you want to share on the topic of diversity? Is there anything you think I missed?

NOTES

INTRODUCTION

1 "West University" is a pseudonym.

2 "Christ College" is a pseudonym.

3 Coley, "Reconciling Religion and LGBT Rights"; Coley, "Theologies of Exclusion"; Coley, "Have Christian Colleges and Universities."

4 Diaz, "Florida Gov. Ron DeSantis Signs a Bill."

5 Scholars have studied LGBTQ+ students' experiences in higher education but less within the umbrella of "diversity."

6 Chun and Evans, "Affirmative Action at a Crossroads." Asian Americans are also considered a panethnic group. Readers will notice that I primarily discuss them as a racialized group in relationship to university diversity practices and policies and refer to some of Asian Americans' own stances as panethnic, for example, when Asian American groups posit themselves as pan-Asian to include various Asian ethnic groups. For more on the relationship between racialization and ethnicity, see Brown and Jones, "Rethinking Panethnicity and the Race-immigration Divide."

7 Poon and Segoshi, "Racial Mascot Speaks."

8 Acker, "Inequality Regimes," 443.

9 Acker, "Inequality Regimes," 443. Acker focused on race, class, and gender in response to scholarship on intersectionality.

10 I draw on Joan Acker's inequality regimes to define an equity regime ("Inequality Regimes," 443).

11 Berrey, *Enigma of Diversity*; Bonilla-Silva, *Racism Without Racists*; Melamed, "Diversity"; Mills, *Black Rights/White Wrongs*.

12 Ishimaru and Galloway, "Hearts and Minds First," 333.

13 Brayboy et al., "Equality and Justice for All?," 159.

14 Stevens et al., "Sieve, Incubator, Temple, Hub."

15 Hout, "Social and Economic Returns"; Torche, "Effect of Maternal Stress."

16 Armstrong and Hamilton, *Paying for the Party*.

17 Jack, *Privileged Poor*.

18 Silver, *Cost of Inclusion*.

19 Ray, "Theory of Racialized Organizations."

20 Corces-Zimmerman et al., "Historic Scaffolds"; Gusa, "White Institutional Presence."

21 Acker, "Hierarchies, Jobs, Bodies"; Coley et al., "Gendered Organizations."

22 Thomas, *Diversity Regimes*, 13.
23 Berrey, "Why Diversity Became Orthodox"; J. Kim, "From Bakke to Grutter"; Moses and Chang, "Toward a Deeper Understanding."
24 Jayakumar et al., "Reclaiming Diversity."
25 J. Kim, "From Bakke to Grutter."
26 Berrey, *Enigma of Diversity*; J. Kim, "From Bakke to Grutter"; Moses and Chang, "Toward a Deeper Understanding."
27 Garces, "Aligning Diversity, Quality, and Equity."
28 Garces, "Aligning Diversity, Quality, and Equity"; Jayakumar et al., "Reclaiming Diversity"; Ross, "Innocence and Affirmative Action."
29 Mayorga-Gallo, "White-Centering Logic."
30 Mayorga-Gallo, "White-Centering Logic"; Mueller, "Producing Colorblindness." For a discussion of the three pillars of White supremacy, see A. Smith, "Indigeneity, Settler Colonialism, White Supremacy"; and for the role of White supremacy in political theory and practice, see Mills, *Racial Contract*.
31 Doane, "Beyond Color-Blindness"; Mayorga-Gallo, "White-Centering Logic"; Melamed, "Diversity."
32 Douds, "Diversity Contract."
33 Bonilla-Silva, *Racism Without Racists*.
34 Edelman et al., "Diversity Rhetoric"; Embrick, "Diversity Ideology"; Melamed, "Diversity"; Thomas, *Diversity Regimes*.
35 Berrey, "Why Diversity Became Orthodox"; J. Kim, "From Bakke to Grutter"; Melamed, "Diversity"; Edelman et al., "Diversity Rhetoric"; Berrey, *Enigma of Diversity*; Embrick, "Diversity Ideology."
36 Edelman et al., "Diversity Rhetoric."
37 Edelman et al., "Diversity Rhetoric"; Embrick, "Diversity Ideology."
38 Hurtado, "Campus Racial Climate"; Hurtado et al., "Assessing the Value"; Hurtado et al., "Climate for Diversity"; Museus and Harris, "Success Among College Students."
39 Longman, *Diversity Matters*; Redden, "Christian Colleges Grow More Diverse."
40 Longman, *Diversity Matters*.
41 Curtis, *Myth of Colorblind Christians*; Hawkins, *Bible Told Them So*.
42 Alumkal, "American Evangelicalism"; Curtis, *Myth of Colorblind Christians*; Emerson and Smith, *Divided by Faith*; A. Smith, *Unreconciled*.
43 Butler, *White Evangelical Racism*; Curtis, *Myth of Colorblind Christians*; Tranby and Hartmann, "Critical Whiteness Theories."
44 Oyakawa, "Racial Reconciliation."
45 Chan et al., "Racial and Religious Convergences and Divergences."
46 Longman, *Diversity Matters*; Paredes-Collins, "Institutional Priority for Diversity"; Yancey, *Neither Jew nor Gentile*.
47 Avery, "LGBTQ Students at Christian Colleges"; Pappano, "At Christian Colleges"; Young, "To Condemn or Not to Condemn"; Burke, "False Dichotomy."
48 Moon, "Beyond the Dichotomy."

49 Moon et al., "Alpha, Omega, and the Letters in Between."
50 Sumerau et al., "Contemporary Religion."
51 Schilt and Westbrook, "Doing Gender, Doing Heteronormativity"; Collier and Daniel, "Production of Trans Illegality."
52 Mahmood, *Religious Difference*; Kahn and Lloyd, *Race and Secularism in America.*
53 J. Scott, *Sex and Secularism.*
54 Taylor, *Secular Age*; Asad, *Formations of the Secular.*
55 Asad, *Formations of the Secular*; J. Scott, *Sex and Secularism*; Gorski, "Historicizing the Secularization Debate"; Gorski and Altınordu, "After Secularization?"
56 For examples of the way secular policies transform religion, see Wenger, "Religious Freedom."
57 Gersen, "Uncomfortable Truth."
58 Monte and Shin, "20.6 Million People"; National Center for Education Statistics, "Indicator 20." The Asian American alone category makes up around 6 percent of the US. This figure is a little over 7 percent when Asian Americans of mixed racial identities are included.
59 Pak et al., *Asian Americans in Higher Education.*
60 National Center for Education Statistics, "Indicator 19"; National Center for Education Statistics, "Indicator 23."
61 National Center for Education Statistics, "Indicator 27."
62 Lee and Zhou, *Asian American Achievement Paradox.*
63 Kao et al., *Education and Immigration.*
64 S. Lee, "Over-Represented and De-Minoritized"; Pak et al., *Asian Americans in Higher Education.*
65 Lee and Zhou, *Asian American Achievement Paradox*; but see Wu, *Color of Success.*
66 Lewis, "Culture of Poverty"; Lewis, *Five Families.*
67 Lee and Zhou, *Asian American Achievement Paradox*; Wu, *Color of Success.*
68 C. Kim, "Racial Triangulation."
69 Bonilla-Silva, "From Bi-Racial to Tri-Racial."
70 Kao et al., *Education and Immigration*; Lee and Zhou, *Asian American Achievement Paradox*; Museus, *Asian American Students*; Museus and Park, "Continuing Significance of Racism"; Ngo and Lee, "Complicating the Image"; Pak et al., *Asian Americans in Higher Education*; Pang et al., "Asian American and Pacific Islander Students"; Tran, "Asian American Diversity and Growth."
71 Pak et al., *Asian Americans in Higher Education.*
72 Teranishi et al., "Asian American and Native American Pacific Islander Serving Institutions"; Vue et al., "Asian Americans in STEM."
73 Museus, *Asian American Students.* For exceptions, see Warikoo, *Diversity Bargain*; Park, *When Diversity Drops.*
74 Ahmed, "Language of Diversity"; Berrey, *Enigma of Diversity*; Mayorga-Gallo, "White-Centering Logic"; Moore and Bell, "Maneuvers of Whiteness"; Petts, "It's All in the Definition"; Rajasekar et al., "Diversity Discourse"; Thomas, *Diversity*

Regimes; Turner, *Suddenly Diverse*; Warikoo, *Diversity Bargain*; Jayakumar et al., "Reclaiming Diversity."

75 Greathouse et al., "Queer-Spectrum and Trans-Spectrum Student Experiences"; Rankin and Garvey, "Identifying, Quantifying, and Operationalizing."

76 Rankin and Garvey, "Identifying, Quantifying, and Operationalizing."

77 Rankin and Garvey, "Identifying, Quantifying, and Operationalizing"; Jourian, "Evolving Nature."

78 Campus Pride, "Tracking Retention"; Rankin and Garvey, "Identifying, Quantifying, and Operationalizing"; Greathouse et al., "Queer-Spectrum and Trans-Spectrum Student Experiences."

79 Rankin and Garvey, "Identifying, Quantifying, and Operationalizing."

80 Steele, "Common App Revises Application Questions"; Steele, "Common App to Update Gender Identity Questions"; Rankin and Garvey, "Identifying, Quantifying, and Operationalizing"; Jaschik, "Beyond Male/Female."

81 Cegler, "Targeted Recruitment."

82 Greathouse et al., "Queer-Spectrum and Trans-Spectrum Student Experiences."

83 Marine, "Stonewall's Legacy."

84 Greathouse et al., "Queer-Spectrum and Trans-Spectrum Student Experiences."

85 Jones, "LGBT Identification."

86 Jones, "LGBT Identification"; Conron, "LGBT Youth Population."

87 Pew Research Center, "Majority of Public Favors Same-Sex Marriage"; Evans et al., "Voices from the Stories Untold"; Greathouse et al., "Queer-Spectrum and Trans-Spectrum Student Experiences"; Marine, "Stonewall's Legacy"; Rankin et al., *2010 State of Higher Education*; Renn, "LGBT and Queer Research."

88 Byrd, *Behind the Diversity Numbers*; Hurtado et al., "Model for Diverse Learning Environments."

89 Barton, *Pray the Gay Away*; Marine, "Stonewall's Legacy"; Levine and Love, "Religiously Affiliated Institutions"; Rockenbach and Crandall, "Faith and LGBTQ Inclusion"; Coley, *Gay on God's Campus*; Kay and Wolff, "LGBTQ Students."

90 US Department of Education, "Sex Discrimination."

91 Caputo and Marcus, "How Some Religious Colleges Avoid Rules."

92 White House, "Executive Order." As of writing this, the second Trump administration has not begun, but it is likely that Title IX protections will be rolled back.

93 College Pulse, "LGBTQ+ Student Divide."

94 College Pulse, "LGBTQ+ Student Divide"; Craig et al., "Fighting for Survival"; Wheeler, "What Is It Like?"; Wolff et al., "Sexual Minority Students."

95 Wolff and Himes, "Purposeful Exclusion."

96 Redden, "Being LGBTQ+ on a Christian Campus."

97 The Christian colleges in Coley's sample are those that maintain religious ties. Coley, "Reconciling Religion and LGBT Rights"; Coley, "Theologies of Exclusion."

98 Coley, personal communication, November 5, 2018.

99 Greathouse et al., "Queer-Spectrum and Trans-Spectrum Student Experiences"; Marine, "Stonewall's Legacy"; Renn, "LGBT and Queer Research"; Heiden-Rootes

et al., "National Survey"; Wolff et al., "Transgender and Gender-Nonconforming Student Experiences"; Wolff et al., "Sexual Minority Students"; Kay and Wolff, "LGBTQ Students."

100 Rankin et al., "Retrospective of LGBT Issues"; Mathies et al., "Hearing 'That's so Gay' and 'No Homo'"; Silverschanz et al., "Slurs, Snubs, and Queer Jokes."

101 Ahmed, "Language of Diversity"; Berrey, *Enigma of Diversity*; Mayorga-Gallo, "White-Centering Logic"; Moore and Bell, "Maneuvers of Whiteness"; Petts, "It's All in the Definition"; Rajasekar et al., "Diversity Discourse"; Thomas, *Diversity Regimes*; Turner, *Suddenly Diverse*; Warikoo, *Diversity Bargain*.

102 Thomas, *Diversity Regimes*.

103 Monte and Shin, "20.6 Million People." Asian Americans make up around 15 percent of the state in which West University is located in and 10 percent of the state in which Christ College is located in.

104 Coley, "Reconciling Religion and LGBT Rights"; Coley, "Theologies of Exclusion."

105 Caputo and Marcus, "How Some Religious Colleges Avoid Rules."

106 Edwards, "Bring Race to the Center"; Edwards et al., "Race, Religious Organizations, and Integration"; Emerson and Smith, *Divided by Faith*; Kahn and Lloyd, *Race and Secularism in America*; Mahmood, *Religious Difference*; Marti, "Affinity, Identity, and Transcendence"; Park, *When Diversity Drops*.

107 I chose to interview students who were employed in diversity leadership positions or who participated in university-sanctioned positions to examine how they navigated their university's diversity discourse and practices and their own views. Although I chose to study student leaders in university-sanctioned leadership positions, it is important to remember that many students participate in leadership and activism outside these positions. Therefore, there are many students who are working toward diversity outside of university positions who are not captured in this study.

108 Duran et al., "Interdisciplinary Return."

109 Tompkins, "Asterisk"; Duran et al., "Interdisciplinary Return."

110 Museus, *Asian American Students*.

CHAPTER 1. THREE DEFINITIONS OF DIVERSITY

1 Thomas, *Diversity Regimes*.

2 Bell and Hartmann, "Diversity in Everyday Discourse."

3 Embrick, "Diversity Ideology."

4 James Thomas makes a similar argument about the flattening of diversity in his book *Diversity Regimes*.

5 Warikoo, *Diversity Bargain*; Warikoo and de Novais, "Colour-Blindness and Diversity."

6 This refers to Max Weber's *The Methodology of the Social Sciences*. Ideal types are primarily useful for illustrating characteristics and do not necessarily mean that a social phenomenon will empirically embody all described characteristics.

7 Alba et al., "Beyond the Melting Pot"; Glazer, "America's Ethnic Pattern"; Glazer and Moynihan, *Beyond the Melting Pot*; Hirschman, "America's Melting Pot Reconsidered."
8 Alba et al., "Beyond the Melting Pot."
9 Chang, "Reconsidering the Diversity Rationale"; Aguirre and Martinez, "Diversity Rationale in Higher Education"; Chang and Ledesma, "Diversity Rationale."
10 Hollinger, *Postethnic America*; Morning, "Race."
11 Morning, "Race"; Omi and Winant, *Racial Formation in the United States.*
12 American Sociological Association, "Culture." Sociologists are also clear that culture is not innate or essential to a group. In other words, culture is formed and transformed, and people draw on culture as repertoires, narratives, frames, and more to make sense of themselves and the world around them.
13 Bonilla-Silva, *Racism Without Racists*; Skrentny, "Culture and Race/Ethnicity."
14 Melamed, "Diversity"; Melamed, "Racial Capitalism"; Bonilla-Silva, *Racism Without Racists.*
15 For a similar argument, see Thomas, *Diversity Regimes.*
16 Berrey, "Why Diversity Became Orthodox"; Stevens and Roksa, "Diversity Imperative in Elite Admissions."
17 Hurtado et al., *Enacting Diverse Learning Environments*; Hurtado et al., "Assessing the Value of Climate Assessments"; Hurtado et al., "Model for Diverse Learning Environments"; Milem et al., *Making Diversity Work on Campus.*
18 Hurtado et al., *Enacting Diverse Learning Environments.*
19 Hurtado et al., "Model for Diverse Learning Environments"; Museus, "Role of Ethnic Student Organizations"; Yi, "Institutional Climate and Student Departure."
20 Byrd, *Behind the Diversity Numbers.*
21 Ridgeway, *Framed by Gender*; Schneider, *Psychology of Stereotyping.*
22 Foucault, *"Society Must Be Defended."*
23 Common Data Set Initiative, "Common Data Set Initiative."
24 Rankin and Garvey, "Identifying, Quantifying, and Operationalizing."
25 Mora, "Cross-Field Effects and Ethnic Classification."
26 Hacking, "Making People Up."
27 Warikoo, *Diversity Bargain*, 54.
28 Alex's and Dani's distinctions between equality and equity reflect those described in the introduction and by educational scholars: Brayboy et al., "Equality and Justice for All?"; Ishimaru and Galloway, "Hearts and Minds First."
29 Kanter, *Men and Women of the Corporation*; Zimmer, "Tokenism and Women in the Workplace. For examples of the spread, see Flores, "Racialized Tokens"; E. Scott, "Beyond Tokenism"; Turco, "Cultural Foundations of Tokenism."
30 Kanter, "Some Effects of Proportions," 966.
31 Emerson and Smith, *Divided by Faith.*
32 Tranby and Hartmann, "Critical Whiteness Theories."
33 Chan et al., "Racial and Religious Convergences and Divergences."

34 Chan et al., "Racial and Religious Convergences and Divergences"; Oyakawa, "Racial Reconciliation."
35 Curtis, *Myth of Colorblind Christians*; Oyakawa, "Racial Reconciliation"; A. Smith, *Unreconciled*; Tranby and Hartmann, "Critical Whiteness Theories."
36 Coley, *Gay on God's Campus*.
37 Natasha Warikoo also found in her study that none of the Asian Americans she interviewed drew on a power analysis framework. Warikoo, *Diversity Bargain*.
38 An, "Asian Americans in American History"; Rodríguez and Ip, "Hidden in History."
39 Trieu and Lee, "Asian Americans."
40 Bell and Hartmann, "Diversity in Everyday Discourse"; Embrick, "Diversity Ideology."
41 Warikoo, *Diversity Bargain*.
42 Buckley and Park, "When You Don't Really Focus on It."

CHAPTER 2. ASSUMPTIONS OF EQUALITY IN CREED AND LIBERALISM

1 These diversity statements highlight diversity discourse as it is propagated through language rather than through visual materials, such as photographs of diverse student bodies often found on university websites or pamphlets. It is possible that students may have had different responses to visual diversity discourse.
2 Asad, *Formations of the Secular*; J. Scott, *Sex and Secularism*.
3 Foste et al., "Articulating Diversity on Campus"; Ahmed, "You End Up Doing the Document"; J. Wilson et al., "Mission and Diversity Statements."
4 Foste et al., "Articulating Diversity on Campus"; Thomas, *Diversity Regimes*; Ahmed, "You End Up Doing the Document."
5 I crafted these statements by drawing on existing diversity statements. I crafted the first statement by drawing on diversity and community values statements from large land-grant universities on the West Coast, which West University represents. Evangelical Christian universities vary tremendously. The second statement drew on diversity and community values statements from colleges and universities in the Council for Christian Colleges and Universities (CCCU), with which Christ College is affiliated.
6 Bonilla-Silva, *Racism Without Racists*; Mayorga-Gallo, "White-Centering Logic"; Melamed, "Diversity"; Bell and Hartmann, "Diversity in Everyday Discourse."
7 Warikoo, *Diversity Bargain*.
8 Oyakawa, "Racial Reconciliation."
9 Diefendorf and Pascoe primarily address love through issues of racial inequality, but their assessments can be applied to other forms of social inequality in which love is touted over systemic change ("In the Name of Love").
10 Mayorga-Gallo, "White-Centering Logic."
11 Brown, *Regulating Aversion*; Mills, *Black Rights/White Wrongs*.
12 Berrey, "Why Diversity Became Orthodox"; J. Kim, "From Bakke to Grutter."

13 Bowman, "Promoting Participation"; Gurin et al., "Diversity and Higher Education"; Gurin et al., "Benefits of Diversity"; Milem, "Educational Benefits of Diversity."
14 Franklin, "Racial Microaggressions"; Franklin, "Coping with Racial Battle Fatigue"; Smith et al., "Racial Battle Fatigue"; Sue, "Race Talk"; Chan and Isaac, "Racialized Fear."
15 Sue, "Race Talk."
16 Carrillo Arciniega, "Selling Diversity to White Men"; Thomas, "Economization of Diversity"; Berrey, *Enigma of Diversity*.
17 Warikoo, *Diversity Bargain*.
18 Mayorga-Gallo, "White-Centering Logic"; Melamed, "Diversity"; Warikoo, *Diversity Bargain*.
19 Foste et al., "Articulating Diversity on Campus."

CHAPTER 3. EQUALITY WITHOUT EQUITY IN SPEECH AT WEST UNIVERSITY

1 Speaker identities were removed to maintain the confidentiality of West University.
2 Responding to controversies over the event, a West University spokesman stressed the university's content-neutral approach.
3 Heim, "How a Rally of White Nationalists."
4 *UVA Today*, "Sullivan Issues Message."
5 Chemerinsky and Gillman, *Free Speech on Campus*.
6 Speech that is not protected is that which can incite lawless actions, true threats to bodily harm, and fighting words. Hate speech is notoriously difficult to define. For some common features in how hate speech is defined, see Sellars, "Defining Hate Speech."
7 powell, "Worlds Apart"; Baer, *What Snowflakes Get Right*.
8 Foundation for Individual Rights and Expression, "Using FIRE's Spotlight Database."
9 College Pulse, "2020 College Free Speech Rankings"; College Pulse, "2024 College Speech Rankings."
10 Chemerinsky and Gillman, *Free Speech on Campus*; powell, "Worlds Apart"; Delgado, "First Amendment Formalism"; Lawrence, "If He Hollers Let Him Go"; Matsuda, "Public Response to Racist Speech."
11 Soucek, "Speech First, Equality Last."
12 For examples, see Tourjée, "Trans Student Harassed"; Landsbaum, "Alt-Right Troll"; UC Berkeley, "Free Speech?"
13 An example of this occurred at UC San Diego. G. Schneider, "Compton Cookout"; *UCSD Guardian*, "Third Racist Incident"; *UCSD Guardian*, "Campus Reacts to Racial Slur."
14 Research shows that minorities indeed experience harm when they experience hate speech. Gelber and McNamara, "Evidencing the Harms of Hate Speech."

15 There was some disagreement between the university and the Republican student group about who would foot the security bill. In the end, West University footed the bill.
16 Eliot, "Money Talks"; Gecker, "Cost of Free Speech."
17 A study of university administrators found that administrators feared that the lack of neutrality would result in legal repercussions. Garces et al., "Repressive Legalism."
18 Chemerinsky and Gillman, *Free Speech on Campus*; Soucek, "Speech First, Equality Last"; Boch, "Increasing American Political Tolerance"; Chong, "Free Speech and Multiculturalism"; Chong and Levy, "Competing Norms."
19 Binder and Kidder argue that liberal students and activists channel their activism inward—that is, into the university—rather than outward (*Channels of Student Activism*). By providing resources, the diversity board and DEI office encourage this inward-facing activism.
20 Kidder and Binder found that conservative students are more likely than liberal students to espouse an absolutist approach to speech ("Politics of Speech on Campus"). In this regard, Victoria and Quinn are more similar to conservative students.
21 Quinn's allusion to neutrality also reflects a broader legal framework of free speech that emphasizes "viewpoint neutrality," in which speech cannot be regulated based on its content except in very narrowly defined conditions.
22 I conducted my interviews in 2017–18. Student and university conflicts over Palestine and Israel have only intensified since Israel's invasion of Gaza in October 2023. This is also true at West University, where student protests have racked the university.
23 Flores et al., "Gender Identity Disparities."
24 Sellars, "Defining Hate Speech"; Greenawalt, "Free Speech Justifications."
25 While students presented political conservatives and marginalized people in opposition, it is important to remember that some marginalized people espouse politically conservative beliefs.
26 Chan and Isaac, "Racialized Fear"; Sue, "Race Talk."
27 Sue, "Race Talk."
28 Walls and Hall, "Focus Group Study"; Chan and Isaac, "Racialized Fear."
29 Niehaus, "Self-Censorship or Just Being Nice"; College Pulse, "2020 College Free Speech Rankings."
30 College Pulse, "2020 College Free Speech Rankings"; Chan and Isaac, "Racialized Fear."
31 For example, White people may avoid discussions of race. See DiAngelo, *White Fragility*; Sue, "Race Talk."
32 Binder and Kidder found that conservative students were interested in and engaged in intergroup dialogue discussions (*Channels of Student Activism*). Differences could be due to differences in university contexts and student experiences.
33 Chemerinsky and Gillman, *Free Speech on Campus*.

34 Moore and Bell, "Right to Be Racist in College."
35 Garces et al., "Repressive Legalism."
36 Soucek, "Speech First, Equality Last."

CHAPTER 4. EQUALITY WITHOUT INCLUSION FOR LGBTQ+ STUDENTS AT CHRIST COLLEGE

1 Augustine-Adams, "Religious Exemptions to Title IX."
2 US Department of Education, "Exemptions from Title IX."
3 Augustine-Adams, "Religious Exemptions to Title IX."
4 White House, "Executive Order"; US Department of Education, "Sex Discrimination."
5 Coley, "Mobilizing for Religious Freedom"; Kazyak et al., "Logics of Freedom"; Richardson, "Managing Religion."
6 Garvey et al., "Generational Perceptions of Campus Climate"; Museus, "Role of Ethnic Student Organizations"; Nicolazzo et al., "Exploration of Trans* Kinship"; Pitcher et al., "Affirming Policies"; Poteat et al., "Gay–Straight Alliances."
7 Diamant, "Half of U.S. Christians Say"; Murphy, "Most U.S. Christian Groups."
8 Sumerau et al., "Contemporary Religion."
9 Coley et al., "Gendered Organizations."
10 Coley, "Mobilizing for Religious Freedom"; Russo, "Religious Freedom."
11 Coley, "Mobilizing for Religious Freedom."
12 Augustine-Adams, "Religious Exemptions to Title IX"; Kazyak et al., "Logics of Freedom"; Richardson, "Managing Religion."
13 This is similar to the rhetoric used by conservative Christians who do not draw on theological reasons for opposing LGBTQ+ students but focus on their own mistreatment and perceive LGBTQ+ individuals as troublemakers. McDowell and Ward, "Tables Are Turning."
14 Kazyak et al., "Logics of Freedom."
15 Coley, *Gay on God's Campus*; Renn, "LGBT Student Leaders."
16 Chang, "Reconsidering the Diversity Rationale"; Chang and Ledesma, "Diversity Rationale"; Warikoo, *Diversity Bargain*.
17 Chang and Ledesma, "Diversity Rationale."
18 Foste and Ng, "Didn't Mean to Mean It That Way."
19 Given Christ College's focus on reconciliation, it is also possible that administrators perceive experiences of discrimination as interpersonal conflicts that can be resolved through interpersonal strategies like communication.
20 Seelman, "Transgender Adults' Access"; Seelman et al., "Experiences of Transgender and Gender Non-Conforming Students."
21 Fain, "College Enrollment Declines Continue."
22 Zylstra, "Tuition Is Rising."
23 Coley, *Gay on God's Campus*; Coley, "Mobilizing for Religious Freedom."
24 Garvey and Rankin, "Making the Grade?"; Greathouse et al., "Queer-Spectrum and Trans-Spectrum Student Experiences"; Rankin et al., *2010 State of Higher*

Education; Renn, "LGBT and Queer Research"; Seelman, "Transgender Adults' Access."

CHAPTER 5. ASIAN AMERICANS AND THE LIMITS OF REPRESENTATION

1 Student organization names have been replaced with pseudonyms.

2 Hurtado et al., *Enacting Diverse Learning Environments*; Hurtado et al., "Model for Diverse Learning Environments"; Milem et al., *Making Diversity Work on Campus.*

3 Astin et al., *Power of Protest*; Astin and Bayer, "Antecedents and Consequents"; Hurtado et al., "Model for Diverse Learning Environments"; Museus et al., "Modeling Racial Differences."

4 Byrd, *Behind the Diversity Numbers.*

5 Bonilla-Silva, *Racism Without Racists.*

6 Thomas and Thomas, *Child in America.*

7 Participants quoted in this chapter who are not Asian American are identified with their racial or ethnic identities. Because Asian American students are the primary focus of this chapter, I do not repeatedly identify Asian American participants as Asian Americans. I identify some participants as Asian American if they discuss Asian Americans in the third person such that it is not clear that they themselves are Asian American.

8 Byrd, *Behind the Diversity Numbers*; Bonilla-Silva, *Racism Without Racists*; Chan, "Does Diversity Include Me?"

9 Museus, "Role of Ethnic Student Organizations."

10 Guiffrida, "African American Student Organizations"; Harper and Quaye, "Student Organizations as Venues."

11 Bell and Hartmann, "Diversity in Everyday Discourse"; Doane, "Beyond Color-Blindness."

12 Buckley and Park, "Hard to Tell."

13 Byrd, *Behind the Diversity Numbers.*

14 S. Lee, "Over-Represented and De-Minoritized"; Pak et al., "Asian Americans in Higher Education."

15 C. Kim, "Racial Triangulation"; C. Kim, *Asian Americans.*

16 C. Kim, *Asian Americans*; Wu, *Color of Success.*

17 There is inequality in educational outcomes among Asian Americans by ethnic group. Museus, *Asian American Students*; Kao et al., *Education and Immigration.*

18 Notably, students like Peter and Orlando discuss Asian American success in the aggregate. Scholars of Asian America point to the vast inequalities among Asian ethnic groups and the need to disaggregate the group, not only to dispel harmful stereotypes about Asian American success but also to shed a light on overlooked disenfranchised groups.

19 S. Lee, *Unseen Unheard Minority*; Liang and Sedlacek, "Attitudes of White Student Services Practitioners"; Suzuki, "Revisiting the Model Minority Stereotype."

20 S. Lee, "Over-Represented and De-Minoritized."

21 The term "yellow peril" is often attributed to the German Kaiser Wilhelm II. In the late nineteenth century and early twentieth century, White Western powers feared the economic and military power of Eastern countries like China and Japan. In the United States, "yellow peril" was associated with fear of Asian immigration. Kawai, "Stereotyping Asian Americans"; E. Lee, *At America's Gates*; E. Lee, "Yellow Peril."

22 S. Lee, "Over-Represented and De-Minoritized"; Ng et al., "Contesting the Model Minority"; Takagi, *Retreat from Race.*

23 See Chung, "Racism"; Museus and Kiang, "Deconstructing the Model Minority Myth."

24 Passel and Cohn, "U.S. Population Projections."

25 Bonilla-Silva, "From Bi-Racial to Tri-Racial."

26 C. Kim, "Racial Triangulation"; C. Kim, *Asian Americans.*

27 Hyun, *Breaking the Bamboo Ceiling*; F. Lee, "Asian American and Pacific Islander Faculty."

28 Hyun, *Breaking the Bamboo Ceiling.*

29 Liang et al., "Developing Asian American Leaders"; Liu and Sedlacek, "Differences in Leadership."

30 Balón, "Asian Pacific American College Students"; Balón and Shek, "Beyond Representation."

31 Balón and Shek, "Beyond Representation"; Chung, "Racism." This scholarship draws inspiration from Edward Said's *Orientalism.*

32 Balón and Shek, "Beyond Representation."

33 Balón, "Asian Pacific American College Students"

34 C. Kim, "Racial Triangulation." Despite a history of Asian activism and leadership, this history remains invisible. Asian Americans often do not become aware of this history until they take a class on Asian American history or become engaged in Asian affinity groups. Trieu and Lee, "Asian Americans."

35 Hurtado et al., *Enacting Diverse Learning Environments*; Hurtado et al., "Model for Diverse Learning Environments"; Milem et al., *Making Diversity Work on Campus.*

36 Buckley and Park, "Hard to Tell."

37 Byrd, *Behind the Diversity Numbers.*

38 Poon et al., "Asian Americans."

CHAPTER 6. LGBTQ+ STUDENTS

1 At the time of my interviews, students used a mix of "gender-neutral bathrooms" and "gender-inclusive bathrooms" to describe bathrooms. West University now uses the term "all gender" and "gender-inclusive" restrooms. Similarly, respondents commonly used the term "preferred name." West University now uses the term "lived name."

2 Seelman, "Recommendations of Transgender Students"; Seelman et al., "Experiences of Transgender and Gender Non-Conforming Students"; Bartholomaeus and Riggs, "Whole-of-School Approaches"; Beemyn, "Making Campuses More Inclusive."

3 Kimberlé Crenshaw provides an example of how this works through the various types of discriminatory laws facing Black women. The law saw them as either women or Black but did not see them as Black women. Crenshaw, "Mapping the Margins."

4 Cech and Rothwell, "LGBT Workplace Inequality"; Meyer, "Intersectional Analysis"; Vaccaro and Koob, "Critical and Intersectional Model"; Miller, "Toward Intersectional Identity Perspectives."

5 Seelman, "Transgender Adults' Access."

6 Pryor et al., "Searching for Home."

7 Z Nicolazzo and colleagues draw on Dean Spade's notion of administrative violence (Nicolazzo et al., "From Best to Intentional Practices"; Spade, *Normal Life*).

8 Nicolazzo et al., "From Best to Intentional Practices," 233.

9 "Center for Racial Reconciliation" is a pseudonym.

10 Emerson and Smith, *Divided by Faith*; Oyakawa, "Racial Reconciliation"; Alumkal, "American Evangelicalism"; A. Smith, *Unreconciled.*

11 Alumkal, "American Evangelicalism"; Emerson and Smith, *Divided by Faith*; Wadsworth, *Ambivalent Miracles.*

12 Curtis, *Myth of Colorblind Christians.*

13 Coley et al., "Gendered Organizations"; Acker, "From Sex Roles to Gendered Institutions."

14 Barbee and Schrock, "Un/Gendering Social Selves"; Pryor, "Out in the Classroom."

15 Whitehead, "Male and Female He Created Them"; Upenieks and Bonhag, "Masculine God Imagery"; Baker and Whitehead, "God's Penology"; Whitehead, "Gender Ideology and Religion."

16 Collins and Bilge, *Intersectionality*; Collins, "Intersectionality's Definitional Dilemmas"; Crenshaw, "Mapping the Margins."

17 Collins, "Tie That Binds"; Collins, "Intersectionality's Definitional Dilemmas"; Crenshaw, "Mapping the Margins."

18 Beattie et al., "What Do We Know."

19 "Advance" is a pseudonym.

20 See hooks, *Feminist Theory*; McDermott and Ferguson, "Sociology of Whiteness"; Ferber, "Construction of Black Masculinity." Josh recognized the problem of focusing on White individuals in other parts of our interview, but he did not describe race here. Instead, he focused on sexuality and gender relative to patriarchy, which nonetheless also intersects with Whiteness.

21 Stryker, "Transgender History"; Schilt and Westbrook, "Doing Gender, Doing Heteronormativity."

22 Boykin, *One More River to Cross*; Cech and Rothwell, “LGBT Workplace Inequality”; Kafer, “Compulsory Bodies”; Meyer, “Intersectional Analysis”; Sears et al., *LGBT People’s Experiences*; B. Wilson et al., “Racial Differences.”

CHAPTER 7. ASIAN AMERICAN STUDENTS

1 “East University” is a pseudonym.

2 Brett described to me obtaining funding from the DEI office for LGBTQ+ religious students to attend a conference.

3 Students do not need to be Christian to enroll at Christ College. Yet, to a Christian university, events like Christmas and Easter are likely to be commemorated as a cultural norm.

4 When churches attempt to diversify, they often turn to diversifying musical worship practices. Marti, *Worship Across the Racial Divide*.

5 Chan et al., “Racial and Religious Convergences and Divergences.”

6 Longman, *Diversity Matters*.

7 Museus, “Role of Ethnic Student Organizations.”

8 Numerous scholars show how White identity tends to be invisible. Some prominent examples include Frankenberg, *White Women, Race Matters*; Lipsitz, *Possessive Investment in Whiteness*; McIntosh, “White Privilege.”

9 D’Souza, “New Segregation on Campus”; Sidanius et al., “Ethnic Enclaves.”

10 It should also be noted that bicultural identity does not need to refer to immigrants or ethnic minorities. More broadly, it refers to anyone who has internalized two cultures. For this study, I am primarily interested in how bicultural identity and different power differentials in structural expressions of culture manifest themselves in how students run their organizations in higher education. Darder, *Culture and Power*; Huynh et al., “Bicultural Identity Integration.”

11 Chung, “Critical Biculturalist Approach.”

12 Chung, “Critical Biculturalist Approach”; Darder, *Culture and Power*; Huynh et al., “Bicultural Identity Integration.”

13 Gusa, “White Institutional Presence”; Corces-Zimmerman et al., “Historic Scaffolds.”

14 I continue to follow AAW on social media. In recent years, it has become more politically assertive on matters, such as condemning anti-Asian hate and supporting Black Lives Matter and Palestine in the Israel-Palestine conflict.

15 Mueller, “Producing Colorblindness”; Mueller, “Advancing a Sociology of Ignorance”; Mayorga-Gallo, “White-Centering Logic.”

16 Chung, “Critical Biculturalist Approach”; Darder, *Culture and Power*.

17 Phe and Yap, “40 Years After Vincent Chin.”

18 Guiffrida, “African American Student Organizations”; Museus, “Role of Ethnic Student Organizations”; Harper and Quaye, “Student Organizations as Venues”; Manzano et al., “Asian American Student Engagement”; Trieu, “It Was About Claiming Space”; Trieu and Lee, “Asian Americans.”

19 Inkelas, "Does Participation in Ethnic Cocurricular Activities"; Manzano et al., "Asian American Student Engagement"; Museus, "Role of Ethnic Student Organizations"; Trieu, "It Was About Claiming Space."
20 D'Souza, "New Segregation on Campus"; Sidanius et al., "Ethnic Enclaves."
21 Alumkal, "American Evangelicalism"; Wadsworth, *Ambivalent Miracles.*
22 Curtis, *Myth of Colorblind Christians*; Hawkins, *Bible Told Them So.*
23 Alumkal, "American Evangelicalism."
24 C. Kim, *Asian Americans.*
25 Poon et al., "Asian Americans"; Poon and Segoshi, "Racial Mascot Speaks"; J. Lee, "Asian Americans."
26 S. Lee, "Over-Represented and De-Minoritized"; Li and Nicholson, "When 'Model Minorities' Become 'Yellow Peril'"; Tessler et al., "Anxiety of Being Asian American"; A. Kim, "Prosecuting Chinese 'Spies.'"
27 S. Lee, *Unseen Unheard Minority*; J. Lee, "Asian Americans"; Wu, *Color of Success*; Poon and Segoshi, "Racial Mascot Speaks"; Poon et al., "Asian Americans."
28 Budiman and Ruiz, "Key Facts About Asian Americans"; Monte and Shin, "20.6 Million People."
29 Budiman and Ruiz, "Key Facts About Asian Americans"; Besheer and Rotolo, "Religion Among Asian Americans."
30 Budiman and Ruiz, "Key Facts About Asian Americans."
31 Museus, "Role of Ethnic Student Organizations."
32 Chung, "Critical Biculturalist Approach."
33 Levin et al., "Effects of Ingroup and Outgroup Friendships." Studies find mixed results in the effect of student organizations on interracial friendships. Park, "Clubs and the Campus Racial Climate"; Saenz et al., "Factors Influencing Positive Interactions"; Saenz, "Breaking the Segregation Cycle"; Stearns et al., "Interracial Friendships."
34 Berrey, *Enigma of Diversity*; Warikoo, *Diversity Bargain.*

CONCLUSION

1 Warikoo, *Diversity Bargain.*
2 Diaz, "Florida Gov. Ron DeSantis"; Iyer and Boyette, "DEI Funding Battle."
3 Razek and Rose, "University of Wisconsin System Board Approves Deal."
4 Diaz, "Florida Gov. Ron DeSantis."
5 Post, "Woke Wars."
6 Aspinall, "Students and Faculty Unite."
7 Lyons, "At Conservative Schools"; Schroeder, "Seminary Presidents Reaffirm BFM."
8 Benjamin, *Imagination.*
9 Fish, *There's No Such Thing as Free Speech.*
10 Charles Lawrence describes some of the different ways courts have ruled in favor for speech and issues of equality ("If He Hollers Let Him Go").
11 Leonardo and Porter, "Pedagogy of Fear."

12 Matsuda, "Public Response to Racist Speech"; Baer, *What Snowflakes Get Right.*
13 Leonardo and Porter, "Pedagogy of Fear"; McClelland et al., "Learning in the Ivory Tower"; Evans et al., "Body Made Flesh."
14 Binder and Kidder, *Channels of Student Activism.*
15 Binder and Wood, *Becoming Right*; Binder and Kidder, *Channels of Student Activism.*
16 For example, there were some students in Binder and Kidder's study who successfully created dialogue groups for students (*Channels of Student Activism*).
17 Frantell et al., "Intergroup Dialogue"; Gurin et al., *Dialogue Across Difference.*
18 Moore and Bell, "Limits of Community."
19 Moore and Bell, "Limits of Community," 1773.
20 Moore and Bell, "Limits of Community."
21 Baer, *What Snowflakes Get Right*; Garces et al., "Repressive Legalism."
22 Lawrence, "If He Hollers Let Him Go."
23 Garces et al., "Repressive Legalism."
24 Gender complementarianism is the view that men and women are created equal but have different roles. In the family, this often means that men "lead" and women "submit." Bartkowski, *Remaking the Godly Marriage*; Bartkowski, *Promise Keepers.*
25 Coley, "Reconciling Religion and LGBT Rights"; Coley, "Theologies of Exclusion."
26 Emerson and Smith, *Divided by Faith*; Park et al., "Equal Opportunity Beliefs"; Perry and Whitehead, "Christian America in Black and White"; Oyakawa, "Racial Reconciliation"; Edgell and Tranby, "Religious Influences."
27 Tranby and Hartmann, "Critical Whiteness Theories."
28 These experiences mirror those of other LGBTQ+ students on campuses where LGBTQ+ student organizations are available. Wolff et al., "Transgender and Gender-Nonconforming Student Experiences"; Kay and Wolff, "LGBTQ Students."
29 Coley, "Have Christian Colleges and Universities."
30 Although students told me that Christ College's counseling services are affirming and do not practice conversion therapy, around 4 to 10 percent of LGBTQ+ students attending Christian colleges reported that their universities tried to change their sexual orientation or gender identity. College Pulse, "LGBTQ+ Student Divide"; Craig et al., "Fighting for Survival"; Wolff et al., "Sexual Minority Students."
31 Gushee, "Christian Higher Ed Can't Win."
32 Green, "Christian Liberal-Arts School"; Post, "Grove City College"; Post, "Woke Wars."
33 The sociologist Christian Smith argues that evangelicals thrive from seeing themselves as embattled (*American Evangelicalism*).
34 Kay and Wolff, "LGBTQ Students."
35 Survey design is tricky, as roommate matching surveys that disclose too much risk outing students to potentially discriminatory administrators.
36 Bonilla-Silva, "From Bi-Racial to Tri-Racial"; C. Kim, "Racial Triangulation"; C. Kim, *Asian Americans.*

37 C. Kim, *Asian Americans.*

38 Bonilla-Silva, *Racism Without Racists.*

39 Corces-Zimmerman et al., "Historic Scaffolds"; Gusa, "White Institutional Presence."

40 Corces-Zimmerman et al., "Historic Scaffolds."

41 For example, HBCUs draw on a similar diversity discourse as predominantly White institutions. Okuwobi et al., "Diversity Displays."

42 Ahmed, *On Being Included*; Berrey, *Enigma of Diversity*; Thomas, *Diversity Regimes*; Warikoo, *Diversity Bargain.*

43 Embrick, "Diversity Ideology."

44 Denson et al., "Do Diversity Courses Improve College Student Outcomes?"; Adida et al., "Do Equity, Diversity and Inclusion (EDI) Requirements."

45 Mackenzie, "Teaching Societal Issues."

46 Other states also passed bans on affirmative action before the Supreme Court's ruling, but my comments here focus on California, given that my cases are on the West Coast.

47 Some researchers have observed that California has effectively produced a two-tiered system, in which Black and Hispanic students enroll in less selective public universities. Antonovics and Backes, "Were Minority Students Discouraged"; Hinrichs, "Effects of Affirmative Action Bans."

48 It should be noted that while ELC increased minority admissions for a few years, these increases have been minimized after changes to the ELC in 2012. University of California Office of the President, "Eligibility in the Local Context (ELC) Program"; Bleemer, "Diversity in University Admissions." Texas's Top 10% plan also had limited gains for its flagship universities. Klasik and Cortes, "Uniform Admissions, Unequal Access."

49 Bernstein, "How U.C. Berkeley Tried."

50 Bleemer, "Affirmative Action"; Park, *When Diversity Drops.*

51 Bastedo et al., "Holistic Admissions."

52 Baker and Bastedo, "What If We Leave It Up to Chance?"

53 Belasco et al., "Test-Optional Movement"; Paris et al., "Impact of Optional"; Buckley et al., *Measuring Success*; Saboe and Terrizzi, "SAT Optional Policies."

54 The Office of the President at the University of California has compiled research to provide insight into the consequences and alternatives to affirmative action in the state. These can be found at ucop.edu. I have listed several studies and overviews here: Colin and Cook, "Future of College Admissions"; Zwick, "College Admissions"; Baker and Bastedo, "What If We Leave It Up to Chance?"; Bastedo et al., "Holistic Admissions"; Bastedo et al., "How Well Do Contextualized Admissions Measures"; Buckley et al., *Measuring Success*; Black, Cortes, and Lincove, "Efficacy Versus Equity"; Klasik and Cortes, "Uniform Admissions, Unequal Access"; Reardon et al., "What Levels of Racial Diversity"; Bleemer, "Diversity in University Admissions."

55 Pak et al., "Asian Americans in Higher Education"; Teranishi, *Asians in the Ivory Tower*; National Center for Education Statistics, "Fast Facts."
56 Poon and Segoshi, "Racial Mascot Speaks"; Poon et al., "Asian Americans."
57 Nguyen et al., "Beyond Compositional Diversity."
58 Poon, "Asian Americans."
59 Tran, "Asian American Diversity and Growth."
60 Tian and Ruiz, "Key Facts"; Pak et al., "Asian Americans in Higher Education."
61 National Science Foundation, "Diversity and STEM"; Vue et al., "Asian Americans in STEM"; Yang, "I'm Almost Always the Only Hmong American Scientist."
62 Hatfield, "Relatively Few Asian Americans."
63 An, "Asian Americans in American History."
64 Yam, "DeSantis Criticized."
65 Dawson, *Behind the Mule.*
66 LGBTQ+ students wanted quantitative measures that provided insight into their outcomes so that these could be marshaled to support equity and access.

BIBLIOGRAPHY

Acker, Joan. "From Sex Roles to Gendered Institutions." *Contemporary Sociology* 21, no. 5 (1992): 565–69. https://doi.org/10.2307/2075528.

Acker, Joan. "Hierarchies, Jobs, Bodies: A Theory of Gendered Organizations." *Gender & Society* 4, no. 2 (1990): 139–58. https://doi.org/10.1177/089124390004002002.

Acker, Joan. "Inequality Regimes: Gender, Class, and Race in Organizations." *Gender & Society* 20, no. 4 (2006): 441–64. https://doi.org/10.1177/0891243206289499.

Adida, Claire L., Adeline Lo, Inbok Rhee, and Sam Williams. "Do Equity, Diversity and Inclusion (EDI) Requirements Change Student Political Attitudes?" *Politics, Groups, and Identities* 20 no. 4 (2024): 958–967. https://doi.org/10.1080/21565503.2023.2227437.

Aguirre, Adalberto, and Rubén Martinez. "The Diversity Rationale in Higher Education: An Overview of the Contemporary Legal Context." *Social Justice* 30, no. 1 (91) (2003): 138–52.

Ahmed, Sara. "The Language of Diversity." *Ethnic and Racial Studies* 30, no. 2 (2007): 235–56. https://doi.org/10.1080/01419870601143927.

Ahmed, Sara. *On Being Included: Racism and Diversity in Institutional Life*. Duke University Press, 2012.

Ahmed, Sara. "'You End Up Doing the Document Rather than Doing the Doing': Diversity, Race Equality and the Politics of Documentation." *Ethnic and Racial Studies* 30, no. 4 (2007): 590–609. https://doi.org/10.1080/01419870701356015.

Alba, Richard, Alejandro Portes, Philip Kasinitz, Nancy Foner, Elijah Anderson, and Nathan Glazer. "Beyond the Melting Pot 35 Years Later: On the Relevance of a Sociological Classic for the Immigration Metropolis of Today." *International Migration Review* 34, no. 1 (2000): 243–279.

Alumkal, Antony W. "American Evangelicalism in the Post-Civil Rights Era: A Racial Formation Theory Analysis." *Sociology of Religion* 65, no. 3 (2004): 195–213. https://doi.org/10.2307/3712249.

American Sociological Association. "Culture." Accessed August 19, 2021. www.asanet.org.

An, Sohyun. "Asian Americans in American History: An AsianCrit Perspective on Asian American Inclusion in State U.S. History Curriculum Standards." *Theory & Research in Social Education* 44, no. 2 (2016): 244–76. https://doi.org/10.1080/00933104.2016.1170646.

Antonovics, Kate, and Ben Backes. "Were Minority Students Discouraged from Applying to University of California Campuses After the Affirmative Action Ban?" *Education Finance and Policy* 8, no. 2 (2013): 208–50. https://doi.org/10.1162/EDFP_a_00090.

Armstrong, Elizabeth A., and Laura T. Hamilton. *Paying for the Party*. Harvard University Press, 2013.

Asad, Talal. *Formations of the Secular: Christianity, Islam, Modernity*. Stanford University Press, 2003.

Aspinall, Sidney. "Students and Faculty Unite to Change Anti-LGBTQ Policies at Seattle Pacific University." KNKX Public Radio, December 28, 2022, sec. Education. www.knkx.org.

Astin, Alexander W., Helen S. Astin, Alan E. Bayer, and Ann S. Bisconti. *The Power of Protest*. Jossey-Bass, 1975.

Astin, Alexander W., and Alan E. Bayer. "Antecedents and Consequents of Disruptive Campus Protests." *Measurement and Evaluation in Guidance* 4, no. 1 (1971): 18–30. https://doi.org/10.1080/00256307.1971.12022476.

Augustine-Adams, Kif. "Religious Exemptions to Title IX." *University of Kansas Law Review* 65, no. 2 (2016): 327–414. https://doi.org/10.17161/1808.25554.

Avery, Dan. "LGBTQ Students at Christian Colleges Face More Harassment, Survey Finds." *NBC News*, March 22, 2021. www.nbcnews.com.

Baer, Ulrich. *What Snowflakes Get Right*. Oxford University Press, 2019.

Baker, Dominique J., and Michael N. Bastedo. "What If We Leave It Up to Chance? Admissions Lotteries and Equitable Access at Selective Colleges." *Educational Researcher* 51, no. 2 (2022): 134–45. https://doi.org/10.3102/0013189X211055494.

Baker, Joseph O., and Andrew L. Whitehead. "God's Penology: Belief in a Masculine God Predicts Support for Harsh Criminal Punishment and Militarism." *Punishment and Society* 22, no. 2 (2020): 135–60. https://doi.org/10.1177/1462474519850570.

Balón, Daniello Garma. "Asian Pacific American College Students on Leadership: Culturally Marginalized from the Leader Role?" *National Association of Student Personnel Administrators (NASPA) NetResults*, 2005, 4.

Balón, Daniello Garma, and Yen Ling Shek. "Beyond Representation: Confronting the New Frontier for Asian American Leadership." In *The Misrepresented Minority: New Insights on Asian Americans and Pacific Islanders, and the Implications for Higher Education*, 311–26. Stylus, 2013.

Barbee, Harry, and Douglas Schrock. "Un/Gendering Social Selves: How Nonbinary People Navigate and Experience a Binarily Gendered World." *Sociological Forum* 34, no. 3 (2019): 572–93. https://doi.org/10.1111/socf.12517.

Bartholomaeus, Clare, and Damien W. Riggs. "Whole-of-School Approaches to Supporting Transgender Students, Staff, and Parents." *International Journal of Transgenderism* 18, no. 4 (2017): 361–66. https://doi.org/10.1080/15532739.2017.1355648.

Bartkowski, John P. *The Promise Keepers: Servants, Soldiers, and Godly Men*. Rutgers University Press, 2004.

Bartkowski, John P. *Remaking the Godly Marriage: Gender Negotiation in Evangelical Families*. Rutgers University Press, 2001.

Barton, Bernadette. *Pray the Gay Away: The Extraordinary Lives of Bible Belt Gays*. New York University Press, 2012.

Bastedo, Michael N., Joseph E. Howard, and Allyson Flaster. "Holistic Admissions After Affirmative Action: Does 'Maximizing' the High School Curriculum Matter?" *Educational Evaluation and Policy Analysis* 38, no. 2 (2016): 389–409. https://doi.org/10.3102/0162373716642407.

Bastedo, Michael N., Mark Umbricht, Emma Bausch, Bo-Kyung Byun, and Yiping Bai. "How Well Do Contextualized Admissions Measures Predict Success for Low-Income Students, Women, and Underrepresented Students of Color?" *Journal of Diversity in Higher Education*, 2023. https://doi.org/10.1037/dhe0000499.

Beattie, Irenee R., Nella Van Dyke, and Natasha Hagaman. "What Do We Know About LGBQ+ College Student Academic Experiences and Outcomes?" *Sociology Compass* 15, no. 3 (2021). https://doi.org/10.1111/soc4.12862.

Beemyn, Brett Genny. "Making Campuses More Inclusive of Transgender Students." *Journal of Gay & Lesbian Issues in Education* 3, no. 1 (2005): 77–87. https://doi.org/10.1300/J367v03n01_08.

Belasco, Andrew S., Kelly O. Rosinger, and James C. Hearn. "The Test-Optional Movement at America's Selective Liberal Arts Colleges: A Boon for Equity or Something Else?" *Educational Evaluation and Policy Analysis* 37, no. 2 (2015): 206–23. https://doi.org/10.3102/0162373714537350.

Bell, Joyce M., and Douglas Hartmann. "Diversity in Everyday Discourse: The Cultural Ambiguities and Consequences of 'Happy Talk.'" *American Sociological Review* 72, no. 6 (2007): 895–914. https://doi.org/10.1177/000312240707200603.

Benjamin, Ruha. *Imagination: A Manifesto*. Norton, 2024.

Bernstein, Sharon. "How U.C. Berkeley Tried to Buoy Enrollment of Black Students Without Affirmative Action." *Reuters*, June 20, 2023. www.reuters.com.

Berrey, Ellen C. *The Enigma of Diversity: The Language of Race and the Limits of Racial Justice*. University of Chicago Press, 2015.

Berrey, Ellen C. "Why Diversity Became Orthodox in Higher Education, and How It Changed the Meaning of Race on Campus." *Critical Sociology* 37, no. 5 (2011): 573–96. https://doi.org/10.1177/0896920510380069.

Besheer, Mohamed, and Michael Rotolo. "Religion Among Asian Americans." Pew Research Center's Religion & Public Life Project, October 11, 2023. www.pewresearch.org.

Binder, Amy J., and Jeffrey L. Kidder. *The Channels of Student Activism: How the Left and Right Are Winning (and Losing) in Campus Politics Today*. University of Chicago Press, 2022.

Binder, Amy J., and Kate Wood. *Becoming Right: How Campuses Shape Young Conservatives*. Princeton University Press, 2012.

Black, Sandra E., Kalena E. Cortes, and Jane Arnold Lincove. "Efficacy Versus Equity: What Happens When States Tinker with College Admissions in a Race-Blind Era?" *Educational Evaluation and Policy Analysis* 38, no. 2 (2016): 336–63. https://doi.org/10.3102/0162373716629006.

Bleemer, Zachary. "Affirmative Action, Mismatch, and Economic Mobility After California's Proposition 209." *Quarterly Journal of Economics* 137, no. 1 (2021): 115–60. https://doi.org/10.1093/qje/qjab027.

Bleemer, Zachary. "Diversity in University Admissions: Affirmative Action, Percent Plans, and Holistic Review." Center for Studies in Higher Education, UC Berkeley, July 1, 2019.

Boch, Anna. "Increasing American Political Tolerance: A Framework Excluding Hate Speech." *Socius* 6 (2020): 2378023120903959. https://doi.org/10.1177/2378023120903959.

Bonilla-Silva, Eduardo. "From Bi-Racial to Tri-Racial: Towards a New System of Racial Stratification in the USA." *Ethnic and Racial Studies* 27, no. 6 (2004): 931–50. https://doi.org/10.1080/0141987042000268530.

Bonilla-Silva, Eduardo. *Racism Without Racists: Color-Blind Racism and the Persistence of Racial Inequality in America*. 4th ed. Lanham, MD: Rowman and Littlefield, 2013.

Bowman, Nicholas A. "Promoting Participation in a Diverse Democracy: A Meta-Analysis of College Diversity Experiences and Civic Engagement." *Review of Educational Research* 81, no. 1 (2011): 29–68. https://doi.org/10.3102/0034654310383047.

Boykin, Keith. *One More River to Cross: Black and Gay in America*. Reprint ed. New York: Anchor, 1997.

Brayboy, Bryan Mckinley Jones, Angelina E. Castagno, and Emma Maughan. "Equality and Justice for All? Examining Race in Education Scholarship." *Review of Research in Education* 31, no. 1 (2007): 159–94. https://doi.org/10.3102/0091732X07300046159.

Brown, Hana, and Jennifer A. Jones. "Rethinking Panethnicity and the Race-Immigration Divide: An Ethnoracialization Model of Group Formation." *Sociology of Race and Ethnicity* 1, no. 1 (2015): 181–91. https://doi.org/10.1177/2332649214558304.

Brown, Wendy. *Regulating Aversion: Tolerance in the Age of Identity and Empire*. Princeton University Press, 2009.

Buckley, Jack, Lynn Letukas, and Ben Wildavsky. *Measuring Success: Testing, Grades, and the Future of College Admissions*. Johns Hopkins University Press, 2018.

Buckley, Jessica Belue, and Julie J. Park. "'Hard to Tell': Students Making Assumptions about Compositional Socioeconomic Diversity on Campus." *Journal of Diversity in Higher Education* 14, no. 1 (2021): 110–22. https://doi.org/10.1037/dhe0000159.

Buckley, Jessica Belue, and Julie J. Park. "'When You Don't Really Focus on It': Campus Climate for Social Class Diversity and Identity Awareness." *Journal of College Student Development* 60, no. 3 (2019): 271–89. https://doi.org/10.1353/csd.2019.0026.

Budiman, Abby, and Neil G. Ruiz. "Key Facts About Asian Americans, a Diverse and Growing Population." Pew Research Center, April 29, 2021. www.pewresearch.org/.

Burke, Kelsy. "The False Dichotomy of Sex and Religion in America." *Sociology of Religion* 83, no. 4 (2022): 417–33. https://doi.org/10.1093/socrel/srab062.

Butler, Anthea D. *White Evangelical Racism: The Politics of Morality in America*. University of North Carolina Press, 2021.

Byrd, W. Carson. *Behind the Diversity Numbers: Achieving Racial Equity on Campus*. Harvard Education Press, 2021.

Campus Pride. "Tracking Retention & Academic Success: Listing of Colleges and Universities with LGBTQ Identity Questions as an Option on Admission Applications & Enrollment Forms." November 28, 2014. www.campuspride.org.

Caputo, Ibby, and Jon Marcus. "How Some Religious Colleges Avoid Rules Prohibiting Discrimination Based on Sexual Orientation." *The Atlantic*, July 7, 2016. www.theatlantic.com.

Carrillo Arciniega, Luzilda. "Selling Diversity to White Men: How Disentangling Economics from Morality Is a Racial and Gendered Performance." *Organization* 28, no. 2 (2021): 228–46. https://doi.org/10.1177/1350508420930341.

Cech, Erin A., and William R. Rothwell. "LGBT Workplace Inequality in the Federal Workforce: Intersectional Processes, Organizational Contexts, and Turnover Considerations." *ILR Review* 73, no. 1 (2020): 25–60. https://doi.org/10.1177/0019793919843508.

Cegler, Tyler. "Targeted Recruitment of GLBT Students by Colleges and Universities." *Journal of College Admission*, Spring 2012.

Chan, Esther. "Does Diversity Include Me? Colorblindness and Racial Triangulation Among Asian Americans on Two College Campuses." *Ethnic and Racial Studies* 43, no. 12 (2020): 2217–35. https://doi.org/10.1080/01419870.2019.1671598.

Chan, Esther, and Victoria Isaac. "Racialized Fear, Fatigue, Pessimism, and Colorblindness: Hindrances to Racial Dialogue on Fifteen Christian Colleges in the US." *Ethnic and Racial Studies* 47, no. 6 (2024): 1–23. https://doi.org/10.1080/01419870.2023.2237563.

Chan, Esther, Isaiah Jeong, and Elijah Jeong. "Racial and Religious Convergences and Divergences Among Christian Students' Approaches to Color-Blindness, Color-Cognizance, and Race in Christian Organizations." *Journal for the Scientific Study of Religion* 62, no. 1 (2023): 164–83. https://doi.org/10.1111/jssr.12823.

Chang, Mitchell J. "Reconsidering the Diversity Rationale." *Liberal Education* 91, no. 1 (2005): 6–13.

Chang, Mitchell J., and Maria C. Ledesma. "The Diversity Rationale: Its Limitations for Educational Practice." In *Diversity in American Higher Education*, edited by Lisa M. Stulberg and Sharon Weinberg. Routledge, 2011.

Chemerinsky, Erwin, and Howard Gillman. *Free Speech on Campus*. Yale University Press, 2018.

Chong, Dennis. "Free Speech and Multiculturalism in and out of the Academy." *Political Psychology* 27, no. 1 (2006): 29–54. https://doi.org/10.1111/j.1467-9221.2006.00448.x.

Chong, Dennis, and Morris Levy. "Competing Norms of Free Expression and Political Tolerance." *Social Research: An International Quarterly* 85, no. 1 (2018): 197–227. https://doi.org/ 10.1353/sor.2018.0010.

Chun, Edna, and Alvin Evans. "Affirmative Action at a Crossroads: *Fisher* and Forward." *ASHE Higher Education Report* 41, no. 4 (2015): 1–126. https://doi.org/10.1002/aehe.20022.

Chung, Jennifer Y. "A Critical Biculturalist Approach to Ethnic Student Organizations." *Journal of Diversity in Higher Education* 8, no. 1 (2015): 30–42. https://doi.org/10.1037/a0038345.

Chung, Jennifer Y. "Racism and Asian American Student Leadership." *Equity & Excellence in Education* 47, no. 2 (2014): 117–32. https://doi.org/10.1080/10665684.2014.900392.

Coley, Jonathan S. *Gay on God's Campus: Mobilizing for LGBT Equality at Christian Colleges and Universities*. University of North Carolina Press, 2018.

Coley, Jonathan S. "Have Christian Colleges and Universities Become More Inclusive of LGBTQ Students Since *Obergefell v. Hodges*?" *Religions* 11, no. 9 (2020): 461. https://doi.org/10.3390/rel11090461.

Coley, Jonathan S. "Mobilizing for Religious Freedom: Educational Opportunity Structures and Outcomes of Conservative Christian Campus Activism." *Research in Social Movements, Conflicts and Change* 44 (2021): 175–200. https://doi.org/10.1108/S0163-786X20210000044012.

Coley, Jonathan S. "Reconciling Religion and LGBT Rights: Christian Universities, Theological Orientations, and LGBT Inclusion." *Social Currents* 4, no. 1 (2017): 87–106. https://doi.org/10.1177/2329496516651639.

Coley, Jonathan S. "Theologies of Exclusion: Christian Universities and Discrimination Against Sexual Minorities." *Sociological Spectrum* 38, no. 6 (2018): 422–37. https://doi.org/10.1080/02732173.2018.1564097.

Coley, Jonathan S., Daniel R. Morrison, Lexie L. Taylor, Jessica L. Schachle-Gordon, and Gabby Gomez. "Gendered Organizations as Heterosexualized Organizations: The Case of Housing, Roommate, and Visitation Policies at Christian Colleges and Universities." *Socius* 9 (2023). https://doi.org/10.1177/23780231231217819.

Colin, Elise, and Bryan J. Cook. "The Future of College Admissions Without Affirmative Action." Urban Institute, June 23, 2023. www.urban.org.

College Pulse. "The LGBTQ+ Student Divide: The State of Sexual and Gender Minority Students at Taxpayer-Funded Christian Colleges." March 2021. https://collegepulse.com.

College Pulse. "2020 College Free Speech Rankings: What's the Climate for Free Speech on America's College Campuses." 2020. www.thefire.org.

College Pulse. "2024 College Speech Rankings: What Is the State of Free Speech on America's College Campuses." 2024. www.thefire.org.

Collier, Megan, and Meghan Daniel. "The Production of Trans Illegality: Cisnormativity in the U.S. Immigration System." *Sociology Compass* 13, no. 4 (2019). https://doi.org/10.1111/soc4.12666.

Collins, Patricia Hill. "Intersectionality's Definitional Dilemmas." *Annual Review of Sociology* 41, no. 1 (2015): 1–20. https://doi.org/10.1146/annurev-soc-073014-112142.

Collins, Patricia Hill. "The Tie That Binds: Race, Gender and US Violence." *Ethnic and Racial Studies* 21, no. 5 (1998): 917–38. https://doi.org/10.1080/014198798329720.

Collins, Patricia Hill, and Sirma Bilge. *Intersectionality*. Polity, 2016.

Common Data Set Initiative. "Common Data Set Initiative." Accessed November 7, 2021. https://commondataset.org.

Conron, Kerith J. "LGBT Youth Population in the United States." Williams Institute, UCLA, 2020. https://williamsinstitute.law.ucla.edu.

Corces-Zimmerman, Chris, Devon Thomas, and Nolan Cabrera. "Historic Scaffolds of Whiteness in Higher Education." In *Whiteness, Power, and Resisting Change in US*

Higher Education, edited by Kenneth R. Roth and Zachary S. Ritter, 9–31. Palgrave, 2021. https://doi.org/10.1007/978-3-030-57292-1_2.

Craig, Shelley L., Ashley Austin, Mariam Rashidi, and Marc Adams. "Fighting for Survival: The Experiences of Lesbian, Gay, Bisexual, Transgender, and Questioning Students in Religious Colleges and Universities." *Journal of Gay & Lesbian Social Services* 29, no. 1 (2017): 1–24. https://doi.org/10.1080/10538720.2016.1260512.

Crenshaw, Kimberlé. "Mapping the Margins: Intersectionality, Identity Politics, and Violence against Women of Color." *Stanford Law Review* 43, no. 6 (1991): 1241–99. https://doi.org/10.2307/1229039.

Curtis, Jesse. *The Myth of Colorblind Christians: Evangelicals and White Supremacy in the Civil Rights Era*. New York: New York University Press, 2021.

Darder, Antonia. *Culture and Power in the Classroom*. 2nd ed. Routledge, 2012.

Dawson, Michael C. *Behind the Mule: Race and Class in African-American Politics*. Princeton University Press, 1994.

Delgado, Richard. "First Amendment Formalism Is Giving Way to First Amendment Legal Realism." *Harvard Civil Rights-Civil Liberties Law Review* 29 (1994): 169–74.

Denson, Nida, Nicholas A. Bowman, Georgia Ovenden, K. C. Culver, and Joshua M. Holmes. "Do Diversity Courses Improve College Student Outcomes? A Meta-Analysis." *Journal of Diversity in Higher Education* 14, no. 4 (2021): 544–56. https://doi.org/10.1037/dhe0000189.

Diamant, Jeff. "Half of U.S. Christians Say Casual Sex Between Consenting Adults Is Sometimes or Always Acceptable." Pew Research Center, August 31, 2020. www.pewresearch.org.

DiAngelo, Robin. *White Fragility: Why It's So Hard for White People to Talk About Racism*. Beacon, 2018.

Diaz, Jaclyn. "Florida Gov. Ron DeSantis Signs a Bill Banning DEI Initiatives in Public Colleges." *NPR*, May 15, 2023. www.npr.org.

Diefendorf, Sarah, and CJ Pascoe. "In the Name of Love: White Organizations and Racialized Emotions." *Social Problems*, April 26, 2023. https://doi.org/10.1093/socpro/spad019.

Doane, Ashley ("Woody"). "Beyond Color-Blindness: (Re)Theorizing Racial Ideology." *Sociological Perspectives* 60, no. 5 (2017): 975–91. https://doi.org/10.1177/0731121417719697.

Douds, Kiara Wyndham. "The Diversity Contract: Constructing Racial Harmony in a Diverse American Suburb." *American Journal of Sociology* 126, no. 6 (2021): 1347–88. https://doi.org/10.1086/714499.

D'Souza, Dinesh. "The New Segregation on Campus." *American Scholar* 60, no. 1 (1991): 17–30.

Duran, Antonio, Reginald A. Blockett, and Z Nicolazzo. "An Interdisciplinary Return to Queer and Trans* Studies in Higher Education: Implications for Research and Practice." In *Higher Education: Handbook of Theory and Research*, edited by Laura W. Perna. Springer, 2020. https://doi.org/10.1007/978-3-030-11743-6_9-1.

Edelman, Lauren B., Sally Riggs Fuller, and Iona Mara-Drita. "Diversity Rhetoric and the Managerialization of Law." *American Journal of Sociology* 106, no. 6 (2001): 1589–1641. https://doi.org/10.1086/321303.

Edgell, Penny, and Eric Tranby. "Religious Influences on Understandings of Racial Inequality in the United States." *Social Problems* 54, no. 2 (2007): 263–88. https://doi.org/10.1525/sp.2007.54.2.263.

Edwards, Korie L. "Bring Race to the Center: The Importance of Race in Racially Diverse Religious Organizations." *Journal for the Scientific Study of Religion* 47, no. 1 (2008): 5–9. https://doi.org/10.1111/j.1468-5906.2008.00387.x.

Edwards, Korie L., Brad Christerson, and Michael O. Emerson. "Race, Religious Organizations, and Integration." *Annual Review of Sociology* 39, no. 1 (2013): 211–28. https://doi.org/10.1146/annurev-soc-071312-145636.

Eliot, Krissy. "Money Talks: What's a Fair Price for Free Speech?" Cal Alumni Association, November 17, 2017. https://alumni.berkeley.edu.

Embrick, David G. "The Diversity Ideology in the Business World: A New Oppression for a New Age." *Critical Sociology* 37, no. 5 (2011): 541–56. https://doi.org/10.1177/0896920510380076.

Emerson, Michael O., and Christian Smith. *Divided by Faith: Evangelical Religion and the Problem of Race in America*. Oxford University Press, 2000.

Evans, John, Brian Davies, and Emma Rich. "The Body Made Flesh: Embodied Learning and the Corporeal Device." *British Journal of Sociology of Education* 30, no. 4 (2009): 391–406. https://doi.org/10.1080/01425690902954588.

Evans, Rosalind, Julie L. Nagoshi, Craig Nagoshi, Jeffrey Wheeler, and Jeremiah Henderson. "Voices from the Stories Untold: Lesbian, Gay, Bisexual, Trans, and Queer College Students' Experiences with Campus Climate." *Journal of Gay & Lesbian Social Services* 29, no. 4 (2017): 426–44. https://doi.org/10.1080/10538720.2018.1378144.

Fain, Paul. "College Enrollment Declines Continue." *Inside Higher Ed*, May 30, 2019. www.insidehighered.com.

Ferber, Abby. "The Construction of Black Masculinity: White Supremacy Now and Then." *Journal of Sport & Social Issues* 31 (2007): 11–24. https://doi.org/10.1177/0193723506296829.

Fish, Stanley. *There's No Such Thing as Free Speech: And It's a Good Thing, Too*. Oxford University Press, 1994.

Flores, Andrew R., Ilan H. Meyer, Lynn Langton, and Jody L. Herman. "Gender Identity Disparities in Criminal Victimization: National Crime Victimization Survey, 2017–2018." *American Journal of Public Health* 111, no. 4 (2021): 726–29. https://doi.org/10.2105/AJPH.2020.306099.

Flores, Glenda Marisol. "Racialized Tokens: Latina Teachers Negotiating, Surviving and Thriving in a White Woman's Profession." *Qualitative Sociology* 34, no. 2 (2011): 313–35. https://doi.org/10.1007/s11133-011-9189-x.

Foste, Zak, Antonio Duran, and Zach Hooten. "Articulating Diversity on Campus: A Critical Discourse Analysis of Diversity Statements at Historically White Institutions." *Journal of Diversity in Higher Education*, 16, no. 5 (2023): 575–88. https://doi.org/10.1037/dhe0000354.

Foste, Zak, and Jennifer Ng. "'Didn't Mean to Mean It That Way': The Reduction of Microaggressions to Interpersonal Errors of Communication among University Resident Assistants." *Journal of Diversity in Higher Education* 15, no. 5 (2022): 548–59. https://doi.org/10.1037/dhe0000297.

Foucault, Michel. *"Society Must Be Defended": Lectures at the Collège de France, 1975–1976*. Picador, 2003.

Foundation for Individual Rights and Expression. "Using FIRE's Spotlight Database." Accessed January 24, 2024. www.thefire.org.

Frankenberg, Ruth. *White Women, Race Matters: The Social Construction of Whiteness*. University of Minnesota Press, 1993.

Franklin, Jeremy D. "Coping with Racial Battle Fatigue: Differences and Similarities for African American and Mexican American College Students." *Race Ethnicity and Education* 22, no. 5 (2019): 589–609. https://doi.org/10.1080/13613324.2019.1579178.

Franklin, Jeremy D. "Racial Microaggressions, Racial Battle Fatigue, and Racism-Related Stress in Higher Education." *Journal of Student Affairs at New York University* 12, no. 44 (2016): 44–55.

Frantell, Keri A., Joseph R. Miles, and Anne M. Ruwe. "Intergroup Dialogue: A Review of Recent Empirical Research and Its Implications for Research and Practice." *Small Group Research* 50, no. 5 (2019): 654–95. https://doi.org/10.1177/1046496419835923.

Garces, Liliana M. "Aligning Diversity, Quality, and Equity: The Implications of Legal and Public Policy Developments for Promoting Racial Diversity in Graduate Studies." *American Journal of Education* 120, no. 4 (2014): 457–80. https://doi.org/10.1086/676909.

Garces, Liliana M., Brianna Davis Johnson, Evelyn Ambriz, and Dwuana Bradley. "Repressive Legalism: How Postsecondary Administrators' Responses to On-Campus Hate Speech Undermine a Focus on Inclusion." *American Educational Research Journal* 58, no. 5 (2021): 1032–69. https://doi.org/10.3102/00028312211027586.

Garvey, Jason C., and Susan R. Rankin. "Making the Grade? Classroom Climate for LGBTQ Students Across Gender Conformity." *Journal of Student Affairs Research and Practice* 52, no. 2 (2015): 190–203. https://doi.org/10.1080/19496591.2015.1019764.

Garvey, Jason C., Laura A. Sanders, and Maureen A. Flint. "Generational Perceptions of Campus Climate Among LGBTQ Undergraduates." *Journal of College Student Development* 58, no. 6 (2017): 795–817. https://doi.org/10.1353/csd.2017.0065.

Gecker, Jocelyn. "Cost of Free Speech at UC Berkeley Is Estimated $600,000 to Deal with Protests as Ben Shapiro Speaks." *NBC Bay Area*, September 17, 2017. www.nbcbayarea.com.

Gelber, Katharine, and Luke McNamara. "Evidencing the Harms of Hate Speech." *Social Identities* 22, no. 3 (2016): 324–41. https://doi.org/10.1080/13504630.2015.1128810.

Gersen, Jeannie Suk. "The Uncomfortable Truth About Affirmative Action and Asian-Americans." *New Yorker*, August 10, 2017. www.newyorker.com.

Glazer, Nathan. "America's Ethnic Pattern: 'Melting Pot' or 'Nation of Nations' (1953)." In *When Ideas Mattered: A Nathan Glazer Reader*, 15–28. Routledge, 2016.

Glazer, Nathan, and Daniel P. Moynihan. *Beyond the Melting Pot: The Negroes, Puerto Ricans, Jews, Italians, and Irish of New York City*. 2nd ed. MIT Press, 1970.

Gorski, Philip S. "Historicizing the Secularization Debate: Church, State, and Society in Late Medieval and Early Modern Europe, ca. 1300 to 1700." *American Sociological Review* 65, no. 1 (2000): 138–67. https://doi.org/10.2307/2657295.

Gorski, Philip S., and Ateş Altınordu. "After Secularization?" *Annual Review of Sociology* 34, no. 1 (2008): 55–85. https://doi.org/10.1146/annurev.soc.34.040507.134740.

Greathouse, Maren, Allison BrckaLorenz, Mary Hoban, Ronald Huseman, Susan Rankin, and Ellen Bara Stolzenberg. "Queer-Spectrum and Trans-Spectrum Student Experiences in American Higher Education." Rutgers Tyler Clementi Center, 2018. https://tylerclementi.org.

Green, Emma. "The Christian Liberal-Arts School at the Heart of the Culture Wars." *New Yorker*, April 3, 2023. www.newyorker.com.

Greenawalt, Kent. "Free Speech Justifications." *Columbia Law Review* 89, no. 1 (1989): 119–55. https://doi.org/10.2307/1122730.

Guiffrida, Douglas A. "African American Student Organizations as Agents of Social Integration." *Journal of College Student Development* 44, no. 3 (2003): 304–19. https://doi.org/10.1353/csd.2003.0024.

Gurin, Patricia, Eric Dey, Sylvia Hurtado, and Gerald Gurin. "Diversity and Higher Education: Theory and Impact on Educational Outcomes." *Harvard Educational Review* 72, no. 3 (2002): 330–67. https://doi.org/10.17763/haer.72.3.01151786u134n051.

Gurin, Patricia, Biren (Ratnesh) A. Nagda, and Gretchen E. Lopez. "The Benefits of Diversity in Education for Democratic Citizenship." *Journal of Social Issues* 60, no. 1 (2004): 17–34. https://doi.org/10.1111/j.0022-4537.2004.00097.x.

Gurin, Patricia, Biren (Ratnesh) A. Nagda, and Ximena Zuniga. *Dialogue Across Difference: Practice, Theory, and Research on Intergroup Dialogue*. Russell Sage Foundation, 2013.

Gusa, Diane Lynn. "White Institutional Presence: The Impact of Whiteness on Campus Climate." *Harvard Educational Review* 80, no. 4 (2010): 464–90.

Gushee, David P. "Christian Higher Ed Can't Win the LGBTQ Debate Unless It Transforms." *Religion News Service*, December 3, 2019. https://religionnews.com.

Hacking, Ian. "Making People Up." In *The Science Studies Reader*, edited by Mario Biagioli. Routledge, 1999.

Harper, Shaun R., and Stephen John Quaye. "Student Organizations as Venues for Black Identity Expression and Development Among African American Male Student Leaders." *Journal of College Student Development* 48, no. 2 (2007): 127–44. https://doi.org/10.1353/csd.2007.0012.

Harvey, Jennifer. *Dear White Christians: For Those Still Longing for Racial Reconciliation*. Eerdmans, 2014.

Hatfield, Jenn. "Relatively Few Asian Americans Say They're Well-Informed About Asian History in the U.S." Pew Research Center, June 29, 2023. www.pewresearch.org.

Hawkins, J. Russell. *The Bible Told Them So: How Southern Evangelicals Fought to Preserve White Supremacy*. Oxford University Press, 2021.

Heiden-Rootes, Katie, Ashley Wiegand, Danielle Thomas, Rachel M. Moore, and Kristin A. Ross. "A National Survey on Depression, Internalized Homophobia, College Religiosity, and Climate of Acceptance on College Campuses for Sexual Minority Adults." *Journal of Homosexuality* 67, no. 4 (2020): 435–51. https://doi.org/10.1080/00918369.2018.1550329.

Heim, Joe. "How a Rally of White Nationalists and Supremacists at the University of Virginia Turned into a 'Tragic, Tragic Weekend.'" *Washington Post*, August 14, 2017. www.washingtonpost.com.

Hinrichs, Peter. "The Effects of Affirmative Action Bans on College Enrollment, Educational Attainment, and the Demographic Composition of Universities." *Review of Economics and Statistics* 94, no. 3 (2012): 712–22.

Hirschman, Charles. "America's Melting Pot Reconsidered." *Annual Review of Sociology* 9 (1983): 397–423. https://doi.org/10.1146/annurev.so.09.080183.002145.

Hollinger, David A. *Postethnic America*. 10th ed. Basic Books, 1995.

hooks, bell. *Feminist Theory: From Margin to Center*. Pluto, 2000.

Hout, Michael. "Social and Economic Returns to College Education in the United States." *Annual Review of Sociology* 38, no. 1 (2012): 379–400. https://doi.org/10.1146/annurev.soc.012809.102503.

Hurtado, Sylvia. "A Campus Racial Climate: Contexts of Conflict." *Journal of Higher Education* 63, no. 5 (1992): 539–69. https://doi.org/10.2307/1982093.

Hurtado, Sylvia, Cynthia L. Alvarez, Chelsea Guillermo-Wann, Marcela Cuellar, and Lucy Arellano. "A Model for Diverse Learning Environments: The Scholarship on Creating and Assessing Conditions for Student Success." In *Higher Education: Handbook of Theory and Research*, edited by John C. Smart and Michael B. Paulsen. Springer, 2012.

Hurtado, Sylvia, Deborah Faye Carter, and Diana Kardia. "The Climate for Diversity: Key Issues for Institutional Self-Study." *New Directions for Institutional Research* 1998, no. 98 (1998): 53–63. https://doi.org/10.1002/ir.9804.

Hurtado, Sylvia, Kimberly A. Griffin, Lucy Arellano, and Marcela Cuellar. "Assessing the Value of Climate Assessments: Progress and Future Directions." *Journal of Diversity in Higher Education* 1, no. 4 (2008): 204–21. https://doi.org/10.1037/a0014009.

Hurtado, Sylvia, Jeffrey Milem, Alma R. Clayton-Pedersen, and Walter Allen. *Enacting Diverse Learning Environments: Improving the Climate for Racial/Ethnic Diversity in Higher Education*. ASHE-ERIC Higher Education Report 26. ERIC Clearinghouse on Higher Education, 1999.

Huynh, Que-Lam, Angela-MinhTu D. Nguyen, and Verónica Benet-Martínez. "Bicultural Identity Integration." In *Handbook of Identity Theory and Research*, edited by Seth J. Schwartz, Koen Luyckx, and Vivian L. Vignoles. Springer, 2011.

Hyun, Jane. *Breaking the Bamboo Ceiling: Career Strategies for Asians*. HarperCollins, 2009.

Inkelas, Karen Kurotsuchi. "Does Participation in Ethnic Cocurricular Activities Facilitate a Sense of Ethnic Awareness and Understanding? A Study of Asian Pacific American Undergraduates." *Journal of College Student Development* 45, no. 3 (2004): 285–302. https://doi.org/10.1353/csd.2004.0037.

Ishimaru, Ann M., and Mollie K. Galloway. "Hearts and Minds First: Institutional Logics in Pursuit of Educational Equity." *Educational Administration Quarterly* 57, no. 3 (August 2021): 470–502. https://doi.org/10.1177/0013161X20947459.

Iyer, Kaanita, and Boyette. "DEI Funding Battle Paralyzes Wis. Budget Negotiations." *Inside Higher Ed*, June 15, 2023. www.insidehighered.com.

Jack, Anthony Abraham. *The Privileged Poor: How Elite Colleges Are Failing Disadvantaged Students*. Harvard University Press, 2019.

Jaschik, Scott. "Beyond Male/Female." *Inside Higher Ed*, April 25, 2016. www.insidehighered.com.

Jayakumar, Uma M., Liliana M. Garces, and Julie J. Park. "Reclaiming Diversity: Advancing the Next Generation of Diversity Research Toward Racial Equity." In *Higher Education: Handbook of Theory and Research*, edited by Michael B. Paulsen. Springer, 2018.

Jones, Jeffrey M. "LGBT Identification in U.S. Ticks Up to 7.1%." Gallup, February 17, 2022. https://news.gallup.com.

Jourian, T. J. "Evolving Nature of Sexual Orientation and Gender Identity: Evolving Nature of Sexual Orientation and Gender Identity." *New Directions for Student Services* 2015, no. 152 (2015): 11–23. https://doi.org/10.1002/ss.20142.

Kafer, Alison. "Compulsory Bodies: Reflections on Heterosexuality and Able-Bodiedness." *Journal of Women's History* 15, no. 3 (2003): 77–89. https://doi.org/10.1353/jowh.2003.0071.

Kahn, Jonathon S., and Vincent W. Lloyd, eds. *Race and Secularism in America*. Columbia University Press, 2016.

Kanter, Rosabeth Moss. *Men and Women of the Corporation*. Rev. ed. Basic Books, 1993.

Kanter, Rosabeth Moss. "Some Effects of Proportions on Group Life: Skewed Sex Ratios and Responses to Token Women." *American Journal of Sociology* 82, no. 5 (1977): 965–90. https://doi.org/10.1086/226425.

Kao, Grace, Elizabeth Vaquera, and Kimberly Goyette. *Education and Immigration*. Wiley, 2013.

Kawai, Yuko. "Stereotyping Asian Americans: The Dialectic of the Model Minority and the Yellow Peril." *Howard Journal of Communications* 16, no. 2 (2005): 109–30. https://doi.org/10.1080/10646170590948974.

Kay, Theresa Stueland, and Joshua R. Wolff. "LGBTQ Students in Nonaffirming Religious Institutions." In *Affirming LGBTQ+ Students in Higher Education*, edited by David P. Rivera, Roberto L. Abreu, and Kirsten A. Gonzalez. American Psychological Association, 2022.

Kazyak, Emily, Kelsy Burke, and Mathew Stange. "Logics of Freedom: Debating Religious Freedom Laws and Gay and Lesbian Rights." *Socius* 4 (2018): 2378023118760413. https://doi.org/10.1177/2378023118760413.

Kidder, Jeffrey L., and Amy J. Binder. "The Politics of Speech on Campus." *Sociological Forum* 36, no. 2 (2021): 338–58. https://doi.org/10.1111/socf.12681.

Kim, Andrew Chongseh. "Prosecuting Chinese 'Spies': An Empirical Analysis of the Economic Espionage Act." *Cardozo Law Review* 40, no. 2 (2018): 749–822.

Kim, Claire Jean. *Asian Americans in an Anti-Black World*. Cambridge University Press, 2023.

Kim, Claire Jean. "The Racial Triangulation of Asian Americans." *Politics and Society* 27, no. 1 (1999): 105–38.

Kim, Joon K. "From Bakke to Grutter: Rearticulating Diversity and Affirmative Action in Higher Education." *Multicultural Perspectives* 7, no. 2 (2005): 12–19. https://doi.org/10.1207/s15327892mcp0702_3.

Klasik, Daniel, and Kalena E. Cortes. "Uniform Admissions, Unequal Access: Did the Top 10% Plan Increase Access to Selective Flagship Institutions?" *Economics of Education Review* 87 (2022). https://doi.org/10.1016/j.econedurev.2021.102199.

Landsbaum, Claire. "Alt-Right Troll Uses Campus Visit to Openly Mock a Transgender Student." *The Cut*, December 15, 2016. www.thecut.com.

Lawrence, Charles R., III. "If He Hollers Let Him Go: Regulating Racist Speech on Campus." *Duke Law Journal* 1990, no. 3 (1990): 431–83.

Lee, Erika. *At America's Gates: Chinese Immigration during the Exclusion Era, 1882–1943*. University of North Carolina Press, 2004.

Lee, Erika. "The 'Yellow Peril' and Asian Exclusion in the Americas." *Pacific Historical Review* 76, no. 4 (2007): 537–62. https://doi.org/10.1525/phr.2007.76.4.537.

Lee, Fiona. "Asian American and Pacific Islander Faculty and the Bamboo Ceiling: Barriers to Leadership and Implications for Leadership Development." *New Directions for Higher Education* 2019, no. 186 (June 2019): 93–102. https://doi.org/10.1002/he.20326.

Lee, Jennifer. "Asian Americans, Affirmative Action and the Rise in Anti-Asian Hate." *Daedalus* 150, no. 2 (J2021): 180–98. https://doi.org/10.1162/daed_a_01854.

Lee, Jennifer, and Min Zhou. *The Asian American Achievement Paradox*. Russell Sage Foundation, 2015.

Lee, Sharon S. "Over-Represented and De-Minoritized: The Racialization of Asian Americans in Higher Education." *InterActions: UCLA Journal of Education and Information Studies* 2, no. 2 (2006).

Lee, Sharon S. *An Unseen Unheard Minority: Asian American Students at the University of Illinois*. Rutgers University Press, 2021.

Leonardo, Zeus, and Ronald K. Porter. "Pedagogy of Fear: Toward a Fanonian Theory of 'Safety' in Race Dialogue." *Race Ethnicity and Education* 13, no. 2 (2010): 139–57. https://doi.org/10.1080/13613324.2010.482898.

Levin, Shana, Colette van Laar, and Jim Sidanius. "The Effects of Ingroup and Outgroup Friendships on Ethnic Attitudes in College: A Longitudinal Study." *Group Processes & Intergroup Relations* 6, no. 1 (2003): 76–92. https://doi.org/10.1177/1368430203006001013.

Levine, Heidi, and Patrick G. Love. "Religiously Affiliated Institutions and Sexual Orientation." In *Toward Acceptance: Sexual Orientation Issues on Campus*, edited by Vernon A. Wall and Nancy J. Evans. University Press of America, 2000.

Lewis, Oscar. "The Culture of Poverty." *Scientific American* 215, no. 4 (1966): 19–25.

Lewis, Oscar. *Five Families: Mexican Case Studies in the Culture of Poverty*. Basic Books, 1975.

Li, Yao, and Harvey L. Nicholson Jr. "When 'Model Minorities' Become 'Yellow Peril'—Othering and the Racialization of Asian Americans in the COVID-19 Pandemic." *Sociology Compass* 15, no. 2 (2021): e12849. https://doi.org/10.1111/soc4.12849.

Liang, Christopher T. H., Sunny Lee, and Marie P. Ting. "Developing Asian American Leaders." *New Directions for Student Services* 2002, no. 97 (2002): 81–90. https://doi.org/10.1002/ss.41.

Liang, Christopher T. H., and William Sedlacek. "Attitudes of White Student Services Practitioners Toward Asian Americans." *NASPA Journal* 40, no. 3 (2003): 30–42. https://doi.org/10.2202/0027-6014.1253.

Lipsitz, George. *The Possessive Investment in Whiteness: How White People Profit from Identity Politics*. Temple University Press, 2018.

Liu, William, and William Sedlacek. "Differences in Leadership and Co-Curricular Perception among Entering Male and Female Asian-Pacific-American College Students." *Journal of The First-Year Experience & Students in Transition* 11, no. 2 (1999): 93–113.

Longman, Karen A. *Diversity Matters: Race, Ethnicity, and the Future of Christian Higher Education*. Abilene Christian University Press, 2017.

Lyons, Sierra. "At Conservative Schools, Anti-Critical Race Theory Still Looms Large." *NPR*, October 6, 2022. www.npr.org.

Mackenzie, Ann Haley. "Teaching Societal Issues in the Science Classroom." *Science Teacher* 89, no. 6 (2022). www.nsta.org.

Mahmood, Saba. *Religious Difference in a Secular Age: A Minority Report*. Princeton University Press, 2015.

Manzano, Lester J., OiYan A. Poon, and Vanessa S. Na. "Asian American Student Engagement in Student Leadership and Activism." *New Directions for Student Services* 2017, no. 160 (2017): 65–79. https://doi.org/10.1002/ss.20244.

Marine, Susan. "Stonewall's Legacy: Bisexual, Gay Lesbian, and Transgender Students in Higher Education." *ASHE Higher Education Report* 37, no. 4 (2011): 1–145. https://doi.org/10.1002/aehe.3704.

Marti, Gerardo. "Affinity, Identity, and Transcendence: The Experience of Religious Racial Integration in Diverse Congregations." *Journal for the Scientific Study of Religion* 48, no. 1 (2009): 53–68. https://doi.org/10.1111/j.1468-5906.2009.01429.x.

Marti, Gerardo. *Worship Across the Racial Divide: Religious Music and the Multiracial Congregation*. Oxford University Press, 2011.

Mathies, Nicole, Todd Coleman, Raymond Mckie, Michael Woodford, Erin Leigh Courtice, Robb Travers, and Kristen Renn. "Hearing 'That's So Gay' and 'No Homo' on Academic Outcomes for LGBQ+ College Students." *Journal of LGBT Youth* 16 (2019): 1–23. https://doi.org/10.1080/19361653.2019.1571981.

Matsuda, Mari J. "Public Response to Racist Speech: Considering the Victim's Story." *Michigan Law Review* 87, no. 8 (1989): 2320–81. https://doi.org/10.2307/1289306.

Mayorga-Gallo, Sarah. "The White-Centering Logic of Diversity Ideology." *American Behavioral Scientist* 63, no. 13 (2019): 1789–1809. https://doi.org/10.1177/0002764219842619.

McClelland, Jerry, Karin Dahlberg, and Jane Plihal. "Learning in the Ivory Tower: Students' Embodies Experience: College Teaching." *College Teaching* 50, no. 1 (2002): 4–8. https://doi.org/10.1080/87567550209595863.

McDermott, Monica, and Annie Ferguson. "Sociology of Whiteness." *Annual Review of Sociology* 48, no. 1 (2022): 257–76. https://doi.org/10.1146/annurev-soc-083121-054338.

McDowell, Amy, and Pace T. Ward. "'The Tables Are Turning': The Evangelical Defense of Anti-LGBTQ+ Religious Liberty." *Sociology of Religion* 84, no. 4 (2023): 406–25. https://doi.org/10.1093/socrel/srad007.

McIntosh, Peggy. "White Privilege: Unpacking the Invisible Knapsack (1989)." In *On Privilege, Fraudulence, and Teaching as Learning*. Routledge, 2019. https://doi.org/10.4324/9781351133791-4.

Melamed, Jodi. "Diversity." In *Keywords for American Cultural Studies*, edited by Bruce Burgett and Glenn Hendler, 3rd ed. New York University Press, 2020.

Melamed, Jodi. "Racial Capitalism." *Critical Ethnic Studies* 1, no. 1 (2015): 76–85. https://doi.org/10.5749/jcritethnstud.1.1.0076.

Meyer, Doug. "An Intersectional Analysis of Lesbian, Gay, Bisexual, and Transgender (LGBT) People's Evaluations of Anti-Queer Violence." *Gender & Society* 26, no. 6 (2012): 849–73. https://doi.org/10.1177/0891243212461299.

Milem, Jeffrey F. "The Educational Benefits of Diversity: Evidence from Multiple Sectors." In *Compelling Interest: Examining the Evidence on Racial Dynamics in Higher Education*, edited by Mitchell J. Chang, Daria Witt, James Jones, and Kenji Hakuta. Stanford University Press 2003.

Milem, Jeffrey F., Mitchell J. Chang, and Anthony Lising Antonio. *Making Diversity Work on Campus: A Research-Based Perspective*. Association of American Colleges and Universities, 2005.

Miller, Ryan A. "Toward Intersectional Identity Perspectives on Disability and LGBTQ Identities in Higher Education." *Journal of College Student Development* 59, no. 3 (2018): 327–46. https://doi.org/10.1353/csd.2018.0030.

Mills, Charles W. *Black Rights/White Wrongs: The Critique of Racial Liberalism*. Oxford University press, 2017.

Mills, Charles W. *The Racial Contract*. Cornell University Press, 2014.

Monte, Lindsay M., and Hyon B. Shin. "20.6 Million People in the U.S. Identify as Asian, Native Hawaiian or Pacific Islander." US Census Bureau, May 25, 2022. www.census.gov.

Moon, Dawne. "Beyond the Dichotomy: Six Religious Views of Homosexuality." *Journal of Homosexuality* 61, no. 9 (2014): 1215–41. https://doi.org/10.1080/00918369.2014.926762.

Moon, Dawne, Theresa W. Tobin, and J. E. Sumerau. "Alpha, Omega, and the Letters in Between: LGBTQI Conservative Christians Undoing Gender." *Gender & Society* 33, no. 4 (2019): 583–606. https://doi.org/10.1177/0891243219846592.

Moore, Wendy Leo, and Joyce M. Bell. "The Limits of Community: Deconstructing the White Framing of Racist Speech in Universities." *American Behavioral Scientist* 63, no. 13 (2019): 1760–75. https://doi.org/10.1177/0002764219842615.

Moore, Wendy Leo, and Joyce M. Bell. "Maneuvers of Whiteness: 'Diversity' as a Mechanism of Retrenchment in the Affirmative Action Discourse." *Critical Sociology* 37, no. 5 (2011): 597–613. https://doi.org/10.1177/0896920510380066.

Moore, Wendy Leo, and Joyce M. Bell. "The Right to Be Racist in College: Racist Speech, White Institutional Space, and the First Amendment." *Law & Policy* 39, no. 2 (2017): 99–120. https://doi.org/10.1111/lapo.12076.

Mora, G. Cristina. "Cross-Field Effects and Ethnic Classification: The Institutionalization of Hispanic Panethnicity, 1965 to 1990." *American Sociological Review* 79, no. 2 (2014): 183–210. https://doi.org/10.1177/0003122413509813.

Morning, Ann. "Race." *Contexts* 4, no. 4 (2005). https://doi.org/10.1525/ctx.2005.4.4.44.

Moses, Michele S., and Mitchell J. Chang. "Toward a Deeper Understanding of the Diversity Rationale." *Educational Researcher* 35, no. 1 (2006): 6–11. https://doi.org/10.3102/0013189X035001006.

Mueller, Jennifer C. "Advancing a Sociology of Ignorance in the Study of Racism and Racial Non-Knowing." *Sociology Compass* 12, no. 8 (2018): e12600. https://doi.org/10.1111/soc4.12600.

Mueller, Jennifer C. "Producing Colorblindness: Everyday Mechanisms of White Ignorance." *Social Problems* 64, no. 2 (2017): 219–332. https://doi.org/10.1093/socpro/spw061.

Murphy, Caryle. "Most U.S. Christian Groups Grow More Accepting of Homosexuality." Pew Research Center, December 18, 2015. www.pewresearch.org.

Museus, Samuel D. *Asian American Students in Higher Education*. Routledge, 2014.

Museus, Samuel D. "The Role of Ethnic Student Organizations in Fostering African American and Asian American Students' Cultural Adjustment and Membership at Predominantly White Institutions." *Journal of College Student Development* 49, no. 6 (2008): 568–86. https://doi.org/10.1353/csd.0.0039.

Museus, Samuel D., and Frank Harris. "Success Among College Students of Color: How Institutional Culture Matters." In *Managing Diversity: (Re)Visioning Equity on College Campuses*, edited by T. E. Dancy III. Peter Lang, 2010.

Museus, Samuel D., Uma M. Jayakumar, and Thomas Robinson. "Modeling Racial Differences in the Effects of Racial Representation on 2-Year College Student Success." *Journal of College Student Retention: Research, Theory & Practice* 13, no. 4 (2012): 549–72. https://doi.org/10.2190/CS.13.4.g.

Museus, Samuel D., and Peter N. Kiang. "Deconstructing the Model Minority Myth and How It Contributes to the Invisible Minority Reality in Higher Education Research." *New Directions for Institutional Research* 2009, no. 142 (2009): 5–15. https://doi.org/10.1002/ir.292.

Museus, Samuel D., and Julie J. Park. "The Continuing Significance of Racism in the Lives of Asian American College Students." *Journal of College Student Development* 56, no. 6 (2015): 551–69. https://doi.org/10.1353/csd.2015.0059.

National Center for Education Statistics. "Fast Facts: Asian American and Pacific Islander Heritage Month." 2023. https://nces.ed.gov.

National Center for Education Statistics. "Indicator 19: College Participation Rates." 2019. https://nces.ed.gov.

National Center for Education Statistics. "Indicator 20: Undergraduate Enrollment." 2019. https://nces.ed.gov.

National Center for Education Statistics. "Indicator 23: Postsecondary Graduation Rates." 2019. https://nces.ed.gov.

National Center for Education Statistics. "Indicator 27: Educational Attainment." 2019. https://nces.ed.gov.

National Science Foundation. "Diversity and STEM: Women, Minorities, and Persons with Disabilities 2023." January 30, 2023. https://ncses.nsf.gov.

Ng, Jennifer C., Sharon S. Lee, and Yoon K. Pak. "Contesting the Model Minority and Perpetual Foreigner Stereotypes: A Critical Review of Literature on Asian Americans in Education." *Review of Research in Education* 31, no. 1 (2007): 95–130. https://doi.org/10.3102/0091732X07300046095.

Ngo, Bic, and Stacey J. Lee. "Complicating the Image of Model Minority Success: A Review of Southeast Asian American Education." *Review of Educational Research* 77, no. 4 (2007): 415–53. https://doi.org/10.3102/0034654307309918.

Nguyen, Mike Hoa, Jason Chan, Bach Mai Dolly Nguyen, and Robert T. Teranishi. "Beyond Compositional Diversity: Examining the Campus Climate Experiences of Asian American and Pacific Islander Students." *Journal of Diversity in Higher Education* 11, no. 4 (2018): 484–501. https://doi.org/10.1037/dhe0000071.

Nicolazzo, Z, Susan B. Marine, and Rachel Wagner. "From Best to Intentional Practices: Reimagining Implementation of Gender-Inclusive Housing." *Journal of Student Affairs Research and Practice* 55, no. 2 (2018): 225–36. https://doi.org/10.1080/19496591.2018.1399896.

Nicolazzo, Z, Erich N. Pitcher, Kristen A. Renn, and Michael Woodford. "An Exploration of Trans* Kinship as a Strategy for Student Success." *International Journal of Qualitative Studies in Education* 30, no. 3 (2017): 305–19. https://doi.org/10.1080/09518398.2016.1254300.

Niehaus, Elizabeth. "Self-Censorship or Just Being Nice: Understanding College Students' Decisions About Classroom Speech." University of California National Center for Free Speech and Civic Engagement, 2021.

Okuwobi, Oneya, Deborwah Faulk, and Vincent J. Roscigno. "Diversity Displays and Organizational Messaging: The Case of Historically Black Colleges and Universities." *Sociology of Race and Ethnicity* 7, no. 3 (2021): 384–400. https://doi.org/10.1177/2332649220980480.

Omi, Michael, and Howard Winant. *Racial Formation in the United States: From the 1960s to the 1990s*. Routledge, 1994.

Oyakawa, Michelle. "Racial Reconciliation as a Suppressive Frame in Evangelical Multiracial Churches." *Sociology of Religion* 80, no. 4 (2019): 496–517. https://doi.org/10.1093/socrel/srz003.

Pak, Yoon K., Dina C. Maramba, and Xavier J. Hernandez. "Asian Americans in Higher Education: Charting New Realities." *ASHE Higher Education Report* 40, no. 1 (2014): 1–136. https://doi.org/10.1002/aehe.20013.

Pak, Yoon K., Dina C. Maramba, and Xavier J. Hernandez. *Asian Americans in Higher Education: Charting New Realities*. Wiley, 2014.

Pang, Valerie Ooka, Peggy P. Han, and Jennifer M. Pang. "Asian American and Pacific Islander Students: Equity and the Achievement Gap." *Educational Researcher* 40, no. 8 (2011): 378–89. https://doi.org/10.3102/0013189x11424222.

Pappano, Laura. "At Christian Colleges, a Collision of Gay Rights and Traditional Values." *New York Times*, June 5, 2018. www.nytimes.com.

Paredes-Collins, Kristin. "Institutional Priority for Diversity at Christian Institutions." *Christian Higher Education* 8, no. 4 (2009): 280–303. https://doi.org/10.1080/15363750902821197.

Paris, Joseph H., Benjamin Torsney, Sara Fiorot, and Catherine Pressimone Beckowski. "The Impact of Optional: Investigating the Effects of Test-Optional Admissions Policies." *Journal of College Access* 7, no. 2 (2022): article 3.

Park, Jerry Z., Joyce C. Chang, and James C. Davidson. "Equal Opportunity Beliefs Beyond Black and White American Christianity." *Religions* 11, no. 7 (2020): 348. https://doi.org/10.3390/rel11070348.

Park, Julie J. "Clubs and the Campus Racial Climate: Student Organizations and Interracial Friendship in College." *Journal of College Student Development* 55, no. 7 (2014): 641–60. https://doi.org/10.1353/csd.2014.0076.

Park, Julie J. *When Diversity Drops: Race, Religion, and Affirmative Action in Higher Education*. Rutgers University Press, 2013.

Passel, Jeffrey, and D'Vera Cohn. "U.S. Population Projections: 2005–2050." Pew Research Center, February 11, 2008. www.pewresearch.org.

Perry, Samuel L., and Andrew L. Whitehead. "Christian America in Black and White: Racial Inequality, Religious-National Group Boundaries, and Explanations for Racial Inequality." *Sociology of Religion* 80, no. 3 (2019): 277–98. https://doi.org/10.1093/socrel/sry046.

Petts, Amy L. "It's All in the Definition: Color-Blind Interpretations of School Diversity." *Sociological Forum* 35, no. 2 (2020): 465–87. https://doi.org/10.1111/socf.12590.

Pew Research Center. "Majority of Public Favors Same-Sex Marriage, but Divisions Persist." U.S. Politics & Policy, May 14, 2019. www.pewresearch.org.

Phe, Nicole P., and Elaine Yap. "40 Years After Vincent Chin." *National Law Review*, May 20, 2022. https://natlawreview.com.

Pitcher, Erich N., Trace P. Camacho, Kristen A. Renn, and Michael R. Woodford. "Affirming Policies, Programs, and Supportive Services: Using an Organizational Perspective to Understand LGBTQ+ College Student Success." *Journal of Diversity in Higher Education* 11, no. 2 (2018): 117–32. https://doi.org/10.1037/dhe0000048.

Poon, OiYan A. "Asian Americans, 'Critical Mass,' and Campus Racial Climate: A CRT Case Study." In *Asian American Education: Identities, Racial Issues, and Languages*, edited by Russell Endo and Xue Lan Rong. IAP, 2011.

Poon, OiYan A., and Megan S. Segoshi. "The Racial Mascot Speaks: A Critical Race Discourse Analysis of Asian Americans and Fisher vs. University of Texas." *Review of Higher Education* 42, no. 1 (2018): 235–67. https://doi.org/10.1353/rhe.2018.0029.

Poon, OiYan A., Megan S. Segoshi, Lilianne Tang, Kristen L. Surla, Caressa Nguyen, and Dian D. Squire. "Asian Americans, Affirmative Action, and the Political Economy of Racism: A Multidimensional Model of Raceclass Frames." *Harvard Educational Review* 89, no. 2 (2019): 201–26. https://doi.org/10.17763/1943-5045-89.2.201.

Post, Kathryn. "Grove City College Condemns 'Alleged Drift into CRT Advocacy.'" *Christianity Today*, April 25, 2022. www.christianitytoday.com.

Post, Kathryn. "'Woke Wars' Infiltrate Christian Colleges, Prof Under Fire for Racial Justice Unit." *Religion News Service*, February 24, 2023. https://religionnews.com.

Poteat, V. Paul, Katerina O. Sinclair, Craig D. DiGiovanni, Brian W. Koenig, and Stephen T. Russell. "Gay–Straight Alliances Are Associated with Student Health: A Multischool Comparison of LGBTQ and Heterosexual Youth." *Journal of Research on Adolescence* 23, no. 2 (2013): 319–30. https://doi.org/10.1111/j.1532-7795.2012.00832.x.

powell, john a. "Worlds Apart: Reconciling Freedom of Speech and Equality." *Kentucky Law Journal* 85, no. 1 (1996): 9–95.

Pryor, Jonathan T. "Out in the Classroom: Transgender Student Experiences at a Large Public University." *Journal of College Student Development* 56, no. 5 (2015): 440–55. https://doi.org/10.1353/csd.2015.0044.

Pryor, Jonathan T., David Ta, and Jeni Hart. "Searching for Home: Transgender Students and Experiences with Residential Housing." *College Student Affairs Journal* 34, no. 2 (2016): 43–60. https://doi.org/10.1353/csj.2016.0011.

Rajasekar, Neeraj, Matthew Aguilar-Champeau, and Douglas Hartmann. "Diversity Discourse as Racialized and Double-Edged: Findings from a National Survey." *Sociology of Race and Ethnicity* 8, no. 2 (2022): 315–32. https://doi.org/10.1177/23326492221078303.

Rankin, Susan, Warren J. Blumenfeld, Genevieve Weber, and Somjen Frazer. *2010 State of Higher Education for Lesbian, Gay, Bisexual & Transgender People*. Campus Pride, 2010. www.campuspride.org.

Rankin, Susan, and Jason C. Garvey. "Identifying, Quantifying, and Operationalizing Queer-Spectrum and Trans-Spectrum Students: Assessment and Research in Student Affairs." *New Directions for Student Services* 2015, no. 152 (2015): 73–84. https://doi.org/10.1002/ss.20146.

Rankin, Susan, Jason C. Garvey, and Antonio Duran. "A Retrospective of LGBT Issues on US College Campuses: 1990–2020." *International Sociology* 34, no. 4 (2019): 435–54. https://doi.org/10.1177/0268580919851429.

Ray, Victor. "A Theory of Racialized Organizations." *American Sociological Review* 84, no. 1 (2019): 26–53. https://doi.org/10.1177/0003122418822335.

Razek, Raja, and Andy Rose. "University of Wisconsin System Board Approves Deal for $800 Million in State Funding That Cuts Back Diversity Initiatives." *CNN*, December 14, 2023. www.cnn.com.

Reardon, Sean F., Rachel Baker, Matt Kasman, Daniel Klasik, and Joseph B. Townsend. "What Levels of Racial Diversity Can Be Achieved with Socioeconomic-Based Affirmative Action? Evidence from a Simulation Model." *Journal of Policy Analysis and Management* 37, no. 3 (2018): 630–57. https://doi.org/10.1002/pam.22056.

Redden, Elizabeth. "Being LGBTQ+ on a Christian Campus." *Inside Higher Ed*, March 15, 2021. www.insidehighered.com.

Redden, Elizabeth. "Christian Colleges Grow More Diverse." *Inside Higher Ed*, August 15, 2008. www.insidehighered.com.

Renn, Kristen A. "LGBT and Queer Research in Higher Education: The State and Status of the Field." *Educational Researcher* 39, no. 2 (2010): 132–41. https://doi.org/10.3102/0013189X10362579.

Renn, Kristen A. "LGBT Student Leaders and Queer Activists: Identities of Lesbian, Gay, Bisexual, Transgender, and Queer Identified College Student Leaders and Activists." *Journal of College Student Development* 48, no. 3 (2007): 311–30. https://doi.org/10.1353/csd.2007.0029.

Richardson, James T. "Managing Religion and the Judicialization of Religious Freedom." *Journal for the Scientific Study of Religion* 54, no. 1 (2015): 1–19. https://doi.org/10.1111/jssr.12172.

Ridgeway, Cecilia L. *Framed by Gender: How Gender Inequality Persists in the Modern World*. Oxford University Press, 2011.

Rockenbach, Alyssa N., and Rebecca E. Crandall. "Faith and LGBTQ Inclusion: Navigating the Complexities of the Campus Spiritual Climate in Christian Higher Education." *Christian Higher Education* 15, nos. 1–2 (2016): 62–71. https://doi.org/10.1080/15363759.2015.1106355.

Rodríguez, Noreen Naseem, and Rosalie Ip. "Hidden in History: (Re)Constructing Asian American History in Elementary Social Studies Classrooms." In *(Re) Imagining Elementary Social Studies: A Controversial Issues Reader*, edited by Sarah B. Shear, Christina M. Tschida, Elizabeth Bellows, Lisa Brown Buchanan, and Elizabeth E. Saylor. Information Age, 2018.

Ross, Thomas. "Innocence and Affirmative Action." *Vanderbilt Law Review* 43, no. 2 (1990): 297–316.

Russo, Charles J. "Religious Freedom and LGBTQ Rights Are Clashing in Schools and on Campuses—and Courts Are Deciding." *The Conversation*, December 2, 2022. http://theconversation.com.

Saboe, Matt, and Sabrina Terrizzi. "SAT Optional Policies: Do They Influence Graduate Quality, Selectivity or Diversity?" *Economics Letters* 174 (2019): 13–17. https://doi.org/10.1016/j.econlet.2018.10.017.

Saenz, Victor B. "Breaking the Segregation Cycle: Examining Students' Precollege Racial Environments and College Diversity Experiences." *Review of Higher Education* 34, no. 1 (2010): 1–37. https://doi.org/10.1353/rhe.2010.0000.

Saenz, Victor B., Hoi Ning Ngai, and Sylvia Hurtado. "Factors Influencing Positive Interactions Across Race for African American, Asian American, Latino, and White

College Students." *Research in Higher Education* 48, no. 1 (2007): 1–38. https://doi.org/10.1007/s11162-006-9026-3.

Said, Edward W. *Orientalism*. Vintage, 1979.

Schilt, Kristen, and Laurel Westbrook. "Doing Gender, Doing Heteronormativity: 'Gender Normals,' Transgender People, and the Social Maintenance of Heterosexuality." *Gender & Society* 23, no. 4 (2009): 440–64. https://doi.org/10.1177/0891243209340034.

Schneider, David J. *The Psychology of Stereotyping*. Guilford, 2005.

Schneider, Gabe. "The Compton Cookout: A Day Party to Be Remembered (or Not)." *The Triton*, February 15, 2017. https://triton.news.

Schroeder, George. "Seminary Presidents Reaffirm BFM, Declare CRT Incompatible." *Baptist Press*, November 30, 2020. www.baptistpress.com.

Scott, Ellen K. "Beyond Tokenism: The Making of Racially Diverse Feminist Organizations." *Social Problems* 52, no. 2 (2005): 232–54. https://doi.org/10.1525/sp.2005.52.2.232.

Scott, Joan Wallach. *Sex and Secularism*. Princeton University Press, 2018.

Sears, Brad, Christy Mallory, Andrew R. Flores, and Kerith J. Conron. *LGBT People's Experiences of Workplace Discrimination and Harassment*. Williams Institute, 2021. https://williamsinstitute.law.ucla.edu.

Seelman, Kristie L. "Recommendations of Transgender Students, Staff, and Faculty in the USA for Improving College Campuses." *Gender and Education* 26, no. 6 (2014): 618–35. https://doi.org/10.1080/09540253.2014.935300.

Seelman, Kristie L. "Transgender Adults' Access to College Bathrooms and Housing and the Relationship to Suicidality." *Journal of Homosexuality* 63, no. 10 (2016): 1378–99. https://doi.org/10.1080/00918369.2016.1157998.

Seelman, Kristie L., N. Eugene Walls, Kelly Costello, Karly Steffens, Kyle Inselman, Hillary Montague-Asp, and Colorado Trans on Campus Coalition. "The Experiences of Transgender and Gender Non-Conforming Students, Staff, and Faculty at Colleges and Universities in Colorado (Executive Summary)." Colorado Trans on Campus Coalition, 2012.

Sellars, Andrew. "Defining Hate Speech." Berkman Klein Center Research Publication No. 2016-20 (2016).

Sidanius, Jim, Colette Van Laar, Shana Levin, and Stacey Sinclair. "Ethnic Enclaves and the Dynamics of Social Identity on the College Campus: The Good, the Bad, and the Ugly." *Journal of Personality and Social Psychology* 87 (2004): 96–110. https://doi.org/10.1037/0022-3514.87.1.96.

Silver, Blake R. *The Cost of Inclusion: How Student Conformity Leads to Inequality on College Campuses*. University of Chicago Press, 2020.

Silverschanz, Perry, Lilia M. Cortina, Julie Konik, and Vicki J. Magley. "Slurs, Snubs, and Queer Jokes: Incidence and Impact of Heterosexist Harassment in Academia." *Sex Roles* 58, no. 3 (2008): 179–91. https://doi.org/10.1007/s11199-007-9329-7.

Skrentny, John D. "Culture and Race/Ethnicity: Bolder, Deeper, and Broader." *Annals of the American Academy of Political and Social Science* 619, no. 1 (2008): 59–77. https://doi.org/10.1177/0002716208319761.

Smith, Andrea. "Indigeneity, Settler Colonialism, White Supremacy." In *Racial Formation in the Twenty-First Century*, edited by Daniel Martinez HoSang, Oneka LaBennett, and Laura Pulido. University of California Press, 2012.

Smith, Andrea. *Unreconciled: From Racial Reconciliation to Racial Justice in Christian Evangelicalism*. Duke University Press, 2019.

Smith, Christian. *American Evangelicalism: Embattled and Thriving*. University of Chicago Press, 1998.

Smith, William A., Man Hung, and Jeremy D. Franklin. "Racial Battle Fatigue and the MisEducation of Black Men: Racial Microaggressions, Societal Problems, and Environmental Stress." *Journal of Negro Education* 80, no. 1 (2011): 63–82.

Soucek, Brian. "Speech First, Equality Last." *Arizona State Law Journal* 55 (2023): 681–732.

Spade, Dean. *Normal Life: Administrative Violence, Critical Trans Politics, and the Limits of Law*. Duke University Press, 2015.

Stearns, Elizabeth, Claudia Buchmann, and Kara Bonneau. "Interracial Friendships in the Transition to College: Do Birds of a Feather Flock Together Once They Leave the Nest?" *Sociology of Education* 82, no. 2 (2009): 173–95. https://doi.org/10.1177/003804070908200204.

Steele, Emma. "Common App Revises Application Questions on Sex and Gender." Common App, February 24, 2021. www.commonapp.org.

Steele, Emma. "Common App to Update Gender Identity Questions on College Application." Common App, March 2, 2022. www.commonapp.org.

Stevens, Mitchell L., Elizabeth A. Armstrong, and Richard Arum. "Sieve, Incubator, Temple, Hub: Empirical and Theoretical Advances in the Sociology of Higher Education." *Annual Review of Sociology* 34, no. 1 (2008): 127–51. https://doi.org/10.1146/annurev.soc.34.040507.134737.

Stevens, Mitchell L., and Josipa Roksa. "The Diversity Imperative in Elite Admissions." In *Diversity in American Higher Education*, edited by Lisa M. Stulberg and Sharon Lawner Weinberg. Routledge, 2011.

Stryker, Susan. "Transgender History, Homonormativity, and Disciplinarity." *Radical History Review* 2008, no. 100 (2008): 145–57. https://doi.org/10.1215/01636545-2007-026.

Sue, Derald Wing. "Race Talk: The Psychology of Racial Dialogues." *American Psychologist* 68, no. 8 (2013): 663–72. https://doi.org/10.1037/a0033681.

Sumerau, J. E., Ryan T. Cragun, and Lain A. B. Mathers. "Contemporary Religion and the Cisgendering of Reality." *Social Currents* 3, no. 3 (2016): 293–311. https://doi.org/10.1177/2329496515604644.

Suzuki, Bob H. "Revisiting the Model Minority Stereotype: Implications for Student Affairs Practice and Higher Education." *New Directions for Student Services* 2002, no. 97 (2002): 21–32. https://doi.org/10.1002/ss.36.

Takagi, Dana Y. *The Retreat from Race: Asian-American Admissions and Racial Politics*. Rutgers University Press, 1992.

Taylor, Charles. *A Secular Age*. Harvard University Press, 2007.

Teranishi, Robert T. *Asians in the Ivory Tower: Dilemmas of Racial Inequality in American Higher Education*. Teachers College Press, 2010.

Teranishi, Robert T., Dina C. Maramba, and Minh Hoa Ta. "Asian American and Native American Pacific Islander Serving Institutions (AANAPISIs): Mutable Sites for Science, Technology, Engineering, and Math (STEM) Degree Production." In *Fostering Success of Ethnic and Racial Minorities in STEM*, edited by Robert T. Palmer, Dina C. Maramba, and Marybeth Gasman. Routledge, 2013.

Tessler, Hannah, Meera Choi, and Grace Kao. "The Anxiety of Being Asian American: Hate Crimes and Negative Biases During the COVID-19 Pandemic." *American Journal of Criminal Justice* 45 (2020): 1–11. https://doi.org/10.1007/s12103-020-09541-5.

Thomas, James M. *Diversity Regimes: Why Talk Is Not Enough to Fix Racial Inequality at Universities*. Rutgers University Press, 2020.

Thomas, James M. "The Economization of Diversity." *Sociology of Race and Ethnicity* 5, no. 4 (2019): 471–85. https://doi.org/10.1177/2332649218793981.

Thomas, William Isaac, and Dorothy Swaine Thomas. *The Child in America: Behavior Problems and Programs*. Knopf, 1928.

Tian, Ziyao, and Neil G. Ruiz. "Key Facts About Asian Americans Living in Poverty." Pew Research Center, March 27, 2024. www.pewresearch.org.

Tompkins, Avery. "Asterisk." *Transgender Studies Quarterly* 1, nos. 1–2 (2014): 26–27. https://doi.org/10.1215/23289252-2399497.

Torche, Florencia. "The Effect of Maternal Stress on Birth Outcomes: Exploiting a Natural Experiment." *Demography* 48, no. 4 (2011): 1473–91. https://doi.org/10.1007/s13524-011-0054-z.

Tourjée, Diana. "Trans Student Harassed by Milo Yiannopoulos Speaks Out." *Vice*, January 3, 2017. www.vice.com.

Tran, Van C. "Asian American Diversity and Growth." *Annual Review of Sociology* 50 (2024): 581–601. https://doi.org/10.1146/annurev-soc-031021-012617.

Tranby, Eric, and Douglas Hartmann. "Critical Whiteness Theories and the Evangelical 'Race Problem': Extending Emerson and Smith's 'Divided by Faith.'" *Journal for the Scientific Study of Religion* 47, no. 3 (2008): 341–59. https://doi.org/10.1111/j.1468-5906.2008.00414.x.

Trieu, Monica M. "'It Was About Claiming Space': Exposure to Asian American Studies, Ethnic Organization Participation, and the Negotiation of Self among Southeast Asian Americans." *Race Ethnicity and Education* 21, no. 4 (2018): 518–39. https://doi.org/10.1080/13613324.2016.1272564.

Trieu, Monica M., and Hana C. Lee. "Asian Americans and Internalized Racial Oppression: Identified, Reproduced, and Dismantled." *Sociology of Race and Ethnicity* 4, no. 1 (2018): 67–82. https://doi.org/10.1177/2332649217725757.

Turco, Catherine J. "Cultural Foundations of Tokenism: Evidence from the Leveraged Buyout Industry." *American Sociological Review* 75, no. 6 (2010): 894–913.

Turner, Erica O. *Suddenly Diverse: How School Districts Manage Race and Inequality*. University of Chicago Press, 2020.

UC Berkeley. "Free Speech? Hate Speech? Or Both?" January 31, 2017. https://news.berkeley.edu.

UCSD Guardian. "Campus Reacts to Racial Slur." February 22, 2010. https://ucsdguardian.org.

UCSD Guardian. "Third Racist Incident Sends Protesters into Chancellors Complex." February 28, 2010. https://ucsdguardian.org.

University of California Office of the President. "Eligibility in the Local Context (ELC) Program." Accessed April 16, 2024. www.ucop.edu.

Upenieks, Laura, and Rebecca Bonhag. "Masculine God Imagery and Sense of Life Purpose: Examining Contingencies with America's 'Four Gods.'" *Journal for the Scientific Study of Religion* 61, no.1 (2024): 76–102. https://doi.org/10.1111/jssr.12881.

US Department of Education. "Exemptions from Title IX." Investigative Reports; Monitoring Reports. March 8, 2021. https://www2.ed.gov.

US Department of Education. "Sex Discrimination: Overview of the Law." Reference Materials. April 13, 2023. https://www2.ed.gov.

UVA Today. "Sullivan Issues Message to University Community Regarding Aug. 12." August 4, 2017. https://news.virginia.edu.

Vaccaro, Annemarie, and Robert M. Koob. "A Critical and Intersectional Model of LGBTQ Microaggressions: Toward a More Comprehensive Understanding." *Journal of Homosexuality* 66, no. 10 (2019): 1317–44. https://doi.org/10.1080/00918369.2018.1539583.

Vue, Zer, Chia Vang, Neng Vue, Vijayvardhan Kamalumpundi, Taylor Barongan, Bryanna Shao, Sunny Huang, et al. "Asian Americans in STEM Are Not a Monolith." *Cell* 186, no. 15 (2023): 3138–42. https://doi.org/10.1016/j.cell.2023.06.017.

Wadsworth, Nancy. *Ambivalent Miracles: Evangelicals and the Politics of Racial Healing*. University of Virginia Press, 2014.

Walls, Jill K., and Scott S. Hall. "A Focus Group Study of African American Students' Experiences with Classroom Discussions About Race at a Predominantly White University." *Teaching in Higher Education* 23, no. 1 (2018): 47–62. https://doi.org/10.1080/13562517.2017.1359158.

Warikoo, Natasha K. *The Diversity Bargain: And Other Dilemmas of Race, Admissions, and Meritocracy at Elite Universities*. University of Chicago Press, 2016.

Warikoo, Natasha K., and Janine de Novais. "Colour-Blindness and Diversity: Race Frames and Their Consequences for White Undergraduates at Elite US Universities." *Ethnic and Racial Studies* 38, no. 6 (2015): 860–76. https://doi.org/10.1080/01419870.2014.964281.

Weber, Max. *The Methodology of the Social Sciences*. Free Press, 1949.

Wenger, Tisa. *Religious Freedom: The Contested History of an American Ideal*. University of North Carolina Press, 2017.

Wheeler, David R. "What Is It Like to Be Gay at a Christian College?" *The Atlantic*, March 14, 2016. www.theatlantic.com.

White House. "Executive Order on Guaranteeing an Educational Environment Free from Discrimination on the Basis of Sex, Including Sexual Orientation or Gender Identity." March 8, 2021. www.whitehouse.gov.

Whitehead, Andrew L. "Gender Ideology and Religion: Does a Masculine Image of God Matter?" *Review of Religious Research* 54, no. 2 (2012): 139–56. https://doi.org/10.1007/s13644-012-0056-3.

Whitehead, Andrew L. "Male and Female He Created Them: Gender Traditionalism, Masculine Images of God, and Attitudes Toward Same-Sex Unions." *Journal for the Scientific Study of Religion* 53, no. 3 (2014): 479–96. https://doi.org/10.1111/jssr.12130.

Wilson, Bianca D. M., Lauren J. A. Bouton, and Christy Mallory. "Racial Differences Among LGBT Adults in the US." Williams Institute, January 2022. https://williamsinstitute.law.ucla.edu.

Wilson, Jeffery, Katrina Meyer, and Larry McNeal. "Mission and Diversity Statements: What They Do and Do Not Say." *Innovative Higher Education* 37, no. 2 (2012): 125–39. https://doi.org/10.1007/s10755-011-9194-8.

Wolff, Joshua R., and Heather L. Himes. "Purposeful Exclusion of Sexual Minority Youth in Christian Higher Education: The Implications of Discrimination." *Christian Higher Education* 9, no. 5 (2010): 439–60. https://doi.org/10.1080/15363759.2010.513630.

Wolff, Joshua R., Heather L. Himes, Sabrina D. Soares, and Ellen Miller Kwon. "Sexual Minority Students in Non-Affirming Religious Higher Education: Mental Health, Outness, and Identity." *Psychology of Sexual Orientation and Gender Diversity* 3, no. 2 (2016): 201–12. https://doi.org/10.1037/sgd0000162.

Wolff, Joshua R., Theresa Stueland Kay, H. L. Himes, and Jennifer Alquijay. "Transgender and Gender-Nonconforming Student Experiences in Christian Higher Education: A Qualitative Exploration." *Christian Higher Education* 16, no. 5 (2017): 319–38. https://doi.org/10.1080/15363759.2017.1310065.

Wu, Ellen D. *The Color of Success: Asian Americans and the Origins of the Model Minority*. Princeton University Press, 2013.

Yam, Kimmy. "DeSantis Criticized for Mandating Asian American History While Banning Courses on 'Systemic Racism.'" *NBC News*, May 17, 2023. www.nbcnews.com.

Yancey, George A. *Neither Jew nor Gentile: Exploring Issues of Racial Diversity on Protestant College Campuses*. Oxford University Press, 2010.

Yang, Kao Lee. "I'm Almost Always the Only Hmong American Scientist in the Room. Yet I Was Told I Come from a Group Overrepresented in STEM." *STAT*, November 11, 2021. www.statnews.com.

Yi, Pyŏng-sik. "Institutional Climate and Student Departure: A Multinomial Multilevel Modeling Approach." *Review of Higher Education* 31, no. 2 (2008): 161–83. https://doi.org/10.1353/rhe.2007.0076.

Young, Luther, Jr. "To Condemn or Not to Condemn: Perceived Climates Concerning Sexual Orientation in Black Churches." *Sociology of Religion* 83, no.2 (2022): 169–93. https://doi.org/10.1093/socrel/srab031.

Zimmer, Lynn. "Tokenism and Women in the Workplace: The Limits of Gender-Neutral Theory." *Social Problems* 35, no. 1 (1988): 64–77. https://doi.org/10.2307/800667.

Zwick, Rebecca. "College Admissions in Twenty-First-Century America: The Role of Grades, Tests, and Games of Chance." *Harvard Educational Review* 77, no. 4 (2008): 419–29. https://doi.org/10.17763/haer.77.4.u67n84589527t80v.

Zylstra, Sarah Eekhoff. "Tuition Is Rising and Enrollment Is Holding. So Why Are Christian Colleges Struggling?" Gospel Coalition, August 15, 2019. www.thegospelcoalition.org.

INDEX

AAW. *See* Asian Americans at West
absolutism. *See* free speech
abstract equality, 5, 97, 141, 207; in classroom environments, 113–14; color-blind ideology relation to, 134, 143; diversity as difference relation to, 40, 51; in diversity statements, 57; inequality regimes and, 65; language of sin and, 117; power and equity approach relation to, 96; student organizations relation to, 136
access: to education, 212–13; equity as, 44; inclusion relation to, 163–64; for minorities, 220–21; privilege and, 101; to resources, 45, 109, 183–86
accommodation, as tolerance, 119
Acker, Joan, 5
activism: of AAW, 195; at Christian colleges, 127–28; DEI offices relation to, 245n19; oppositional, 43
activist identity, 50, 120–21
administrative officials: diversity statements relation to, 55; donors relation to, 125–27; equity regimes relation to, 169; gender-inclusive bathrooms relation to, 165; model minority myth relation to, 144
admissions, 8, 220–21, 253n48. *See also* affirmative action policies
affirmation, 69–70, 71, 215; faculty relation to, 112–13; RA relation to, 173–74
affirmative action policies, 3, 7–9, 152–53, 208, 220–21, 253n46; Asian Americans relation to, 200–201; Christ College relation to, 21–22; legally protected groups and, 10; UC relation to, 253n54; West University relation to, 20
alternative voices, to hate speech, 93
American College Health Association, 17
anti-Blackness, 200, 205, 218
antisemitism, 95–96
applications, sexual orientation in, 16–17
Armstrong, Elizabeth, 6
Asian American history, 222
"Asian American leadership," 148–49
Asian Americans, 16, 182, 208; at Christ College, 2, 22, 26, 136–38, 141–42, 181, 194, 197; community for, 204; conservative speakers relation to, 87; diversity programs relation to, 141, 143–45, 153; ethnic differences among, 27; ethnic diversity and, 201–2; in higher education, 3, 13, 15, 200–201; LGBTQ+ students, 83; numerical representation of, 28, 39–40, 134–35, 196, 199, 218, 222; as panethnic group, 237n6; politics and, 195; power analysis framework relation to, 50–51; racial diversity relation to, 131–32, 199–200; racial hierarchies and, 14, 15, 201; racial reconciliation and, 198, 202–3; racial triangulation and, 142–43; in student government, 147–48; in student leadership, 149–50; at West University, 20, 23, 26, 130–32, 133, 147, 181, 199, 221

Asian Americans at West (AAW), 26, 35; cultural festival of, 130; culture and, 188–89; dual identity of, 189–90; ethnic diversity in, 203; model minority myth relation to, 50–51; politics relation to, 195–96, 250n14; resource access for, 183–85
Asian ethnic identities, 27; inequality and, 247n18; student organizations for, 135, 222–23
Asiatic Barred Zones Act (1917), 50, 145

Bakke, Allan, 7–8
"bamboo ceiling," 148
beliefs, diversity of, 36–37
Bell, Joyce, 104, 212–13
belonging, 192, 216–17
bicultural identity, 188, 204, 250n10
bicultural organizations, 192–94
Biden administration, 18, 108
biopolitics, 43
Black evangelicals, 49
Black Lives Matter, 98–99, 250n14
Black students, White students relation to, 102
Black Student Union, 192
Board of Trustees, of Christ College, 108, 128, 216
Bonilla-Silva, Eduardo, 14, 146
Brown, Wendy, 73
Byrd, W. Carson, 140

campus climate: compositional diversity relation to, 40; free speech relation to, 102; numerical representation relation to, 23; student organizations relation to, 135
campus controversies, free speech and, 90
CCCU. *See* Council for Christian Colleges and Universities
Chin, Vincent, 195, 199
Chinese Exclusion Act (1882), 50, 145
Chinese immigrants, 13, 145
Christ College, 1, 18, 24–25; affirmative action policies relation to, 21–22; Asian Americans at, 2, 22, 26, 136–38, 141–42, 181, 194, 197; cultural traditions at, 250n3; diversity rationale at, 123–24; exclusion and, 115; heteronormativity at, 112, 172–73; housing arrangements at, 110–11; as inequality regimes, 109, 129; LGBTQ+ reconciliation at, 180; LGBTQ+ students at, 28, 31–32, 75–76, 77, 106–7, 126–29, 169, 175, 216–17; numerical representation at, 134, 138–39; organizational change at, 159; racial diversity at, 131, 137, 185–86; racial reconciliation at, 20, 49–50, 165–67, 185, 197, 246n19; religious diversity at, 107–8; sexuality relation to, 110, 121–23, 128; student leadership at, 151; West University compared to, 19–20, 21; White cultural practices at, 186–87; White students at, 23. *See also* Harbor, at Christ College
Christian colleges, 10; belonging at, 216–17; conversion therapy at, 252n30; DEI relation to, 209–10; donors relation to, 127–28, 129; enrollment at, 129; inclusion relation to, 116, 215; LGBTQ+ reconciliation at, 168; LGBTQ+ student organization at, 18; LGBTQ+ students at, 11, 119, 215; organizational change in, 214; racial reconciliation at, 49–50; religious language at, 68; student organizations at, 186–87
Christianity, 57–58; equity and, 108–9; gender binary relation to, 11–12; LGBTQ+ students relation to, 246n13; oppression relation to, 67, 68; queer identity relation to, 173; racial reconciliation and, 198; reconciliation relation to, 60–61; sexual orientation relation to, 62; White racial dominance relation to, 68; White supremacy relation to, 66, 78

Christian superiority, 64–65
"cisgendering of reality," 111, 115
cisnormativity, 12, 163
civil rights movement, 198, 200
classroom environments: abstract equality in, 113–14; discrimination in, 109–10; equity in, 210–11; exclusion in, 115, 128; microaggressions in, 121; misgendering in, 171–72
Coley, Jonathan, 50, 214
color-blind ideology, 218; abstract equality relation to, 134, 143; counterspeech relation to, 104; inequality regimes relation to, 134; racial diversity and, 138; racial inequality relation to, 132–33; racial reconciliation and, 11, 166; systemic inequality relation to, 153; tolerance relation to, 71
commodification, of POC, 76
Common Application, 16–17, 43
community, 199, 224; for Asian Americans, 204; cultural traditions relation to, 191; diversity rationale relation to, 194; power analysis framework relation to, 209; in student organizations, 188; tolerance relation to, 73
community values: inclusion relation to, 170–71; policies relation to, 169–70
commuter students, 37
compassion, equity and, 70–71
compositional diversity, 23, 40
conformity, "melting pot" relation to, 35
conservative speakers, 211–12; LGBTQ+ students relation to, 87; at public universities, 83–84; security for, 89
conservative students, 101–2; facilitators relation to, 103; free speech relation to, 245n20; intergroup dialogue and, 245n32
conversion therapy, 18, 252n30
Cooperative Institutional Research Program, Freshman Survey of, 17
Corces-Zimmerman, Chris, 218
Council for Christian Colleges and Universities (CCCU), 18, 20, 127, 243n5
counseling services, 122, 215, 252n30
counterspeech, hate speech and, 104–5
creedal beliefs, 61–62
creedal language, inequality regimes and, 78
Crenshaw, Kimberlé, 249n3
critical race theory (CRT): Christian colleges relation to, 209; DEI bans and, 3
cultural essentialist narratives, 153, 208. *See also* model minority myth
cultural mobility, White multiculturalism and, 77
cultural traditions, 182–83, 191, 219–20; at Christ College, 250n3; racial diversity in, 188; Whiteness relation to, 187
culture, 242n12; AAW and, 188–89; of Asian Americans, 39, 141–42; difference of, 38, 181–82; race compared to, 39; racial triangulation relation to, 142–43; student government relation to, 148; student organizations and, 192; Western, 66
culture of poverty narrative, 14
culture wars, 216

dead names, on student identification cards, 160–61
Dear White Christians (Harvey), 61
definitions, inequality relation to, 32, 58
dehumanization, 91
DEI. *See* diversity, equity, and inclusion
DEI bans, 3, 208
DEI offices, 1, 20, 24–25, 85–86; activism relation to, 245n19; counternarratives and, 93, 104; hate speech relation to, 92, 96; legal rhetoric of, 95; legal scholars at, 91; LGBTQ+ students relation to, 166; organizational change relation to, 120–21; protests and, 94; resource access relation to, 184–85
Department of Education, 18, 22, 43

DeSantis, Ron, 222
dialogue spaces: facilitators in, 100; intergroup dialogue in, 212; as safe spaces, 210
difference, 32, 41–42; of culture, 38, 181–82; social, 187, 207; social identity relation to, 40, 91
difference, diversity as, 34–35, 85, 104, 128, 136, 141; abstract equality relation to, 40, 51; Christian colleges relation to, 209; Christianity relation to, 58; diversity rationale relation to, 37, 49; free speech and, 28; inequality relation to, 4, 207; LGBTQ+ students relation to, 215; numerical representation relation to, 152
discrimination: in classroom environments, 109–10; language of love relation to, 115; as learning experiences, 124–25; LGBTQ+ students and, 17–18; public universities relation to, 116; religious, 25; religious freedom relation to, 117–18; sexuality and, 107; in student government, 147–48
diversity. *See specific topics*
diversity, equity, and inclusion (DEI), 1, 12–13, 20; Asian Americans and, 182; Christian colleges relation to, 209–10; education in, 219; equality relation to, 208–9; LGBTQ+ students and, 180; numerical representation and, 132–34, 140
diversity courses, 219
diversity programs: Asian Americans relation to, 141, 143–45, 153; model minority myth relation to, 133–34, 143–45; for racialized minorities, 142
diversity rationale, 8, 191; at Christ College, 123–24; community relation to, 194; diversity as difference relation to, 37, 49; educational benefits of, 76–78, 204; inclusion relation to, 74; in secular diversity statements, 73; student organizations and, 205; White supremacy relation to, 9
diversity statements, 35, 54–56, 64, 207, 243n1; abstract equality in, 57; equality in, 65; sexual orientation in, 62–63; as social documents, 79; Whiteness in, 98–99; White supremacy relation to, 89. *See also* evangelical diversity statements; secular diversity statements
donors, 123, 183–85, 212; administrative officials relation to, 125–27; Christian colleges relation to, 127–28, 129
double liability dilemma, 105
dual identity, of AAW, 189–90. *See also* bicultural organizations

East Asian Americans, 14, 26, 27
education: access to, 212–13; in DEI, 219; Equal Protection Clause and, 85; of marginalized populations, 75–76; oppression and, 101–2; politics and, 195–96, 205; socioeconomic inequality relation to, 6; in student organizations, 189–93
educational benefits, 37, 209; of diversity rationale, 76–78, 204; inclusion relation to, 73–75
educational outcomes: of Asian Americans, 14, 208; for racialized minorities, 143
educational support, for LGBTQ+ students, 177–78
Eligibility in Context Program (ELC), 220, 253n48
elite universities, 6, 13, 77
Embrick, David, 32
Emerson, Michael, 49
emotional labor, of marginalized populations, 101–2
enrollment, 127, 129, 253n47
equality: cultural traditions relation to, 182–83; in definitions, 58; DEI relation to, 208–9; in diversity statements, 65;

equity compared to, 5–6, 31, 97; evangelical diversity statements relation to, 78; free speech relation to, 213–14; language of love and, 108–9; language of sin relation to, 59, 62–64; LGBTQ+ student organization and, 128–29. *See also* abstract equality
Equal Protection Clause, 85, 212–13
equitable dialogue, 100
equity, 28; as access, 44; Christianity and, 108–9; in classroom environments, 210–11; compassion and, 70–71; cultural traditions relation to, 182–83; DEI offices relation to, 95; diversity relation to, 34, 47–48, 51, 52–53, 79; in diversity statements, 57; equality compared to, 5–6, 31, 97; free speech relation to, 97; inclusion relation to, 157–58; intersectionality and, 159, 179–80; model minority myth relation to, 146–47; numerical representation and, 52, 152; organizational change for, 4–5, 205; policies for, 32; power analysis framework relation to, 50, 146, 158–59; racial diversity relation to, 19, 150, 219; religious language relation to, 59; tolerance relation to, 73. *See also* power and equity approach
equity regimes, 5–6, 165, 210; administrative officials relation to, 169; inequality regimes relation to, 79; LGBTQ+ students and, 157, 159; numerical representation relation to, 223; racial reconciliation relation to, 166; Whiteness relation to, 218
ethnic differences, among Asian Americans, 27
ethnic disparities, in STEM, 15
ethnic diversity, 201–2, 203
ethnicity, 36–37, 39
evangelical diversity statements, 56, 243n5; equality relation to, 78; inclusion relation to, 73–75; language of sin in, 64, 117; power analysis framework relation to, 59–60, 68; religious language in, 57–58; secular diversity statements compared to, 72, 74; sexual orientation in, 62–63; sexual orientation relation to, 69–70; White racial perspective in, 65–66, 67
evangelicalism, 20, 55, 59
exclusion, 115, 128, 152, 158
exclusionary policy statements, 115, 216
exclusionary practices, 107, 109–10, 115

facilitators, 100, 103
faculty, 112–14, 217
faith-based admission requirements, 113
Features and Implications of Diversity as Difference, Numerical Representation, and Power and Equity, 33
feminist movement, 178
FIRE. *See* Foundation for Individual Rights in Education
First Amendment. *See* free speech
forgiveness, 54–55, 61–62, 68
Foucault, Michel, 43
Foundation for Individual Rights in Education (FIRE), 85–86
Fourteenth Amendment, Equal Protection Clause of, 85
free speech, 1, 244n6; absolutism, 87–88, 90, 91, 94–95, 99, 210, 214, 245n20; campus climate relation to, 102; campus controversies and, 90; DEI offices relation to, 104; diversity as difference and, 28; equality relation to, 213–14; Equal Protection Clause and, 212–13; equity relation to, 97; hate speech *versus*, 84; inclusion relation to, 115; intolerance relation to, 88; LGBTQ+ students relation to, 19; marginalized populations and, 97; moral responsibility and, 99–100; power analysis framework and, 86, 88, 101; privilege relation to, 98; protests and, 94; at public universities, 83–85,

free speech (*cont.*)
91–92, 210; realist approach to, 85, 89; viewpoint neutrality and, 245n21; at West University, 85–86, 93
Free Speech Week, 89
Freshman Survey, of Cooperative Institutional Research Program, 17

Garces, Liliana, 105
gender binary, 16; Christianity relation to, 11–12; mental health relation to, 172; student leadership relation to, 175
gender complementarianism, 214, 252n24
gender identity, 3, 16–17; "cisgendering of reality" and, 111; power analysis framework and, 44; queer identity relation to, 26; religious freedom and, 129; student leadership relation to, 175; Title IX relation to, 108; visual diversity relation to, 139–40
gender-inclusive bathrooms, 159; housing arrangements and, 164–65; at West University, 162–64, 248n1
gender-inclusive language, 175, 217
generational trauma, 202–3
God's love, 60, 62, 63
good-faith discussions, 212

Hamilton, Laura, 6
Harbor, at Christ College, 1, 25, 47, 113, 129, 157; activist identity in, 120–21; administrative officials relation to, 125–26; affirmation and, 215; exclusionary policy statements relation to, 216; housing arrangements relation to, 111, 124–25; resource access for, 109; as safe spaces, 168
Hart-Celler Act (1965), 50
Harvey, Jennifer, 61
hate speech, 1, 90–91, 244n6; alternative voices to, 93; counterspeech and, 104–5; DEI offices relation to, 92, 96; free speech *versus*, 84; minorities and, 244n14
HBCUs. *See* historically Black colleges and universities
heteronormativity, 7, 171; at Christ College, 112, 172–73; queer identity relation to, 26–27
Heyer, Heather, 84
higher education. *See specific topics*
Hispanic students, 137
historically Black colleges and universities (HBCUs), 218–19
history, 64; of inequality, 51, 52, 59–60, 79; in secular diversity statements, 67
Hmong students, 222
homophobia, 123–24; at Christ College, 180; in classroom environments, 171–72; free speech and, 213; toxic masculinity relation to, 178
"honorary White" grouping, 146
housing arrangements: "cisgendering of reality" and, 115; diversity rationale and, 123–24; exclusion in, 128; gender-inclusive language in, 175, 217; Harbor relation to, 111, 124–25; for LGBTQ+ students, 110–11, 121–22, 164–65; student leadership relation to, 174
hurtful speech, 91–92
hyper-selectivity, 13

ideal types, 34, 241n6
imago dei, 66
immigration, 13, 35, 50, 92
imperialism, 66–67
inclusion, 4–5, 204; access relation to, 163–64; Asian Americans and, 198; at Christian colleges, 116, 215; Christianity and, 108–9; community values relation to, 170–71; diversity rationale relation to, 74; donors relation to, 123, 127–28; equity relation to, 157–58; evangelical diversity statements relation to, 73–75; free speech relation to, 115; LGBTQ+ student organization and, 128–29; for LGBTQ+ students, 122–23; of minori-

ties, 132; numerical representation and, 133, 138, 152; policies for, 32, 117, 174; in power analysis framework, 158–59; RA relation to, 173–74; reconciliation and, 167–68; religious freedom relation to, 115, 116–17; in student organizations, 196; White supremacy relation to, 88
individualism, 49, 215
inequality: Asian ethnic identities and, 247n18; definitions relation to, 32, 58; diversity as difference relation to, 4, 207; free speech relation to, 85; gender, 7; history of, 51, 52, 59–60, 79; numerical representation relation to, 45, 152, 207–8; social, 40, 78, 104–5, 175–76, 209, 217–18; socioeconomic, 6; structural, 49; systemic, 10, 14, 62, 153; toxic masculinity relation to, 178. *See also* racial inequality
inequality regimes, 5, 7, 34, 165, 210, 223; abstract equality and, 65; Christ College as, 109, 129; color-blind ideology relation to, 134; creedal language and, 78; diversity rationale relation to, 204; equity regimes relation to, 79; intersectionality and, 175–76; numerical representation relation to, 52, 152–53; power analysis framework relation to, 53; public universities as, 105; social difference and, 207; tolerance relation to, 69
institutional legitimacy, 184
institutional power, 43
intergroup dialogue, 24, 212, 245n32
interracial relationships, 214–15
intersectionality, 159; learning experiences relation to, 177–78; numerical representation relation to, 223; policies relation to, 161–62; privilege and, 175–76, 179–80; racial triangulation relation to, 205; reconciliation and, 167
intolerance, free speech relation to, 88
invisible identity, 42

Jack, Anthony Abraham, 6

Kahn, Jonathan, 12
Kim, Claire J., 14, 142–43, 200
Knowles, Solange, 48
Korean ethnic student organization, 130, 194–95

learning environment, diversity rationale and, 8
learning experiences, 123; discrimination as, 124–25; intersectionality relation to, 177–78
Lee, Hanna, 50
Lee, Jennifer, 13
Lee, Sharon, 145
legal absolutist approach, 86, 90, 104, 105
legally protected groups, affirmative action policies and, 10
legal rhetoric, of DEI offices, 95
Lewis, Oscar, 14
LGBTQ+ faculty, 217
LGBTQ+ reconciliation, 167–68, 180
LGBTQ+ student organization, 1, 22, 109, 162; at Christian colleges, 18; culture relation to, 39; DEI offices relation to, 184; inclusion and, 128–29; power analysis framework relation to, 50; at West University, 25, 35, 83. *See also* Harbor, at Christ College
LGBTQ+ students, 16, 20, 118; Asian American, 83; at Christ College, 28, 31–32, 75–76, 77, 106–7, 126–29, 169, 175, 216–17; at Christian colleges, 11, 119, 215; Christianity relation to, 246n13; conservative speakers relation to, 87; DEI and, 180; DEI offices relation to, 166; educational support for, 177–78; equity regimes and, 157, 159; exclusionary practices and, 109–10, 115; faculty relation to, 114; housing arrangements for, 110–11, 121–22, 164–65; inclusion for, 122–23; moral responsibility to, 116; nondiscrimination practices for, 214; numerical representation of, 138–39;

LGBTQ+ students (*cont.*)
power analysis framework relation to, 59; religion classes relation to, 113; at religious universities, 17–18; at secular universities, 18–19; visual diversity relation to, 140; at worship services, 172–73
liberalism, 71, 73, 78
life outcomes, of racialized minorities, 145
lifestyle expectations, at Christ College, 110, 112, 115
lived name, 162, 248n1
Lloyd, Vincent, 12
lottery system, 220
love, language of, 79, 243n9; discrimination relation to, 115; equality and, 108–9; in evangelical diversity statements, 72–73
Lunar New Year, 39

Mahmood, Saba, 12
majorities, 51–52, 71–72
marginalization, in classroom environments, 114
marginalized populations, 103; conservative speakers relation to, 87; education of, 75–76; emotional labor of, 101–2; free speech and, 97; power analysis framework and, 90; power and equity approach relation to, 89–90
mathematics, 40–41
Mayorga-Gallo, Sarah, 9
"melting pot," 35–36
mental health, 42; gender binary relation to, 172; of LGBTQ+ students, 128–29; student identification cards relation to, 159
microaggressions, 121, 221
Mills, Charles W., 73
minorities: access for, 220–21; hate speech and, 244n14; inclusion of, 132; numerical representation and, 51–52, 152; racialized, 2, 8, 140, 142–43, 145; in student leadership, 150–51; tolerance relation to, 71–72; White supremacy relation to, 218
misgendering, in classroom environments, 171–72
model minority myth, 14–15, 16, 196, 201, 208; AAW relation to, 50–51; culture and, 142; diversity programs relation to, 133–34, 143–45; equity relation to, 146–47; numerical representation and, 152; privilege relation to, 199–200; racial diversity relation to, 140–41; racial hierarchies and, 221; racial triangulation and, 149–50, 153; student leadership relation to, 147; yellow peril relation to, 145–46
Moon, Dawne, 11
Moore, Wendy Leo, 104, 212–13
moral responsibility, 99–100, 116
multiculturalism, 77, 219
multicultural worship night, 185–86
multiethnic clubs, 186

nationality, 36–37
National Science Foundation (NSF), 15, 222
National Survey of Student Engagement, 17
Nazi extremist groups, 88
Nicolazzo, Z, 165
nonbinary identity, 11–12, 43, 159
nondiscrimination practices, 22, 214
nonselective colleges, 13
nontraditional students, 37
NSF. *See* National Science Foundation
numerical diversity, 40–41, 42, 137
numerical representation, 23, 36, 138; of Asian Americans, 28, 39–40, 134–35, 196, 199, 218, 222; DEI and, 132–34, 140; diversity relation to, 32, 34, 51–52, 79; equity regimes relation to, 223; ethnic diversity relation to, 203; inequality regimes relation to, 52, 152–53; inequality

relation to, 45, 152, 207–8; of LGBTQ+ students, 138–39
numeric metrics: for LGBTQ+ students, 17; racial diversity and, 8; racial hierarchies relation to, 16; representation and, 4

Obama administration, 18, 108
Office of Civil Rights, 18
Okuwobi, Oneya, 214
oppositional activism, 43
oppression, 59, 72; Christianity relation to, 67, 68; education and, 101–2; forgiveness and, 54–55; intersectionality and, 162; language of sin and, 65; White supremacy and, 179
organizational change, 158–59, 180, 218, 224; in Christian colleges, 214; community values relation to, 170; DEI offices relation to, 120–21; for equity, 4–5, 205; power analysis framework and, 208; for racial reconciliation, 169; student leadership and, 121
organizational practice, 7, 12
outside donors, 183–85, 212

pacification, 46–47
panethnic group, 237n6
partying, 6
patriarchy, privilege and, 178
people of color (POC), 27, 41–42, 63, 67, 76. *See also* Asian Americans
perception-based diversity, 42–43
performative policies, 162–63
Perkins, John, 48
"perpetual foreigners," 149–50
perspectives, diversity of, 36
pluralism, evangelicalism relation to, 55
POC. *See* people of color
policies, 9, 50, 108, 220–21; community values relation to, 169–70; for inclusion, 32, 117, 174; intersectionality relation to, 161–62; performative, 162–63; for student identification cards, 160–61; violence in, 165. *See also* affirmative action policies
politics, 43, 195–96, 205, 250n14
Powell, Lewis, Jr., 8
power, 32, 34, 44, 51, 52–53, 79
power analysis framework, 34, 43–44, 143; Asian Americans relation to, 50–51; community relation to, 209; cultural essentialist narratives in, 153; equity in, 50, 146, 158–59; evangelical diversity statements relation to, 59–60, 68; free speech and, 86, 88, 101; inequality regimes relation to, 53; marginalized populations and, 90; privilege and, 45; "seat at the table" and, 48–49; secular diversity statements and, 59–60, 64; student leadership and, 59, 86; tokenism and, 46, 52, 208; tolerance and, 71; White supremacy and, 200
power and equity approach, 93–94, 98, 104; abstract equality relation to, 96; marginalized populations relation to, 89–90
preferred names, 161, 248n1. *See also* lived name
privilege, 77, 100, 178; access and, 101; in classroom environments, 114; engagement relation to, 103; free speech relation to, 98; intersectionality and, 175–76, 179–80; learning experiences relation to, 124–25; model minority myth relation to, 199–200; power analysis framework and, 45; racial hierarchies relation to, 201
pronouns, 27, 217; community values relation to, 170–71; RA relation to, 174
protests, 94, 245n22
public universities: access in, 213; discrimination relation to, 116; enrollment at, 253n47; free speech at, 83–85, 91–92, 210; as inequality regimes, 105; nondiscrimination practices at, 22. *See also* West University

queer identity, 26–27; affirmation for, 215; Christianity relation to, 173; intersectionality and, 178–79; representation of, 176
quotas, 8, 46

RA. *See* residential advisor
race: culture compared to, 39; power analysis framework and, 43–44
race-conscious admissions, 8. *See also* affirmative action
racial binary, 196–97, 205
racial dialogue, 102
racial diversity, 41, 70–71, 196; Asian Americans relation to, 131–32, 199–200; at Christ College, 131, 137, 185–86; at Christian colleges, 10–11; color-blind ideology and, 138; in cultural traditions, 188; equity relation to, 19, 150, 219; model minority myth relation to, 140–41; numeric metrics and, 8; at West University, 130–31, 135; White students relation to, 204–5
racial hierarchies, 146; Asian Americans and, 14, 15, 201; model minority myth and, 221; numeric metrics relation to, 16; racial triangulation and, 141, 143, 153
racial histories, 222
racial identity, 34; religious identity relation to, 61, 198; secularism relation to, 12; visual diversity relation to, 139–40
racial ideology, 9
racial inequality, 7, 15–16, 243n9; affirmative action policies relation to, 8; color-blind ideology relation to, 132–33; culture relation to, 39; diversity rationale and, 9; numerical representation and, 134; power and, 44; racial reconciliation relation to, 166; in religious organizations, 49; White evangelicals relation to, 214–15
racialized minorities, 8, 140; at Christ College, 2; diversity programs for, 142; educational outcomes for, 143; life outcomes of, 145
racial justice, 44
racial reconciliation, 48; Asian Americans and, 198, 202–3; at Christ College, 20, 49–50, 165–67, 185, 197, 246n19; color-blind ideology and, 11, 166; interracial relationships and, 214–15; organizational change for, 169; reparations relation to, 61; systemic inequality and, 62
racial stereotypes, 193. *See also* model minority myth
racial stratification, 146
racial triangulation, 14, 200; culture relation to, 142–43; intersectionality relation to, 205; model minority myth and, 149–50, 153; racial hierarchies and, 141, 143, 153; White supremacy relation to, 16; yellow peril relation to, 145–46
racism, 50, 61, 76, 104–5, 132–33, 213
racist policies, 9
Ray, Victor, 6
realist approach, to free speech, 85, 89
reconciliation, 54–55, 60–61; Christ College relation to, 112, 115; LGBTQ+, 167–68, 180. *See also* racial reconciliation
religion, 12, 55, 63, 107. *See also* Christianity
religion classes, 112–13
religious discrimination, 25
religious diversity, at Christ College, 107–8
religious freedom, 108, 119–20, 129; discrimination relation to, 117–18; inclusion relation to, 115, 116–17
religious identity, 11, 61, 198
religious language: at Christian colleges, 68; equality in, 59; in evangelical diversity statements, 57–58
religious organizations, racial inequality in, 49

religious universities, 3, 60; LGBTQ+ students at, 17–18; secular universities compared to, 22–23; Title IX relation to, 22, 108. *See also* Christ College
reparations, racial reconciliation relation to, 61
representation, 4, 150–51, 176
Republican student organization, 83–84, 103; immigration relation to, 92; outside donors to, 212
residential advisor (RA), 173–74
resource access, 45; for AAW, 183–85; for Harbor, 109; for multicultural worship night, 185–86
resource allocation, 91

safe spaces: dialogue spaces as, 210; Harbor as, 168; for LGBTQ+ students, 75–76; student organizations relation to, 135
same-sex relationships: at Christ College, 22; policies relation to, 117; at religious universities, 17–18
science, technology, engineering, and mathematics (STEM), 15, 222
Scott, Joan, 12
scripture, Whiteness relation to, 67–68
secular diversity statements, 243n5; diversity rationale in, 73; evangelical diversity statements compared to, 72, 74; history in, 67; power analysis framework and, 59–60, 64; tolerance in, 69–70, 78
secularism, 12, 55
secular universities, 18–19, 22–23, 27
security, for conservative speakers, 89
sexuality, 3; Christ College relation to, 110, 121–23, 128; discrimination and, 107; power analysis framework and, 44; religious freedom relation to, 115; visual diversity relation to, 139–40
sexual orientation: in applications, 16–17; in diversity statements, 62–63; evangelical diversity statements relation to, 69–70; Title IX relation to, 108
Shapiro, Ben, 89
Sharpe, Christina, 1
Silver, Blake, 6
sin, language of: abstract equality and, 117; equality relation to, 59, 62–64; God's love relation to, 63; oppression and, 65; White supremacy and, 68
Smith, Christian, 49
social difference, 187, 207
social documents, diversity statements as, 79
social identity, 37; difference relation to, 40, 91; intersectionality and, 167; numerical representation relation to, 133, 152; visual diversity relation to, 140
social inequality, 78, 217–18; Christian colleges relation to, 209; counterspeech and, 104–5; intersectionality relation to, 175–76; stratification and, 40
social justice, 103
socioeconomic inequality, education relation to, 6
Soucek, Brian, 105
statements, of university board, 96
STEM. *See* science, technology, engineering, and mathematics
structural inequality, White supremacy relation to, 49
student diversity board, 24
student government, 147–48
student identification cards, 159–61, 165
student leadership, 25, 241n107; Asian Americans in, 149–50; cultural values relation to, 148; gender identity relation to, 175; housing arrangements relation to, 174; intergroup dialogue and, 24; model minority myth relation to, 147; organizational change and, 121; power analysis framework and, 59, 86; representation in, 133, 150–51; tolerance relation to, 69; at West University, 44, 91, 150

student organizations, 207; abstract equality relation to, 136; for Asian ethnic identities, 135, 222–23; bicultural identity relation to, 250n10; as bicultural organizations, 192–94; at Christian colleges, 186–87; community in, 188; diversity rationale and, 205; education in, 189–93; politics and, 195–96; Republican, 83–84, 92, 103, 212. *See also* Asian Americans at West; LGBTQ+ student organization
student safety, in housing arrangements, 124–25
Students for Fair Admissions v. Harvard (2023), 3, 8–9
Students for Fair Admissions v. UNC (2023), 3, 8–9
subtraction stories, 12
Sullivan, Teresa, 84–85
Sumerau, J. E., 111
systemic exclusion, 158
systemic inequality, 14; affirmative action policies relation to, 10; color-blind ideology relation to, 153; racial reconciliation and, 62
systemic racism: color-blind ideology relation to, 132–33; counterspeech relation to, 104–5; reconciliation relation to, 61

targeting speech, 210–11
Taylor, Charles, 12
test-optional policies, 220–21
theology, sociology compared to, 214
Thomas, James, 7
Title IX, 17–18, 22, 108
tokenism, 45, 47; power analysis framework and, 46, 52, 208; "seat at the table" relation to, 48–49; in student leadership, 150–51
tolerance: accommodation as, 119; community relation to, 73; evangelicalism relation to, 55; majorities relation to, 71–72; in secular diversity statements, 69–70, 78
Tower of Babel, 58
toxic masculinity, homophobia relation to, 178
trans* identity, 11–12, 26–27, 162; affirmation for, 215; conservative speakers relation to, 84; housing arrangements for, 164; LGBTQ+ reconciliation relation to, 168; student identification cards and, 159–61; Title IX and, 18
trans*phobia, 86, 97; at Christ College, 106–7, 180; in classroom environments, 171–72; faculty and, 114; free speech and, 213; as learning experiences, 123–24
Trieu, Monica, 50
Trump, Donald, 1, 94
Trump administration, 18

UC. *See* University of California
UC Berkeley, 89–90
Unite the Right, 84–85
university board, statements of, 96
University of California (UC), 220, 253n54
University of California Davis School of Medicine, 7–8
University of California Regents v. Bakke (1978), 7–8
University of Iowa, 16
University of Virginia, 84–85
University of Wisconsin, 208
US Census statistics, 223

viewpoint neutrality, 245n21
violence, 165, 213
visual diversity, 139–40, 243n1

Warikoo, Natasha, 34, 43–44, 77, 208
Weber, Max, 241n6
Western culture, 66
West University, 28, 31, 69, 159; Asian Americans at, 20, 23, 26, 130–32, 133,

147, 181, 199, 221; Christ College compared to, 19–20, *21*; cultural traditions of, 183; DEI office at, 1, 20, 24, 85–86, 91, 94–95, 104; educational support at, 177–78; free speech at, 85–86, 93; gender-inclusive bathrooms at, 162–64, 248n1; intersectionality at, 178; LGBTQ+ student organization at, 25, 35, 83; power analysis framework at, 44; queer identity at, 176; racial diversity at, 130–31, 135; student identification cards at, 160–61; student leadership at, 44, 91, 150
White cultural practices, 6–7; at Christ College, 186–87; student organizations relation to, 196
White evangelicals, 49, 198, 214–15
White identity, 250n8
White masculinity, 98
White multiculturalism, cultural mobility and, 77
Whiteness, 187, 189, 201, 204; in diversity statements, 98–99; equity regimes relation to, 218; scripture relation to, 67–68
White racial dominance, 11, 68
White racial perspective, 65–66, 67
White respectability, 101
White students, 23, 76, 102, 204–5
White supremacy, 158; Christianity relation to, 66, 78; diversity rationale relation to, 9; diversity statements relation to, 89; evangelicalism and, 59; inclusion relation to, 88; language of sin and, 68; minorities relation to, 218; oppression and, 179; power analysis framework and, 200; racial triangulation relation to, 16; structural inequality relation to, 49
worship services, 172–73, 175

yellow peril, 145–46, 248n21
Yiannopoulos, Milo, 89

Zhou, Min, 13

ABOUT THE AUTHOR

ESTHER CHAN is Assistant Professor of Sociology at the University of Wisconsin–Milwaukee. She teaches courses on sociological research methods, qualitative research methods, and race and ethnicity in the United States. Her research interests include race and ethnicity; religion; science, medicine, and technology; and gender and sexuality.